PIRATES

Predators of the Seas

PIRATES

Predators of the Seas

Angus Konstam and Roger Michael Kean

Introduction by David Cordingly   Foreword by Gail Selinger

www.skyhorsepublishing.com

10 9 8 7 6 5 4 3 2

ISBN-13: 978-1-5107-0285-1

The Library of Congress Cataloging-in-Publication Data is available on file.

Cover design by Rain Saukas
Printed in China
This book is printed on acid-free paper.

For Thalamus Publishing
Project editor: Warren Lapworth
Maps: Roger Kean
Illustrations: Oliver Frey
Four-color work: Thalamus Studios

PICTURE CREDITS
AKG London: 17 (top), 17 (bottom), 36 (top), 48, 51 (middle), 181 (right); Archivo Iconografica/Corbis: 15 (bottom), 46; Bettmann/Corbis: 71, 119, 151; BNP: 121; Blue Lantern Studio/Corbis: 118; Bridgeman Art Library: 51 (top), 214 (bottom); Burstein Collection/Corbis: 68; City Arts Centre/Barry Clifford: 168 (both); Gianni Dagli Orti/Corbis: 70; Delaware Art Museum:2–3, 11, 93, 123, 136, 137, 146–147, 226 (bottom), 234, 236 (bottom); E.Pasquier/Sygma: 225, 227 (both), 228; E.T. Archive: 21 (bottom), 37, 40 (bottom), 52 (bottom), 79; Oliver Frey/Thalamus Studios: 14, 16, 25 (bottom), 33, 34, 36 (bottom), 39, 40 (top), 41, 42 (top), 42 (bottom), 45, 50, 128–129 (all), 130–131 (all), 158, 232;
Raymond Gehman/Corbis: 156; Philippe Giraud/Corbis: 185 (bottom); Richard Hamilton Smith/Corbis: 112; Rune Hellstad/Corbis: 7; Hispanic Society of America: 74; Images.com/Corbis: 10; Jeremy Horner/Corbis: 122; Dave G. Houser/Corbis: 103; Roger Kean/Thalamus Studios: 15 (top), 19; Kimbell Art Museum/Corbis: 57;
Kobal Collection: 231 (bottom); Angus Konstam: 1, 8 (bottom right), 9, 23 (bottom), 64 (top), 81 (bottom), 97, 114, 115, 124, 132, 133, 141, 143, 145, 154, 160, 161, 163, 165, 166–167, 172, 173, 175, 194, 200, 201, 217, 233, 234–235 (top); Bob Krist/Corbis: 100; Danny Lehman/Corbis: 85, 108; Liu Liqun/Corbis: 25 (top); Araldo de Luca/Corbis: 69; Niall MacLeod/Corbis: 150; Mariners' Museum, Virginia: 24, 26, 135, 176, 177 (top), 178, 187, 190–191, 195, 199 (bottom), 205, 223, 224–225, 230 (bottom); MEPL: 42–43, 47, 231 (top); Francis G. Mayer/Corbis: 189; Mel Fisher Maritime Museum: 174; Kevin R. Morris/Corbis: 104; Museum of Arts & Sciences, Florida: 81 (top); N.H.F. Historical Services, USA: 199 (top); National Maritime Museum: 8 (bottom left), 21 (top). 22, 23 (top), 26–27, 58 (both), 62, 65, 66, 75, 76–77, 82 (top), 82–83, 84, 86 (top), 86 (bottom), 90, 99, 112–113, 120–121, 127, 138, 147, 148, 178–179, 183, 184, 188, 196, 204–205, 207, 208, 209, 210 (both), 213, 214 (top), 218, 219, 222; MichaelNicholson/Corbis: 126; Richard T. Nowitz/Corbis: 35, 226 (top); pub. domain: 185 (top), 186; Joel W.Rogers/Corbis: 91; Salamander: 20, 140, 215, 236; Swim Ink 2, LLC/Corbis: 8 (top);
Thalamus Publishing: 18, 51 (bottom), 52 (top), 57, 61 ,64 (bottom), 78 (top), 78 (bottom), 82, (bottom), 88, 92, 98, 102, 105, 106, 110, 111, 117, 142, 153, 155, 157, 159, 162, 164, 170, 177 (bottom), 180, 181 (left), 211, 220, 230 (top); George Thande/Reuters/Corbis: 229 (bottom); Mike White/Thalamus Studos: 12, 12–13; Whydah Society: 167; Michael S. Yamashita/Corbis: 229 (top)

Contents

Foreword

PIRATES! This single word brings to mind a colorful cast of characters, lightning-fast sword fights, blazing ship battles, elaborate clothing, and most exciting of all, treasure! Lots of it.

The majority of people nowadays think pirates sailed exclusively during the European expansion period of the fifteenth through the eighteenth centuries, now called the Golden Age of Piracy. The truth goes further back, well before the Phoenicians, when men first lashed logs together and sailed the waters stealing from others.

These men (and women) have fascinated the general public for generations. Though a small percentage of pirate crews were once honest sailors, runaway slaves, or men forced into naval service, the majority were thieves, escaped convicts, and murderers. They and their heinous acts represented the dark underbelly of the political, social, and economics norms of their countries and their times. The reality is that they took what they wanted, had little if any regard for human life, and answered to nobody but themselves.

Why such a fascination for pirates? Free will. We all have that longing at some time or another to do what we want, when we want, and without consequences. We cheer for those that manage to have such a life, as long as their behavior is not injurious towards us.

With the exception of pirates, the common man of the Golden Age had little or no freedoms at all. Pirates ignored even the smallest of royal edicts. These edicts, issued in the major European countries, dictated many aspects of life, including what fabrics or colors the general populace was allowed or forbidden to wear; there were even laws that regulated the possession of jewelry. With the exception of the wedding band, jewelry was only allowed for the ruling class. If one ignored these proclamations, prison was the likely punishment.

Life was circumscribed in other ways as well. Individuals had few chances to rise above their born station and make a better life for themselves. For the common man, there was no judicial recourse when he was denied earned wages. Stealing a loaf of bread to ward off starvation led to prison, mutilation, or even death. Because life was so much harsher then than it is today, someone in desperate circumstances could easily conclude that there was as much chance of dying on land as there was while pirating. By going "on the account" they had an opportunity for instant wealth and a better life.

Pirates of the Golden Age created their own democracies aboard their ships at a time when captains had absolute rule over a crewman's life or death. Shares of treasure were equally distributed following a successful raid, along with monetary compensation doled out for severe injuries. Pirates were also able to flaunt their ill-gotten gains, unlawful clothing attire, and stolen gems when they went to town, showing their contempt for the restrictive laws of their time.

With the advent of literacy, daily newspapers, and broadsheets, the exploits of pirates disrupting everyday life and commerce became better known to a broader audience than ever before in history. These tales fueled not only terror but also the romantic imaginations of people throughout Europe, the Caribbean, and the American colonies, as they still do to this day.

This easy-to-read book is a treasure trove of well-researched facts. You are introduced to many historical pirates, from the most infamous of men to the most obscure; you will learn why so many felt the urge to go "on the account." The book is also filled with maps, illustrations, and ship diagrams, and no detail is left out. The fascinating narrative will guide the reader from piracy's beginnings (the earliest mention found on clay tablets) to the machine-gunning men of today, dispelling many myths long repeated in books and movies.

This book is a must for any pirate historian or enthusiast.

Gail Selinger, Pirate Historian and Author

Introduction

Pirates have long been associated with the Caribbean Sea and tropical islands, in particular with the islands of the West Indies, and rightly so. The islands provided hundreds of safe anchorages sheltered by offshore reefs, and passing among them were any number of potential victims: merchant vessels laden with rich goods from Europe; ships from Africa with cargoes of ivory, gold, and slaves; Spanish treasure ships loaded with the wealth of Central America. Apart from the mosquitoes and occasional hurricane, the Caribbean was a pirate paradise for men like Blackbeard, the barbaric Edward Teach—of whom it was said, "a greater monster never infested the seas"—and Calico Jack, whose chief claim to fame was not his piratical exploits but the two female members of his crew, Mary Read and Anne Bonny.

But pirates did not restrict their operations to the West Indies or the Spanish Main. As Konstam and Kean graphically demonstrate in this book, pirates operated throughout the world. For centuries, the shipping in the Mediterranean was at the mercy of the Barbary corsairs' oared galleys. In northern Europe, along the shores of the Red Sea, in the Strait of Malacca, indeed wherever trade routes squeezed through straits or between islands, pirates would lurk there, waiting to pounce.

Many of them operated from bases where they were protected by the local populace, but the more intrepid made vast ocean voyages in search of plunder. The infamous Captain Kidd was one of several who sailed across the Atlantic to Madagascar and the Indian Ocean. Bartholomew Roberts made several voyages from Newfoundland to the Caribbean, then across to the west coast of Africa. Others sailed around Cape Horn into the Pacific in search of Spanish treasure ships.

Many of the pirates were fine seamen, and they showed an impressive ability to outwit the authorities. There was an admirable tradition of democracy that enabled crews to vote their captains in and out of office and ensured that plunder was shared equally. But it would be a mistake to conclude that pirates in any way resembled the romantic heroes depicted by Errol Flynn and Douglas Fairbanks Snr., or even the less romantic figure of Johnny Depp's Jack Sparrow. Philip Ashton, a young sailor taken by pirates in 1722, described his captors as "a vile crew of miscreants, to whom it was a sport to do mischief, where prodigious drinking, monstrous cursing and swearing, hideous blasphemies and open defiance of Heaven and contempt of Hell itself was the constant employment...."

Pirate attacks were violent and frequently accompanied by torture and murder. This has been the pattern throughout history, and it continues today, particularly in the South China Sea, off the coasts of West and East Africa, in Brazilian waters, and in the Strait of Malacca—in all these locations pirate attacks are as frequent and as brutal as they were in the West Indies during the 17th and 18th centuries.

David Cordingly

Preface

The worst pirate ever—Johnny Depp's Captain Jack Sparrow, terror of the Caribbean, reworked the mythology and now appears as a waxwork in Madame Tussaud's.

Pirates in recent years have enjoyed an unprecedented surge in popularity, thanks in no small part to the success of the movie series *Pirates of the Caribbean* and Johnny Depp's flamboyant portrayal of Captain Jack Sparrow—the worst pirate some English commodores had ever seen. But there has also been a resurgence in histories of piracy, with Blackbeard enjoying no less than two biographies in the space of a single year. What is it with pirates and why do they so grip our imagination? The very word conjures up a powerful image of swashbuckling heroes flashing ludicrously huge swords, making captives walk the plank, burying treasure on desert islands, and in general having a very rousing time. This popular image of piracy appeals to anyone who feels the constraints of modern urban society. Pirates are our proxies, doing those things that many people would love to do but cannot—living a free life, contemplating very little while lying back against a palm tree on a tropical sandy beach and knocking three bells out of other pirates in a portside tavern.

This jolly perception of piracy is heavily colored by imagery created for books, the stage, television, and movies. Pirates are good business, not only for ticket sales but also in marketing, the symbolism used to sell products from holidays to cars. Pirates have become almost mythical beings, and like any myth there is always a grain of truth behind the creation. Myths, however, have a way of gaining momentum, every generation adding another layer of detail so that soon the truthful grains are buried in the sands of fiction. For example, there is no evidence that pirates made prisoners walk the plank, although they were readily used for pistol practice or simply tortured for an evening's sadistic enjoyment.

The pirates of fiction—Jack Sparrow, Captain Hook, Long John Silver, Captain Blood, and many others— are pale imitations of the real thing (except perhaps Captain Sparrow, who seems to be an imitation of something quite different...). The experiences of real pirates did involve burying treasure, desertion on tropical islands, peg-legs, and even parrots, but shipwreck, disease, betrayal, and an end on the gibbet were more commonly the recurring themes

7

SPEND YOUR HOLIDAYS IN JAMAICA

THE BLUE LAGOON JAMAICA.

LOVELIEST & MOST ROMANTIC TROPICAL ISLE.

Pirates sell—a Jamaica Board of Tourism poster from the late 1940s–early 1950s capitalizes on the Caribbean's romantic association with buccaneers.

The shock discovery that there were also women pirates, like the infamous Bonny and Read (**below right**), was a shot in the arm for the drama and literature concerned with piracy. Mary Read (**below**) was quickly promoted to heroine status in popular imagination, in stark contrast to the reality.

in their invariably short and brutish lives. Hollywood's pirate movies would hardly be complete without a good barroom fight, but in fact almost every port was closed to them. The romantic vision fails to mention that, denied a safe harbor, most starving pirate crews had to prey on other ships in order to survive.

Fiction and films generally portray the pirate as a person who, confronted by their highschool careers advisor, opted for a life of piracy as a choice, just like any other trade. But crime is seldom a simple matter of choice. Men have turned to piracy for as long as man has sailed the sea and whether the pirates operated in ancient galleys, sailing ships, or modern speedboats, many of their reasons for becoming pirates were the same. Far from "yo-ho-ho and a bottle of rum," it was often desperate or disillusioned people who made up the crews of pirate vessels. Some were driven by unemployment and the threat of starvation, others found themselves unfairly on the wrong side of harsh laws. Some, of course, were just downright wicked.

That their average age was 27 tells us much about the short life expectancy of a pirate in the so-called "Golden Age" of piracy at the end of the 17th century. Execution was the expected punishment, yet piracy was an attractive alternative to the other options facing seamen—the misery of a merchantman, the harsh treatment aboard a naval vessel. Although not exclusively so, seamen were the natural recruits to a pirate crew and freedom was a major motivating force. A seaman's pay was extremely poor. Profits went to the ship-owners and shares in naval prize money were usually divided unequally, the officers taking almost all of it. On a pirate ship, profits went to the pirates themselves. Slumped at the bottom of a restrictive social hierarchy, the opportunity to make a quick profit and then retire enticed many sailors into a career of crime on the high seas.

A life at sea was grueling. Apart from the discomfort of appalling living quarters, the extremes of weather and the constant dangers of merciless seas, the food was often rotten, the drinking water frequently foul, and diseases like malaria, dysentery, yellow fever, and scurvy were rife. If the career promised little, at least for a pirate or privateer there was the chance of huge financial rewards.

In times of war, privateers were effectively pirates licensed by a government to harass enemy shipping and capture prizes. Shares from the sale of booty were more fairly divided between the crew of a privateer than was the case in the navy. Profit enticed seamen to become privateers, and peace caused massive unemployment among the maritime community, an example being the situation at the end of the War of the Spanish Succession in 1714. In such circumstances, the logical way of continuing to earn a living for privateering crews was to turn to piracy.

However, the route to piracy for the majority of sailors was occasioned by the capture of their vessel by pirates. For the common sailor with no ransom potential, the future held three choices: instant execution, slavery, or signing up with the pirate captain. It was never a very difficult choice. It also held the advantage that in the case of capture, many pirates were able to claim in their defense that they had been pressed by their captors and joined them unwillingly. Considering that this was the way the navy regularly recruited sailors, it was easy for judges to at least half believe the convicted pirate and, in some cases, show leniency.

In history, piracy always seems to have drawn together very mixed crews—the social castaways of different lands and cultures joined by a common need to survive. In the late 17th and the 18th centuries, pirate crews were composed of men (and a few women) of many nations, social classes, and races. Some 700 pirates were recorded in court archives as being active in the Caribbean in 1715–25, and of these Englishmen were in the majority at 35 percent. English-speaking Americans made up 25 percent, 20 percent were natives of the West Indies, 10 percent were Scottish, and 8 percent came from Wales. The other seafaring nations, such as Sweden, Holland, France, and Spain, only accounted for 2 percent. Some crews included men of African descent, either runaway slaves from American and Caribbean plantations or free American blacks. In 1721 Bartholomew Roberts's crew was made up from 187 white men and 75 black men, most of whom were runaways. Even the misery of a sailing ship and the likely brutal end was preferable to slavery on a West Indian plantation.

Poverty, as displayed in William Hogarth's *Gin Lane*, was the lot of the majority of English people in the early 18th century; no wonder those who could ran away from it. Many thought a life at sea aboard a pirate ship not only an escape but also an opportunity to get rich quick.

Is this man really a pirate?

If there is some confusion as to what a pirate really is, there is certainly as much about what he should be called, and again it is the fault of popular fiction, which hands around definitions with the willful freedom of… well, a pirate. While piracy may be too romantic a term to apply to the bandits in speedboats who attack shipping in the waters of the South China Sea, nevertheless it applies to an Uzi-wielding Indonesian pirate as much as it does to Blackbeard. It is the primary definition: a pirate is a robber who performs his crimes at sea. The tactics and methods may have changed over time, but not the crime. Unfortunately for clarity's sake, modern usage has expanded the word's meaning to include landlubbers, so that perhaps the activity most associated today with the word pirate is the theft of copyrighted material. We are all familiar with the concept of the pirated video tape, from the

Computer Pirate by Philippe Chapelle; by associating the copyright thief with the seafaring pirate cheats clothe their actions in a cloak of romanticism.

Opposite: *Which shall be Captain* by Howard Pyle. More than any other artist, Pyle's work set the style and image of the pirate in the public's mind. A native of Wilmington, Delaware, he was born in 1853 and died while visiting Florence, Italy in 1911. A teacher, author, and painter, Pyle revolutionized the art of illustration with a new dynamic way of presenting dramatic moments in history. His illustrations for *Tales of Pirates and Buccaneers* and *Howard Pyle's Book of Pirates* became the seminal influence in piratical imagery.

news if not the fact. It seems odd that such a sedentary and land-based activity as copyright theft should commonly be defined by a term that in history is firmly associated with a criminal act attached, at least in some way, with the high seas.

Definitions, then, are important to a clear understanding of piracy. In their time, the difference between being seen as a buccaneer, privateer, corsair, or pirate could mean the difference between life and death. In the same way that one nation's hero is another's terrorist, so a pirate in one country could be considered a patriot in another, like Henry Morgan, Sir Francis Drake, or even John Paul Jones. Indeed, it frequently suited a government to sanction a ship's captain to act like a pirate and attack enemy shipping when no state of war existed between the two countries. A pirate in the truest sense attacks any ship, regardless of its nationality.

A pirate robs from others at sea, and acts beyond any law. This was reinforced in the 17th and 18th centuries in England and its colonies when piracy fell under the jurisdiction of Admiralty law and piracy was defined as a crime committed below the low-tide mark around the shores and rivers, estuaries, and high seas. The Lord High Admiral's authority was made visibly manifest as convicted pirates were often hanged on the low-tide mark. Other countries adopted the definition, and the punishment.

In consequence, many pirates went to great lengths to cover their crimes, trying to hide behind the more forgiving appellations of privateer or buccaneer. The term buccaneer evolved in the early 17th century on the Caribbean island of Hispaniola (now Haiti and the Dominican Republic). Here, the French backwoodsmen smoked their meat over a *buccan* or barbecue, and so became known as *boucaniers*. Many early buccaneers were fugitives from Spanish law, which held sway over much of the Caribbean, and they hated all Spaniards. By the mid-17th century, the boucanier hunters began attacking passing Spanish shipping and their success attracted runaway slaves, seamen, and other outlaws. In time, "buccaneer" came to refer to the sea-raiders of the Spanish Main—mainly English and French—who acted as semi-legal pirates, based principally in Port Royal and Tortuga.

By contrast, a privateer acted as a proxy for his country's navy. A contract called *letters of marque* permitted the civilian captain, his ship, and his crew to attack enemy ships during wartime. The primary objective of the privateer was to capture enemy vessels as intact as possible, and return to base with the "prize." In return for issuing the *letters*, the government received a share of the profits of the captured ship and cargo, calculated at one-fifth of the value. In the name of Queen Elizabeth I, the 16th-century English Sea Rovers exemplified privateering and their efforts greatly enriched the queen's coffers at the expense of the Spanish. But despite the glitter of a monarch's name on a contract—although often enough the agreement was verbal and could be denied by royal prerogative before irate ambassadors— there is no disguising that fact that a privateer (or more accurately, a privateersman) was only a licensed pirate who did not attack his own people. Unfortunately, once the state of war had ended, many privateers—unable or unwilling to give up the life of a sea dog—turned to piracy. Sometimes a privateer overstepped not only the spirit but also the clauses of his contract and became a pirate, as in the case of Henry Morgan when he attacked Panama in 1671 (*see pages 112–13*).

The small, fast *flibotes* (fly boats) used by some French buccaneers gave them the alternative name of filibusters, sometimes loosely called freebooters. The term fell into disuse, only to be revived during the 19th century, when "filibuster" described a smuggler or blockade-runner. (And, interestingly a filibuster is the name given to the delaying tactic of a time-consuming speech made in the US Senate in an effort to prevent the passage of a bill or amendment—which might be considered the theft of due process, a form of piracy perhaps.)

From the French term for a privateer, *la course*, Mediterranean pirates came to be known as corsairs. Confusingly, the word was applied to either a pirate or a privateer, depending on the protagonists' viewpoint. For instance, the most famous, the Barbary corsairs of the North African coast, regarded themselves as Muslim privateers fighting their religious enemies under contract from the city-states of the Barbary Coast. Europeans, on the other hand, branded them as little more then filthy pirates (as indeed did the inhabitants of the Barbary Coast whenever the corsairs turned their guns on them).

Throughout the history of sail, pirates have hoped for much, but somewhere deep in their hearts have expected little. Most condemned pirates standing before the judge and jury of the unforgiving 18th-century European courts displayed a fatalism that hinted at the inevitability with which they saw their capture and execution. That was their reality. This book sets out

to examine real pirates throughout history, from the ancient Mediterranean to the waters of the Caribbean, and from the eastern seaboard of America to the South China Sea. Stripped of romanticism, their crimes and their fates are detailed, and the reality revealed.

CHAPTER ONE

The Pirate Ship

The work-seahorses of ages

Piracy on the high seas is as old as navigation itself. Only the type of vessel employed and the weapons and ordnance available to the particular period make any real distinction between the very first pirates and those of recent times. In every event, speed and maneuverability combined with a reasonable cargo capacity for stolen booty have been the most desired qualities of a pirate ship.

Oared craft, sometimes aided by a primitive sail, were used in the first recorded acts of piracy. In the 13th century BC the Sea Peoples of the late Bronze Age and the later Cretan pirates of the 10th century BC both used a kind of galley. Those of the Sea Peoples can be seen in the massive carvings on the walls of mortuary temple of the Egyptian pharaoh Ramesses III at Medinet Habu (*see page 34*). They would have been very similar to the mythical *Argo* that carried Jason and the Argonauts on their voyage to seize the fabled golden fleece of Colchis, itself a combined trading venture and pirate-raid. Jason's story ends in a suitably dramatic Greek manner—he was killed when a piece of timber falling from the *Argo* struck him on the head, making him the first pirate to die by the hand of his own vessel.

Homer mentioned these early Greek pirate ships, describing them as small open-decked galleys with between 10 and 25 oars per side. They must have been the "black ships before Troy" that brought disaster to the Trojans. The collapse in about 1100 BC of the Mediterranean Bronze Age cultures, such as the Mycenaean, brought about a Dark Age. However, maritime commerce continued and during the following 250 years several

Small coastal trading vessels, which relied more on sails than oars, were vulnerable to pirates, although the slightly larger merchant ships called *kerkouroi*, seen here in the background, made better pickings. As a result, they were equipped with a ram at the prow to help fight off pirate ships.

Biremes of classical Greece join battle. Two main tactics can be seen. Using the heavy metal-shod beak, one rams an enemy head-on. In the background another vessel is rowed toward its opponent at battle speed. At the last moment the nearside oars are withdrawn and the ship careers alongside, shearing off the opponent's oars as it passes, rendering it helpless.

new types of vessel made an appearance in contemporary representations. Merchantmen tended to rely far more on sail than manpower, many dropping oars as a means of propulsion altogether, and although broad-beamed galleys that could use oar or sail are depicted, so too are narrower, more sleekly designed craft. Fast enough to overhaul merchantmen or evade capture by heavier warships, these were ideal pirate vessels, and they still had sufficient capacity to carry plunder to their bases in the labyrinthian bays of the Peloponnese and the Aegean islands.

By the eighth century BC the Phoenicians were sailing in fast galleys powered by two tiers of oars, the type of warship known as a *bireme*. Within another two centuries the Greek navies had adopted and adapted the bireme, increasing the number of oars for extra speed, mounting a fighting platform for marines, and adding a heavy-duty ram on the prow to help sink enemy ships. However, this last improvement was not ideal for a pirate ship, which needed to plunder its prey and not sink it first, and so the smaller pirate biremes remained less specialized than their naval opponents in the Greek and Phoenician navies.

For the purposes of making war, the bireme developed into the much larger and more powerful *trireme* by the fifth century BC. The added third bank of oars produced the greater speed required over short distances when attempting to ram another vessel. While excellent as warships, triremes were neither particularly seaworthy nor capable of extended voyages, effectively making them coastal ships. So merchant shipping was left unescorted on the open sea and remained the prey of the smaller and more seaworthy pirate biremes.

Variations on the bireme

The Romans were never a great sea-faring people in the Republican period, but were forced to embrace the sea as a means of defeating the rival power of Carthage in the First Punic War (264–41 BC). The Roman navy deployed a larger version of the Greek trireme known as a *quinquereme*. Despite its name, the quinquereme still had three banks of oars, but used five oarsmen in line, two to each of the two upper tiers, one to the lowest, which gave the vessel enormous short-haul power. Quinqueremes were, if anything, even less seaworthy than the trireme and so, while they gave the Roman navy tactical supremacy of the Mediterranean, they were virtually useless in ridding the seas of the pirates who flourished in this period.

Roman marines leap across a *corvus* from their quinquereme to board a Carthaginian galley. The *corvus* was a form of maneuverable bridge with a spike at the end that slammed down on an enemy ship and allowed Roman legionaries to board and fight as though they were on land (they hated the sea), but its weight made already unstable quinqueremes top heavy and liable to turn turtle.

A variety of ships based on the bireme were available to pirates. The *hemiola,* from the Greek word for one-and-a-half, first appeared in Greek waters during the fourth century BC. A light, fast ship that combined oars and a large square sail, the hemiola was constructed in such a way that its crew could withdraw and stow a central section of the oars to make space for boarding a prize, and lower the mast to create a fighting platform.

The *lembos*, an open-decked bireme, was used by Illyrian pirates in the Adriatic Sea, easily able to dodge the more sluggish Roman triremes and quinqueremes. The Romans, however, later copied the design during the second century BC and used their own version as an anti-piracy craft—the *liburnian* was another adapted pirate bireme that also saw service as a light warship. Liburnians formed the fleet backbone of the Cilician pirates, who were later hired as mercenaries by several nations.

For much of the third and second centuries BC, the island of Rhodes maintained a fleet of *triemiola* to hunt down and destroy pirates. These smaller, faster, open-decked versions of the hemiola also allowed the removal of a number of oars before

Cross-section through a Roman quinquereme showing how the five rowers that gave the vessel its name were arranged.

coming alongside another vessel, ready for boarding. This increased her ability to swamp the pirate ship with marines.

When Pompey the Great fought the Cilician pirates (*see page 42*) in the first century BC, he relied on hired Rhodean biremes and Roman-built liburnians, supported by heavier but slower warships. He was so successful in wiping out the pirate threat in the Mediterranean that although the Roman navy maintained a fleet of fast biremes to prevent any resurgence of piratical activity, they were hardly ever needed after the foundation of the Roman empire at the turn of the millennium.

The oared galley never went out of fashion in the Mediterranean Sea. By the time of the fall of the Western Roman empire in the late fifth century AD, the real power in the Mediterranean was concentrated around Constantinople, capital of the Eastern Roman empire, later known as the Byzantine empire. Byzantium's navy went through phases of success and failure, confronted variously by sea raids from would-be usurpers of the throne, the Arabs from bases in Palestine, Egypt, and even as close as Cyzicus in the Sea of Marmara, the Viking Rus sailing down the Dnieper river and crossing the Black Sea, and from Venetian and Genoese traders.

An incised carving shows a Roman quinquereme of the 1st century BC.

A battle rages on the Bosporus outside the mighty walls of Constantinople, as Greek galleys armed with Greek fire repel attackers. A closely guarded secret, this terrifying flame-throwing device helped the often poorly manned Byzantine navy defeat Arab and Viking raiders over the centuries.

In essence, the galleys used by all nationalities remained substantially unchanged from their Roman predecessors, but the Byzantines had one enormous advantage over their foes. They held the secret to the most terrifying weapon of the time—Greek fire. Deployed onboard small, speedy and maneuverable ships called *dromones*, a liquid fire of unknown composition was sprayed from specially designed pumps onto the enemy. The oil-based flammable liquid stuck to everything it hit, as well as floating on the water's surface, engulfing in flames any who jumped overboard to save themselves. Greek fire saved the day on any number of occasions when the enemy closed in around Constantinople's massive city walls.

During the medieval period, the arrival of northern European ships, built in a quite different manner, almost but never quite extinguished the traditional galley. Indeed, the galley was to see a renaissance in the 16th century.

The ships of medieval Europe

At the start of the Middle Ages, European ships were only capable of making short trading voyages. By the late 15th century, a string of technological breakthroughs produced ships that were capable of carrying European trade to the edges of the known world and beyond. The traditional structure of the bireme and galley that so suited the Mediterranean Sea was quite unfit for the more turbulent waters of

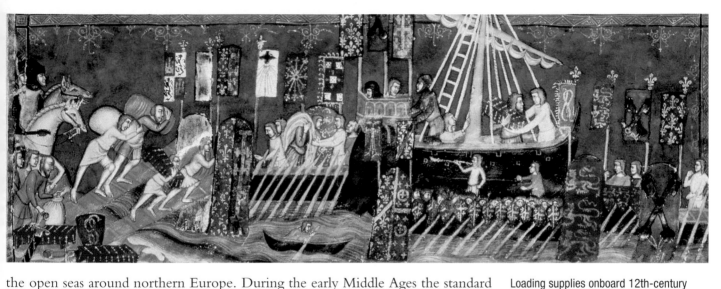

the open seas around northern Europe. During the early Middle Ages the standard trading ship in northern Europe was the *knorr*, a vessel developed from the Viking longships that had dominated European waters since the eighth century (*see illustration, page 50*). The hulls of these astonishingly seaworthy ships were built of overlapping planks fixed to a lightweight, flexible frame, a construction method known as clinker-built. The knorr was pointed at both ends and open-decked. A single mast and square sail provided propulsion, while a steering oar swept over the side acted as a rudder. With their shallow draft, they made ideal river-raiders—using sail or stowable oars—and at the same time took the Vikings clear across the North Atlantic Ocean to Iceland, Greenland, Labrador, and Newfoundland.

Loading supplies onboard 12th-century open-decked knorrs of a French crusading fleet. An added sterncastle may be seen.

As maritime trade grew in 13th-century northern Europe, the knorrs were modified to improve their efficiency and cargo-carrying capacity. A better sail plan and the addition of a foresail or bowsprit gave the vessel more speed, while raised platforms at the bow and stern provided shelter and acted as fighting platforms if the ship were attacked. It was a necessary precaution—as maritime trade grew, so did piracy.

Embarking troops for the Third Crusade (1189–92) onto cogs with their flat sterns and enhanced forecastles and sterncastles.

Increased trade also called for more sophistication than the knorr could provide, and by the mid-13th century it had developed into the *cog*, which rapidly became the dominant ship in northern European waters. A cog had a fixed stern rudder instead of a sweep, so its stern was no longer pointed, and cargo was protected from the elements by an enclosed deck. The square sail plan prevented the cog from sailing close to the wind, but

17

this drawback was eventually overcome when European sailors later met their Mediterranean counterparts. Cogs were the seaworthy trading vessels used by the Hanseatic League, and provided the basis for all warships and pirate vessels of their day. The only difference between a trader and a warship was the size of her crew, and possibly the increased size of her fighting platforms.

When northern European sailors ventured into the Mediterranean they encountered vessels based on Arabic lines; carvel-built designs in which the hull planking is joined edge-to-edge rather than overlapping and fixed to a heavier and more stable frame than on a clinker-built hull. Their triangular lateen sails were quite different, the shape and their rigging allowing them to sail closer to the wind. Italian shipbuilders now took the lead by amalgamating the different designs. They copied the increased hull size of the northern cog but adapted it to carvel-built construction. The result, known as a roundship, was a marriage of northern size to a southern sail plan on a carvel hull.

During the 15th century, a fast sailing ship known as a *caravel* was developed in the Mediterranean. It combined the steering advantage of lateen sails with those of the European-style stern rudder, and the caravel's lightly built carvel hull made the ship fast, responsive, and easily handled by a small crew. A similar evolution from the cog emerged at about the same time in northern Europe, which eventually became the *carrack*. Fighting platforms designed as a part of the construction rather than as afterthoughts made this type of vessel more seaworthy and the previous "castles" at the bow and stern developed into true forecastles and sterncastles, providing solid fighting platforms. The introduction of artillery during the 15th century turned them into formidable warships. The carrack—or *nao* as the Spanish and Portuguese knew them —became the backbone of Europe's merchant fleets and navies.

In the last phase of perfecting the carrack's lines, Europe's shipyards switched from the traditional clinker- to carvel-built hulls because of the artillery component. The increasingly heavy guns of the period had to be mounted inside a ship and low down near the waterline to keep the ship safely trimmed. Cutting gunport holes in the overlapping planks of clinker-built hulls weakened them dangerously, whereas the joins in a carvel hull were simply reinforced and caulked, maintaining the ship's integrity. These large ships combined a strong frame with the streamlined carvel hull, and their cargo capacity was much greater than that of Mediterranean craft of the same period.

A carrack before the wind, from a painting of c.1540. The carrack replaced the cog as the standard late medieval merchantman and pirate ship. Compared to the cog, the carrack had a cloud of sails and a massive sterncastle, which began to provide a degree of comfort for the ship's master at least. The muzzles of cannon can be seen protruding through gunports cut through the carvel–built hull close to the waterline.

Galleys versus sailing ships

In Mediterranean waters of the Renaissance period, the new roundships plied their trade alongside traditional sail-and-oared galleys that had hardly changed their appearance in two thousand years. The rowed galley was still a more useful vessel in the island-crowded and narrow waters of seas like the Adriatic and Aegean than a sailing ship, but was less likely to be found in deep, open waters. But in the 16th century there came a big change. Suddenly, it seemed as if all the navies of the region wanted to recapture the days of antiquity by building fleets of war galleys.

Renaissance galleys looked similar to, and behaved like, earlier Roman ships but had a number of differences. For one, the use of artillery had prompted construction of a strong forecastle to carry from one to five main guns in a forward-facing battery, while swivel guns provided close-range fire. Unlike the larger sailing ships of the era, which carried their armament in large broadside batteries, galleys pointed their bow towards the enemy in order to open fire, in the process presenting a narrow target to the enemy.

The galleys carried one or more masts fitted with lateen sails, allowing them to take advantage of wind to supplement oar propulsion. A typical galley carried 20–30 oars or sweeps, each manned by three, four, or even six rowers, usually slaves or prisoners, seated on wooden benches. This level of power meant the galley was able to go from dead in the water to full speed in a matter of seconds. In the generally light winds of the Mediterranean, this gave the galley a natural advantage over a sailing ship. While the latter might carry a heavier armament and her higher structure served as a defense against attack, the sailing ship was slower and more cumbersome. A nimble galley could dance around a sailing vessel, keeping out of the narrow angle of fire from the enemy's broadsides while bombarding her.

However, Barbary corsairs and other Mediterranean pirates avoided long-range gunnery whenever possible, for an artillery bombardment could seriously damage a potential prize, particularly if it was another galley. The ideal prize was one captured without a running sea battle. For the same reason, ramming was never an attractive proposition; in the standard Barbary tactic the pirates swarmed aboard a grappled prize over its forecastle as soon as they came alongside, then attempted to overpower the vessel's crew in hand-to-hand fighting.

Mediterranean regions developed their own versions of the basic galley design. The Venetians placed the emphasis on speed, favoring long, narrow galleys with racing lines. They were also less stable than their contemporaries. Most of the other Christian states and the Ottoman Turks of the eastern Mediterranean preferred a broader and taller galley, which provided a higher and more stable gun platform.

Compared to a sailing ship with its typical crew complement of a dozen or less, full galleys were expensive to maintain, and only a small number were retained by the navies of the Mediterranean, including the principal Barbary ports. The rest of the galley fleets of the 16th century comprised a smaller version of the galley known

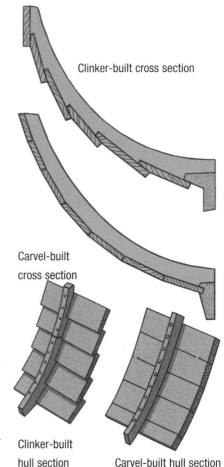

Clinker-built cross section

Carvel-built
cross section

Clinker-built
hull section

Carvel-built hull section

The term "clinker-built" is derived from the clinch-bolts used to fix the overlapping strakes, or planks, to the frame. Only a few shaped frame timbers were fixed to the keel to hold the strakes in place; the remainder of the strengthening skeletal framework was added afterward. By contrast, in a carve-built hull the keel and heavier framework are constructed first, the planks then bent around the finished frame. The term "carvel" was probably derived from the Arabic vessel called a *caravo*, which used this type of construction.

as the *galiot*. These were faster than the larger war galleys, and ideally suited to Mediterranean piracy.

A typical galiot was flush-decked and fitted with a single mast carrying a lateen sail. Between six and 12 oars per side were each manned by an average of two oarsmen, and on true corsair galiots these were free pirates rather than slaves, since the smaller size of the vessel precluded carrying anyone who was unwilling to board an enemy prize. The long-hulled, sleek galiot formed the bulk of the corsair fleets of the Barbary Coast and the Ottoman empire. Larger galleys rowed by slaves were often reserved to the pirate commander as a flagship, generally avoiding naval combat. Some were used in pirate operations, particularly when an amphibious assault was anticipated and land-raiders needed to be carried aboard. A variant of the galiot known as the *tartan*, with its two masts, placed greater emphasis on sail.

Although use of the galley declined throughout the 17th century, slave ships of the 18th century were often ship-rigged galleys and used as pirate ships (*see William Kidd, pages 138–40, and Sam Bellamy, pages 167–69*), and oared corsair craft of various types remained in use along the Barbary Coast until the early 19th century. While the Mediterranean pirates preferred their small galleys, those of rougher northern waters used small caravels to attack enemy shipping, or else relied on the carrack's firepower to dismast and overpower the target. Privately owned ships were in constant demand for hire in national defense as "privateers." These were the ships used to explore the New World and by the pirates who preyed on the wealth discovered there.

The Spanish galleon and English privateer

In the latter half of the 16th century Spanish shipwrights designed the carrack variant that would thereafter be *the* ship of seafaring derring-do in popular imagination—the *galeón*. In the first instance, these ships were designed to carry and protect the annual treasure fleets sailing between the Spanish New World colonies and Spain, but English shipbuilders were quick to imitate and began constructing low, sleek "racing"

A large corsair galley of about 1770, with cutaway section. Its powerful armament of four guns are mounted above the bow, facing forward, and below the gun platform with four swivel guns. Since a galley of this size could carry a large force of fighting men for boarding prizes, slaves would be used to man the 48 oars—24 on each side. Between four and six slaves, usually captured prisoners, worked each oar. It is easy to imagine how crowded such a vessel would be, but the Barbary Coast pirates rarely lived onboard, spending their nights ashore.

galleons, ideally suited as pirate or privateering craft. In the hands of England's famous captains such as Sir Francis Drake they were formidable weapons.

On March 1, 1579, Drake in his small English race-built galleon *Golden Hind* caught up with a small Spanish galleon, the *Cacafuego*. The Spaniard ship, captured with hardly a fight, yielded an astonishingly rich haul of pirate booty. The chase served to show the differences between the two ship types: the Spanish galleon and her English race-built derivative. The typical escort galleon was a vessel of between 300 and 500 tons, although they could displace as much as 1200 tons. Some, like the

Above right: A fleet of Barbary galleys, from a 17th-century engraving.

The *Golden Hind*, an English race-built, square-rigged galleon, took Sir Francis Drake into battle in the Spanish Main. She was about 75 feet long, 20 feet wide, and displaced only 120 tons. Her fast, racy lines and high manueverability combined with 18 guns of various size provided a powerful striking ability. Dutch shipbuilders later followed the basic design of these English privateers, which paved the way for the pirate ships used by buccaneers of the 17th century.

Cacafuego, were even smaller—less than 200 tons—but these were not considered true galleons.

The largest galleons were used as flagships, rather than as escorts for the treasure fleets. These were the ships that formed the backbone of the Spanish Armada, but they were never used against English privateers in the Spanish Main. There the English Sea Rovers met medium-sized galleons and well-armed *nao*s (carracks).

With their high forecastles and massive sterncastles, Spanish galleons were unwieldy. Because they were treasure ships their cargo capacity was large, and as the most prestigious ships sailing between Spain and the New World, they also carried passengers, who usually proved a hindrance if the ship had to go into action. In addition to a powerful armament of artillery, Spanish galleons carried a contingent of soldiers, although circumstances usually limited their value due to a flawed tactical doctrine. The Spanish used gunfire as a prelude to a boarding action, but better English and Dutch gun carriages using four small wheels instead of two large ones were able to deliver a far higher rate of fire—and even the best soldiers in the world were useless in a long-range gunnery duel. Despite these drawbacks, a combination of the convoy system and the imposing appearance of Spanish galleons usually deterred potential attackers, including the most persistent of the English Sea Rovers.

The ships used by the English privateers of the period were designed along completely different principles. Sir John Hawkins used the royal warship *Jesus of Lübeck* in his expedition of 1567, an old carrack of Henry VIII's navy. She was similar to many of the armed warships used by the Spanish, but had been modified by removing much of her superstructure to create a lighter, more seaworthy and speedily maneuverable warship.

A new breed of English shipwrights such as Matthew Baker produced plans for a new type of race-built galleon, designed from the keel upward to be fast, and these became the leading warships of England's recently formed Royal Navy. England, however, relied heavily on privateers to supplement the navy, and many

Model of the classic Spanish *galeón*. These were slow-moving ships, especially on the return journey from the New World, laden with Aztec gold or Inca silver. It was practice to gather a large fleet to sail in convoy for mutual protection from their main foes, the English and Dutch privateers who prowled the Caribbean Sea.

of their ships imitated the royal shipwrights' designs. English race-built galleons combined a far sleeker hull shape than the Spanish galleon with a low super-structure rising gradually toward the quarter-deck, avoiding the towering Spanish superstructures. Sir Francis Drake's *Golden Hind* is a typical example.

The crews of privateers and royal warships were trained to avoid close contact with the enemy and to rely on gunnery to win the battle for them. These were the ships used by English privateers and pirates to raid the Spanish Main and prey on Spanish shipping, from the Pacific to the coast of Spain.

The ideal pirate vessel

During both the buccaneering era (1640–90) and the subsequent "Golden Age" of piracy (1690–1730), pirates in American and Caribbean waters adapted regular cargo vessels for their particular needs. When ships were captured they were sold, destroyed, or turned into pirate vessels. Although men such as Blackbeard and Bartholomew Roberts hunted in large, well-armed ships, most pirates used smaller craft. Certain types of ships were preferred over others. The ideal ship had to be fast enough to catch—or run from—more powerful enemies, so smaller, lighter craft were favored, particularly the *sloop*, ideally suited for the hit-and-run tactics of the pirate trade, and its offspring the *schooner* and *brigantine*. Ideally, they were commodious enough to carry plunder and stores, but space for the men was limited since their crews tended to be larger than was the case for a merchantman.

So much for the theory; there is very little graphic evidence from the time to tell us what a pirate ship looked like, despite Hollywood's sterling efforts to persuade movie-goers. Written evidence indicates that pirates and buccaneers opted for sloops and, to a lesser extent, brigantines, while schooners became steadily more popular during the 18th century. Their specifications show how they were ideally suited to the needs of piracy.

Detail of the Port of Panama from Nicholas Hack's *waggoner* (collection of sea charts) of 1683–4, dedicated to King Charles II of England. Hack's work marked the beginning of modern map-making but, like the pirates who took full advantage of any chart they seized, Hack borrowed most of his detail of "the Great South Sea" from stolen Spanish manuscripts.

Bermudan sloops were highly sought after as pirate vessels. This diagram shows the sleek hull lines of a ship c.1700.

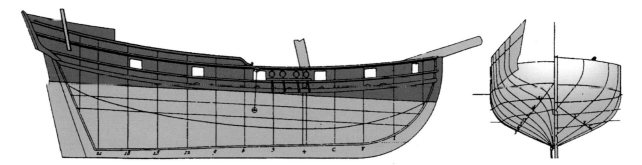

Sloops were the main small workhorse vessel of the 17th and 18th centuries and formed the largest single type of vessel found in American and Caribbean waters. The name describes a range of vessels that were small, single-masted, and carried an enormous spread of sail in proportion to their size. The sail plan was typically a fore-and-aft rig, with a mainsail and a single foresail. This made them fast, quick-turning, and easily handled vessels even in shoaling waters, thanks to their shallow draft. A typical sloop of around 1700 was capable of carrying up to 75 men and 14 small guns.

In the 18th century the term "sloop" also referred to similar small vessels with one, two, or three masts. Jamaican shipbuilders produced a highly regarded sloop with a reputation for seaworthiness and speed, and this became a favorite of the buccaneers. Traditionally constructed of red cedar, they were strong enough to carry an extra armament of guns. By the 18th century, Bermudan shipwrights had also acquired a high reputation for building sloops and schooners. The schooner was an American version of the sloop, for which the shipyards of Baltimore were justly famed, and they became increasingly common in American and Caribbean waters in the later 18th century. A narrow hull and large spread of sail made them fast and sleek, capable of sailing at almost 12 knots (13.8mph) in the right winds. Typically, they also had a shallow draft, allowing pirate schooners to hide amid the shallow waters and shoals of the Bahamas and the Carolina coast. Their principal disadvantage was the lack of hold space that limited both cruising range and storage for plunder. Typically, schooners displaced up to 100 tons and could carry around 75 men and eight small guns.

A model of a two-masted brigantine, showing the shallow draft of this type of sloop that made it an ideal craft for working the shoals off the American coast. Brigantines were able to slip into river estuaries and hide from more powerful warships.

Brigantines were in common use for coastal trading in American waters, and their two masts allowed these vessels to take advantage of different wind conditions. The foremasts carried square-rigged sails, while their mainmasts used a fore-and-aft-rigged mainsail and a square-rigged topsail. Brigantines measured up to 80 feet long, weighed up to 150 tons, and could carry a hundred men and 12 small guns. A variation of the classic brigantine was the *snow*, which had a gaff-rigged sail at the back of the mainmast set on its own spar, or trysail.

Pirate ships of the East

Popular fiction and films promote the notion of the Caribbean and the Spanish Main as the key centers of "real" piracy, but on the other side of the world the South China Sea was every bit as dangerous to the unwary merchantman. Since the earliest days of sailing, the junk has been the universal maritime vessel of the Far East, and by the time Europeans arrived in the region in the late 16th century it had developed into a clearly defined ship type. The name "junk" was first applied by the Portuguese, who named it *junco*, a word they had learned from their subject Indonesian natives, who called the vessels the *djong*.

According to legend, the Chinese were taught how to build a junk by the legendary emperor Fu Hsi, the child of a sea nymph. China's extensive river network encouraged an early flourishing of shipbuilding, including the construction of vessels far larger than their European counterparts. The Chinese even invented the first paddle wheel ship in about AD 500, and evidence points to ships powered by as many as 32 paddles in use by the 12th century. However, while ideal on wide rivers and estuaries, they would have been of doubtful use at sea, but junk captains certainly enjoyed other valuable inventions long before European sailors.

From an early understanding of the principles of magnetism, the world's first primitive compasses seem to have been in use by the Qin dynasty (221-207 BC). They took the form of a piece of lodestone shaped like a ladle balanced on a round or square bronze plate marked with the cardinal points. Proper north–south orienting pointers of an iron ore called magnetite were in use by the third century AD. The first person to use the compass extensively was Chinese explorer Zheng-He, who made seven ocean voyages in AD 1405–33, including visits to India, the east African coast, possibly Egypt and certainly the Red Sea and the Persian Gulf, as well as Malaysia and Indonesia. In the process he introduced China to its greatest period of maritime trade.

An ancient Chinese "ladle" compass.

Sometimes called the "Chinese Columbus," Zheng-He made seven voyages of exploration some 60 years before Columbus set sail across the Atlantic Ocean. The giant junks of Zheng-He's fleet would have dwarfed the European explorer's ship, *Santa Maria* (85 feet), as seen in this comparison. The Chinese junk is over 400 feet in length.

Small coastal junks, like this one of the early 18th century, carried a single mast and sail. The vessel was home to the trader's entire family, who acted as crew and stevedores when in port. As soon as they left the safety of an anchorage, trading junks were at the mercy of pirates. The only way to continue operating was to pay protection money to the local pirate chief.

Junks were steered using a sternpost rudder by 1000 AD, well before they came into use on European ships, as did the use of multiple masts. Earlier still, in about the first century AD, the chain pump was invented to raise river water to high paddy fields, and also gave sailors an effective means of pumping out a ship's bilges. Not least, as far as pirates were concerned, the use of gunpowder gave Chinese junks a powerful medium-range weapons capability, as well as a means of launching distress flares.

In the late 13th century, the Venetian merchant Marco Polo was impressed by the junk, which he saw as superior to anything in his native Venice. He recorded that "they have a single deck, and under this the space is divided into small compartments, more or less according to the size of the vessel, some furnished as a small living quarters for a merchant. They are fitted with only one rudder. They have four masts with as many sails, and some have a further two which can be raised and lowered when necessary." He also noted with wonder that Chinese shipwrights had already invented the watertight compartments that were supposed to make *Titanic* unsinkable: "In addition to the cabins already spoken of, some vessels of the larger sort have their hulls fitted with thirteen partitions which are made of thick planks joined together. The purpose of these is to protect the vessel if she springs a leak by running against a rock."

The junks used by the pirates of the South China Seas in the 17th to 19th centuries were similar to the vessels described by Marco Polo, although usually fitted with only two or three masts. Modern Chinese junks are similar, but adapted for marine engines. This makes the junk the longest-serving vessel type in human history. After Marco Polo, many European travelers reported sighting flotillas of hundreds of heavily armed warships and thousands of trading ships; all junks. Other variations on the basic junk design were reported by Europeans elsewhere in Asia; the *twaqo* of Malaysia and the *rua chalom* of Siam and Burma, plus the junks found in Japanese waters. These were mostly small local craft, but it was the Chinese junk that amazed the European traders of the 17th century. They were also alarmed at the way it was adapted for use as a pirate vessel.

Most pirate junks were converted from captured trading junks. They were armed with both large guns and a type of swivel gun known as a *lantaka*, but like most pirates, their masters aimed to capture a prize without resorting to damaging gunfire. Some of the largest pirate junks were over 100 feet long, with a beam of 20 feet, although most vessels were smaller, typically with an average length of around

Reconstruction showing an armed junk of the early 19th century. Despite the presence of Portuguese and British naval patrols in the Pearl river off Macao and Hong Kong, merchants in the mid-18th century were subjected to such a degree of lawless plundering that peaceful trading junks had to sail heavily armed, so much so that there was frequently nothing but the cargo to distinguish a trading junk from a pirate.

45 feet. At least in 1807 and probably earlier, Chinese pirate junks were run almost as family ventures. The master and some of his crew housed their families onboard, and while the captain occupied a stern cabin, the crew lived in the main hold. Seagoing pirate junks had substantial cargo space, part of which was taken up with a gunpowder magazine and weapons store.

Although Europeans in the 19th century described junks as "craft of primitive appearance," experienced sailors knew that their sail plan was responsive and well suited to the waters of the South China Sea. Junks were invariably seaworthy and, if handled properly, could be frighteningly fast. Pirate crews varied in number from a few dozen on small craft to almost 200 men for larger junks. The large, well-armed crew of a pirate junk was more than a match for the sparsely manned trading junks and later European lightly armed merchantmen they attacked, and they often also outnumbered the crews of imperial warships.

In the 17th century, the later Ming dynasty suddenly closed China's ports, and banned foreign trade and Chinese seagoing missions. This isolationism is attributable to several influences, but principally two: a move of the imperial capital from the seaboard city of Nanjing to Beijing, and a strong revival of Confucian thinking on imperial policy. Nanjing had been the center of maritime trade and naturally encouraged on open, outward-looking government, whereas the Beijing administration lost interest in shipping and foreign trade. Confucian thinking promoted the concept that China had achieved a state of social perfection, thus needed no potentially dangerous outside culture or influence.

The policy was extended to the once-powerful Chinese navy, which lost prestige. And it had a profound effect not only on Chinese trade but also on piracy in the region. The Ming emphasis was placed on using the greatly expanded Grand Canal for internal shipping, protected by the army. In consequence, with a severely depleted and demoralized navy, China's coasts came under attack from Japanese *wako* pirates (*see pages 205–06*).

Free to raid in earnest and, like their European counterparts, often with the blessing of local Japanese rulers, whole swathes of the Chinese coastline were subjected to pirate attacks. The area to the north of Nanjing was even occupied by pirates on a permanent basis. The *wako* pirates were often in cahoots with Portuguese armed traders who, deprived of the formerly lucrative trade with China, happily turned to piracy to fill their holds with those oriental luxuries that had become so popular back home.

Pirate junks under attack from the East India Company paddle-powered warship *Nemesis* in the Pearl estuary, near Hong Kong in 1841. Company officials called them "pirates" but to the Chinese suffering from British imperialism during the Opium Wars, the junk captains were freedom fighters and heroes.

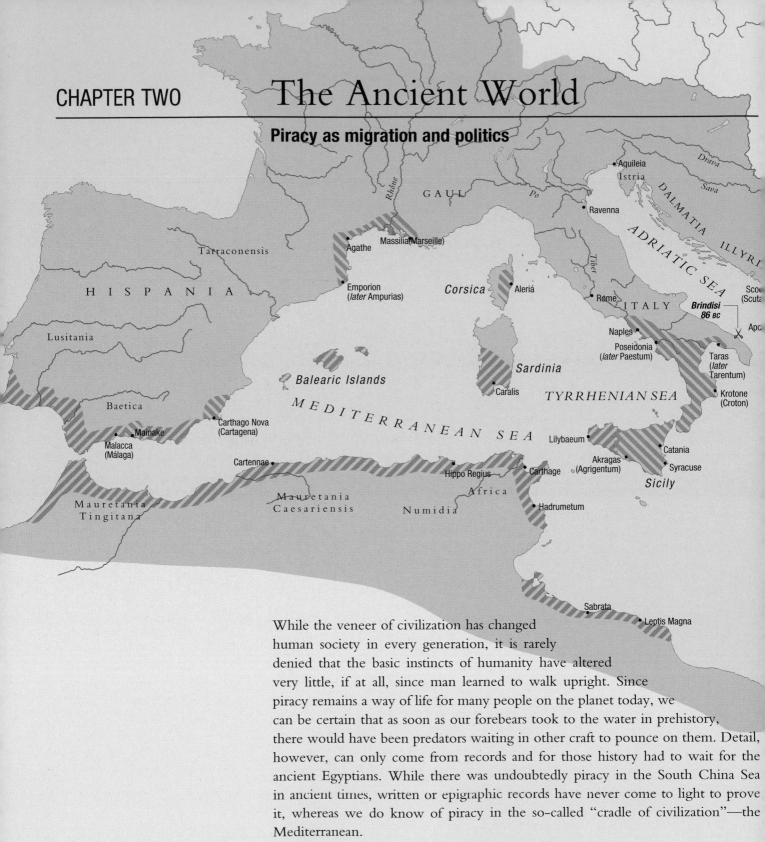

CHAPTER TWO

The Ancient World

Piracy as migration and politics

Aquileia
Istria
Drava
Sava
GAUL
Po
Rhône
DALMATIA ILLYRI
Ravenna
ADRIATIC SEA
Tarraconensis
Agathe
Massilia(Marseille)
Scoc
(Scuta
HISPANIA
Emporion
(*later* Ampurias)
Corsica
Aleriá
Rome
ITALY
Brindisi
86 BC
Apc
Lusitania
Naples
Poseidonia
(*later* Paestum)
Taras
(*later*
Tarentum)
Balearic Islands
Sardinia
Krotone
(Croton)
Caralis
TYRRHENIAN SEA
Baetica
Carthago Nova
(Cartagena)
M E D I T E R R A N E A N   S E A
Lilybaeum
Mainake
Catania
Malacca
(Málaga)
Cartennae
Akragas
(Agrigentum)
Syracuse
Hippo Regius
Carthage
Sicily
Mauretania
Tingitana
Mauretania
Caesariensis
Numidia
Africa
Hadrumetum
Tiber
Sabrata
Leptis Magna

While the veneer of civilization has changed
human society in every generation, it is rarely
denied that the basic instincts of humanity have altered
very little, if at all, since man learned to walk upright. Since
piracy remains a way of life for many people on the planet today, we
can be certain that as soon as our forebears took to the water in prehistory,
there would have been predators waiting in other craft to pounce on them. Detail,
however, can only come from records and for those history had to wait for the
ancient Egyptians. While there was undoubtedly piracy in the South China Sea
in ancient times, written or epigraphic records have never come to light to prove
it, whereas we do know of piracy in the so-called "cradle of civilization"—the
Mediterranean.

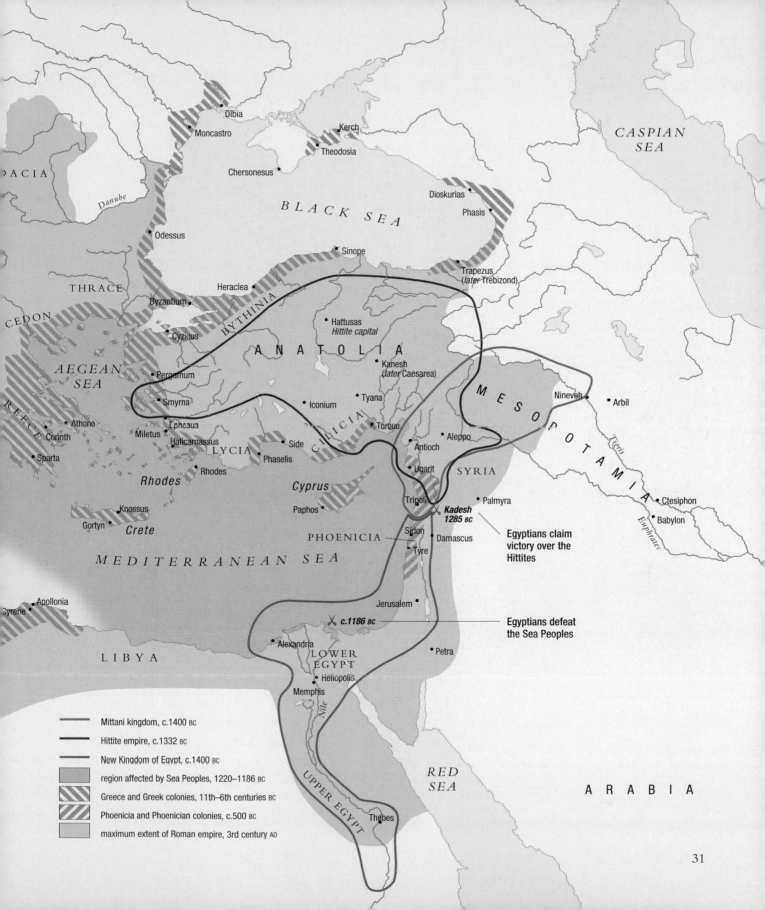

CASPIAN
SEA

Olbia
Moncastro

Kerch
Theodosia

Chersonesus

DACIA

Danube

BLACK SEA

Dioskurias
Phasis

Odessus

Sinope

Trapezus
(*later* Trebizond)

THRACE

Heraclea

BYTHINIA

Hattusas
Hittite capital

CEDON

Byzantium

Cyzicus

ANATOLIA

MESOPOTAMIA

Nineveh

Arbil

AEGEAN
SEA

Pergamum

Kanesh
(*later* Caesarea)

Smyrna

Tyana

Iconium

Ephesus

CILICIA

Tarsus

Aleppo

Athono

Miletus

Halicarnassus

LYCIA

Side

Antioch

Tigris

Corinth

Phaselis

Ugarit

SYRIA

Sparta

Rhodes

Rhodes

Cyprus

Tripoli

Palmyra

Ctesiphon

Knossus

Paphos

Kadesh
1285 BC

Euphrates

Babylon

Gortyn

Crete

PHOENICIA

Sidon

Damascus

Egyptians claim
victory over the
Hittites

MEDITERRANEAN SEA

Tyre

Apollonia

Jerusalem

Cyrene

c.1186 BC

Egyptians defeat
the Sea Peoples

LIBYA

Alexandria

LOWER
EGYPT

Petra

Heliopolis

Memphis

Nile

RED
SEA

ARABIA

UPPER
EGYPT

Thebes

31

It was in the great inner sea—*mare internum*, as the later ancient Romans sometimes referred to it—that the world's first expansion of maritime trade began, and as merchants ventured further afield, sea raiders began to prey on their ships and cargoes. For the next two millennia, as cultures and empires rose and fell, so too did the threat of piracy. In periods when the Egyptians, Greeks, Carthaginians, and Romans were unable to maintain a strong naval presence, pirate communities spread along the Mediterranean's rocky shores and among its numerous islets. Only after the Roman commonwealth claimed the whole of *mare nostrum* ("Our Sea," as late Republican Romans knew the Mediterranean) was piracy was eradicated from the ancient Western world.

The first people identified as pirates who emerged from the pages of history did so before the pyramids were built. They are the Lukka, and records of Ugarit, the Hittites, and Egyptians mention them, although mostly only as part of a list of peoples. Sea raiders based on the coast of Lycia in Asia Minor (modern Turkey), their attacks date from as early as the 14th century BC. In the 13th century the Lukka were briefly allies of their natural enemies the Hittites against Egypt; a poem about the battle of Kadesh during the reign of Ramesses II (c.1279–12) records their presence. An inscription at Thebes of the pharaoh Merneptah (c.1212–02) boasts of his prowess in battle against would-be invaders of Egyptian territory, which include the Lukka. Although these first pirates are not mentioned after the 11th century BC, they clearly demonstrate that piracy was not an invention of the past half-millennium.

The decline of the Lukkan raiders in the 12th century and their subsequent disappearance from history has been explained by their assimilation into the group of maritime nomads known as the Sea Peoples. The appearance of these sea raiders (who are often identified with the Dorians who invaded Greece at this time) brought the Bronze Age cultures of the eastern Mediterranean basin to their knees, and helped usher in a Dark Age of ancient civilization. A concomitant dwindling of maritime trade would surely have resulted in a similar decline in piracy, and while there is historical evidence to support this assumption, pirates can still be traced to bases in Greece, Crete, and even western parts of the Mediterranean throughout the Dark Age. Phoenician and Greek merchants of this period reported pirate attacks, and

Reconstruction of an Egyptian seagoing vessel, based on wall reliefs of the funerary temple of Queen Hatshepsut (c.1498–83 BC) at Deir el-Bahari, on the west bank of the Nile at Thebes (Luxor). These images describe a trading expedition the queen sent to the fabled Land of Punt. Its location is unknown, but believed to be somewhere on the East African coast.

there is even archeological evidence in the form of a wrecked Greek trading ship, its side pierced by arrows.

On the eastern side of the "Fertile Crescent" of Mesopotamia, pirate activity was also recorded in the Persian Gulf, where raiders threatened the flow of maritime trade between India and even as far afield as China. The seventh-century BC Assyrian kings sent expeditions to combat the pirates and restore trade routes.

The mysterious Sea Peoples

As has been stated, some of the earliest reports of piracy can be found at Thebes (modern Luxor) in Egypt. It might be thought surprising that piracy should be recorded at a site hundreds of miles from the sea, but Thebes was the capital of the kingdom of Upper and Lower Egypt, and it was here on the walls of the great temples that the pharaohs posted their victorious claims.

Sea Peoples (*Hau-nebu* in Egyptian) was a collective name given by Egyptian chroniclers to those who invaded the kingdom of Egypt in the late 13th and early 12th centuries BC. It referred to migrating tribes whose various origins remain a mystery but who appeared in the eastern Mediterranean at this time. The Egyptian inscriptions mention six tribes: the Shardana, Denyen, Peleset, Shekelesh, Weshesh, and Tjeker people (but note, not the Lukka, who were clearly seen as a separate entity). The main source of Egyptian information comes from inscriptions in the temple of Karnak (by Merneptah) on the Nile's east bank and on the west bank at Medinet Habu, the funerary temple of Ramesses III. Both mention a link between the Sea Peoples and

Detail of the great sea battle fought by the Sea Peoples and the Egyptian navy of Ramesses III, as rendered on the walls of the pharaoh's funerary temple at Medinet Habu, west bank of the Nile at Luxor. Color has been added to make the figures clearer.

the known Egyptian enemies in Libya and Palestine, indicating a possible alliance formed with the migrating tribes that threatened to destroy Egypt, although Ramesses III claimed that his swift military action prevented such a catastrophe.

Several cataclysmic events in the late Bronze Age Mediterranean world have been credited to the Sea Peoples' mass migration, including the end of Mycenaean Greek civilization, the collapse of the Mitanni kingdom, and the destruction of the Hittite empire in Asia Minor. Several historians suggest that the Tursha and Lycian (Lukka) peoples of Asia Minor formed part of this group, but avoided contact with the Egyptians. The Shardana, Shekelesh, and Peleset tribes possibly originated on the northeast Adriatic coast, although the Shardana have also been linked to Sardinia. The confusion is understandable, since the Karnak inscription says that the Libyans hired mercenaries from what is today Turkey, Sardinia, Sicily, Italy, and Greece—the northern rim of the Egyptians' known world.

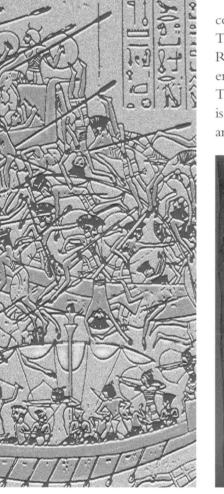

The Medinet Habu inscriptions record a tumultuous sea battle when the confederation of Sea Peoples attempted an invasion after crossing the sea from Palestine. The battle, fought off the Nile delta, has been dated to 1186 BC and the navy of Ramesses III was victorious. These carvings—the earliest known depiction of a naval engagement in the world—provide information about how the battle was fought. The Sea Peoples are shown in smaller boats than their Egyptian foes (although this is probably artistic convention rather than accurate recording). They appear to lack armor and bows, both vital tools in Bronze Age warfare. Unless this was a deliberate Egyptian attempt to make them seem primitive, the depiction supports the idea that they were acting as raiders, intent on easy spoils and quick gains rather than full-scale war.

Given that the inscription is propaganda, the battle is shown as somewhat one-sided, but other evidence suggests that the Sea Peoples were not as vulnerable as they were depicted. Carvings at other Egyptian sites show Sherden (Shardana) warriors wearing armor and helmets and carrying swords and shields. Libya and Egypt were happy to hire them as mercenaries, suggesting that the Sea Peoples were equipped as well as any. Similarly, accounts elsewhere in the eastern Mediterranean describe the Sea Peoples as great warriors and seamen, well armed with long swords and helmets. There is also evidence that they were feared raiders who preyed on shipping and coastal towns, and defeated all the forces sent against them, apart from the Egyptians.

Right: Egyptian bas-relief showing a warrior of the Sea Peoples, c.1200–1100 BC.

Historians argue about Ramesses III's great victory; some contend that the Medinet Habu inscriptions are greatly exaggerated, little more than a poor copy of the earlier ones at Karnak dedicated to Merneptah. But whether Ramesses fought a mere skirmish or a massive battle that comprehensively defeated his enemies, the date marks the end of the Sea People's piratical attacks and their dominance of the eastern Mediterranean basin.

Subsequently, there is evidence that most of the Sea Peoples settled in Palestine, where the Peleset tribe have been credited as the ancestors of the Philistines. While many of these tribes turned to farming rather than raiding, the Tjeker in particular continued to engage in maritime trade throughout the region, but also engaged in piracy. Tjeker settlements located around Dor, in modern Israel, form the earliest recorded pirate havens. However, coastal trade had replaced piracy in the Tjeker economy by the tenth century, and this maritime people were probably the ancestors of the great Mediterranean traders and settlers, the Phoenicians. In their turn, the Phoenicians would colonize whole areas of the western Mediterranean from their mother cities of Tyre and Sidon, the most famous of them being Carthage.

Greek pirates—with and without authority

As Egypt contended with the Sea Peoples, piracy became commonplace in the rest of the eastern Mediterranean. Certain places made natural pirate havens, which were used as bases from which to attack shipping. One of the most successful was the large island of Crete, ideally located astride the ancient world's busiest shipping lanes. In the tenth century BC, the ancient Minoan civilization of Crete was overrun by the Dorians, who had migrated south into Greece on the collapse of the Mycenaean kingdoms. Using Cretan cities as bases, the Dorians engaged in piratical raids on any passing vessels.

Fishermen form a decorative element on a Classical period Greek vase. It might be thought that pirates concentrated their attacks on mercantile shipping, but fishing boats were more commonly plundered than vessels carrying treasure.

The island's reputation was such that in the *Odyssey* Homer describes all Cretans as pirates. Crete's cities were renowned as slave markets and clearing houses for all kinds of contraband. The good times for Cretan pirates lasted for almost 800 years until the reign of lawlessness was brought to an end in the second century BC, when Rhodean anti-pirate patrols cleared the waters of the eastern Mediterranean. Crete's turn would come again in the eighth century AD, as a base for Arab pirates.

After emerging from its Dark Age, Greek culture began to make rapid progress towards true civilization through the growth of politically motivated city-states. Increasing urban organization from the fifth century onward created the need for powerful navies—particularly in the light of the simultaneous rise of a great Persian empire across the Aegean Sea. For the first time since the days of the Egyptian

Hoplites (Greek soldiers) onboard biremes of two different Greek city-states prepare to fight a boarding action.

New Kingdom, piracy could be countered by punitive naval expeditions. The effects of pirate attacks and the attempts to counter piracy by the city-states make frequent appearances in the work of Classical Greek authors such as Herodotus and Thucydides.

However, during the emergent Classical period the roles of pirates and navies were often interchangeable, and a number of the Greek city-states either actively encouraged piracy or used their navies in what were nothing less than pirate raids on neighboring cities. Pirates from Lemnos even raided Athens itself, and an Athenian naval expedition was sent to crush the pirates and occupy the island in the early sixth century BC. Other islands, including Kithnos, Mikonos, and the Sporades, were attacked by the Athenian navy during the fifth century, although these states considered the Athenians as little more than pirate raiders.

The Aetolian League of city-states was formed during the fourth century BC and soon came to dominate the politics of central Greece. Piracy was encouraged as a means of extending the league's power against rival Greek and Persian states. In the following century the situation became so extreme that Aetolian pirates dominated the Aegean, extorting protection payments as tribute from coastal settlements. Their end only came when Rome conquered the Aetolian League in 192 BC. Dispossessed of bases and income, the pirates were forced to look elsewhere for sanctuary and found it across the Mediterranean in Cilicia, from where they would become a headache for their conquerors.

A detail from a Roman floor mosaic shows Odysseus lashed to the mast of his ship so the Sirens' bewitching singing cannot tempt him to leap overboard and swim to his death at their rapacious hands. The other crewmen had their ears stopped to prevent them from hearing the Sirens' voices. The image depicts a late bireme.

A profusion of pirate bases

While the Aetolian League exerted its baleful control over central Greece, further north along the mountainous Adriatic coast piracy formed the main source of income for inhabitants of neighboring Dalmatia and Illyria. A glance at the map overleaf shows that the eastern Adriatic coast is an ideal pirate haven, with its numerous islands and fjord-like inlets. From their well-hidden but also well-protected bases, the pirates raided up and down the Adriatic and into the central Mediterranean, with their activities reaching a peak in the third century BC. With Roman trade on the increase, forward pirate bases were also established on the islands of Corfu, Santa Maura, and Cephalonia, which were ideally located to prey on shipping. The

Romans eventually countered the threat by sending an army into Illyria, defeating the pirates—which effectively meant almost all the inhabitants—and establishing a client government. However, many pirates simply moved north, occupying Dalmatia and the Istrian peninsula, and renewed their attacks on Roman shipping. A revival of piracy in Illyria led to the Roman annexation of the region in 168 BC.

The flatter terrain that lies between Dalmatia and Istria was a valuable cereal-growing area, and attacks from Istrian pirates on Roman grain convoys led to two punitive expeditions and the eventual annexation of the region. Dalmatia was occupied in 180 BC, but its broken coast made pirate bases difficult to locate and attack, and several groups of pirates continued to operate from them until the region was fully conquered by Rome in AD 9.

Greek settlers who formed colonies in the western Mediterranean, particularly in the south of Italy, on Sicily and Sardinia, and along the coasts of southern France and Spain, frequently engaged in piratical activities until the Romans crushed them. The Greeks were in frequent conflict with the Etruscans who attacked Greek shipping during the sixth and fifth centuries BC, although their actions might be considered national policy rather

Aquileia

ISTRIA

DALMATIA

Ravenna

ILLYRIA

ADRIATIC
SEA

Center of Illyrian pirate
empire, reduced by Rome
in 228 and again in 218

Scodra
(Scutari)

Rome

THRACE

ITALY

Dyrrachium
(Scutari)

Pella

Bari

MACEDON

Naples

Apollonia

Brundisium
(Brindisi)

Roman
Illyria

AEGEAN
SEA

EPIRUS

TYRRHENIAN
SEA

AETOLIAN
LEAGUE

IONIAN SEA

Thermon   Delphi

Major pirate havens

Conquered by
Rome, 192 BC;
pirates migrate
to Cilicia

Patrai

Athens

Lipari Islands

Corinth

Olympia

SICILY

Sparta

Syracuse

The central Mediterranean, c.200 BC

Sea of
Crete

MEDITERRANEAN SEA

	kingdom of Macedon
	Aetolian League
	Achaean League
	Roman confederacy

CRETE

than piracy, since the Etruscans wanted to exclude Greek merchants from interfering with their trade monopoly. Indeed, the Greek name for the Etruscans was *Tyrrhenos*, meaning pirates, now enshrined in memory as the name of the sea bordering the western Italian coast.

True pirate bases were located in the Lípari Islands off the northern coast of Sicily, in the Balearic Islands, and on the Ligurian coast of Provence. These survived until the Carthaginians under Hannibal first conquered them, followed by the Romans, who ended organized piracy in the western Mediterranean.

The Cilicians

The Aetolian pirates who had been thrown out of Greece by the Romans had largely migrated to Cilicia, where they no doubt intermarried with the uncivilized natives of that wild, rugged territory. In a very short time, Cilicia became the most celebrated pirate haven of the ancient world, and the Cilicians formed one of the largest pirate bands in history. Located along the southern shore of Asia Minor, in what is now Turkey, and bordered to the north by the Taurus Mountains, Cilicia was mountainous and inhospitable. With no land for growing crops or herding animals—beyond a few goats—Cilicians fished for sustenance and plundered shipping for wealth. Their depredations during the later second and much of the first century BC were so severe that at times maritime trade in the eastern Mediterranean was brought to a complete standstill. Close to the main sea route from Syria to Italy and Greece, and close to the sea lanes of Egypt and Palestine, Cilicia was ideally located for the purposes of piracy. Additionally, of a similar nature to Illyria, numerous rocky inlets, promontories, and hidden anchorages made up its broken coastline.

While the Greek city-states had maintained active naval patrols, Cilicia's pirate operations were controlled and kept to an acceptable level. Alexander the Great (356–23) had done a great deal to suppress them during his conquest of the Persian empire, but the decline in the second century BC of his Macedonian "successor states" to the east coincided with the Punic Wars between Carthage and Rome to the west. As the Hellenistic Seleucid states of Syria and Asia Minor became incapable of maintaining naval patrols along the Cilician coast because of internal warfare, the pirates took full advantage of the naval void in the eastern Mediterranean. Their raiding soon grew into a full-scale industry.

The Romans' victory over the Seleucid empire in 190 BC should have caused alarm among the pirates. Under the terms of the treaty of Apamea, signed two years later, western Asia Minor became a Roman protectorate under the force of Roman arms. However, when the battered Seleucid navy was withdrawn, no Roman fleet was sent to take its place. Seleucid power in Asia Minor was replaced by that of Pontus, its king preferred to ally with the Cilician pirates rather than with Rome. As

Roman merchant vessels made attractive prey to the Cilician pirates, their holds packed with *amphorae* containing valuable commodities. Out at sea, these sailing ships could usually outrun a pirate vessel, but closer to the fretted shores of the eastern Mediterranean, the Adriatic, and around the Peloponnese, they became vulnerable to the fast-rowed galleys of the pirates.

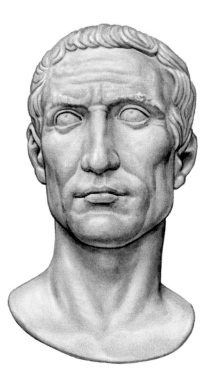

When patrician Romans like the young Julius Caesar became victims of Cilician pirate activity, it was time for the senate to take action and bring the villains to book.

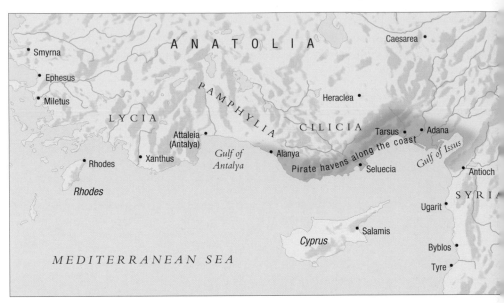

a result, the pirate communities prospered and thousands more flocked to join them.

At first, Rome largely ignored the Cilician attacks, which were restricted to the shores of the eastern Mediterranean. Besides, the rapidly expanding Roman commonwealth desperately needed slaves and Cilician attacks on coastal villages and local shipping fueled the slave markets of Crete and the Aegean. Ironically, the safest pirate havens were Miletus, Ephesus, and Smyrna, all located in the Roman protectorate. As long as a ready supply of skilled slaves was guaranteed, the Roman provincial governors were prepared to turn a blind eye. But this state of affairs could

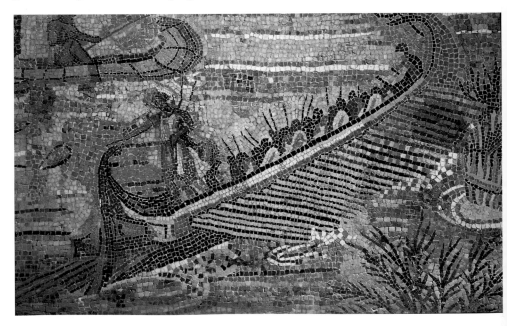

The Cilician pirates used much the same vessels as the Roman navy—indeed, some were appropriated navy ships captured in battle. A bireme features in a Roman mosaic pavement in the Casa dei Vetti, Pompeii.

not last long. By the end of the second century the pirates' depredations were seriously damaging Roman mercantile trade. While the Roman aristocracy cared little for the plight of petty merchants, it was different when the financial concerns of patricians and senators came under threat. The senate passed its first anti-piracy law in 101 BC, which closed the harbors of Rome's Asia protectorate to the pirates. However, this only pushed the Cilicians out into a wider sphere, and they soon began to attack shipping in the western Mediterranean, even plundering off the Italian coast. By this stage, the Cilician pirates virtually represented a state of their own and were happy to earn extra wealth through hiring their service out as naval mercenaries.

In 89 BC King Mithridates of Pontus invaded Roman Asia. While the Pontic army took care of matters on land, Mithridates made an alliance with the Cilicians to give him a navy. This allowed him to besiege the island of Rhodes and transport supplies to support his troops, who had invaded northern Greece. After the defeat of a large Roman naval squadron off Brundisium (Brindisi) in 86, Mithridates even threatened Roman control of the western Mediterranean with his large and well-organized pirate fleets. However, the Roman power of arms reigned supreme on land, and the Pontic army fell before the legions of Cornelius Sulla in the same year.

The peace treaty of 85 restored Asia and Greece to Rome, but few attempts were made to halt the continued piracy of the Cilicians, whose attacks grew in audacity. Even Roman patricians became victims of capture, none more famous than Julius Caesar, although at the time his star had yet to rise. Famously, Caesar joked with his captors that once his ransom was delivered, he would return and wipe them out to the last man. The pirates thought his boasts were very amusing… but he kept his promise. However, if Caesar's celebrity was yet to flower, that of his future triumvir Pompey was well established.

But for the success on land of Sulla, **above**, King Mithridates of Pontus might have brought Rome to her knees through the victories of his hired Cilician pirate navy.

The Mediterranean broom

Gnaeus Pompeius Magnus (Pompey the Great) was considered—not least by himself —to be the finest Roman military commander of his time. In 67 BC he was granted an *imperium* to enforce the *lex Gabinia de piratis persequendis*, a new anti-piracy law. His status demanded substance, and Pompey received it. The senate voted him 6000 talents of gold (a vast fortune), 500 vessels and their crews, 120,000 Roman troops, and the right to tax and raise militia in cities up to 50 miles from any coast. Such power, amounting as it did to a virtual dictatorship, was far from popular, but that his *imperium* was finally granted illustrates how seriously Rome took the pirate threat.

Pompey split his command into 13 divisions, each patrolling its own region. The large military force was land-based or transported by sea, although plenty of marines also formed ships' crews. Each division's legate sought out pirate bases and blockaded them. Army units were then sent in to kill or capture the pirates, seize their ships, and destroy their bases. Reserve units of the main fleet were deployed to prevent any escaping Cilician ships from linking up with other pirate groups. The main concentration of Pompey's campaign was targeted at the Cilician coast, and in several hard-fought battles the pirates were usually outmatched.

As Rome's grip tightened, the pirates of several threatened strongholds made to break out through the blockade, but found themselves confronted by the squadrons Pompey had held in reserve and, repulsed in the ensuing battle, the pirates retreated to the remote fortress of Coracesium, sited on a peninsula of Cilicia. There, it was a simple matter for Pompey to invest Coracesium's land walls and deny the pirates use of the harbor. After a short siege, Coracesium surrendered. Many of the captives were pardoned on payment of a fine or in exchange for information leading to the arrest of any captains or land-based ringleaders; some were executed, others relocated to farmlands. The entire anti-pirate campaign had taken only three months. It resulted in the Mediterranean being cleared of pirates for the first time in human history. Pompey claimed that he had destroyed more than 120 bases and hundreds of pirate vessels, and slain over 10,000 pirates in the course of battles. At home he was a hero, and the senate could claim success in the vast amount of pirate booty that had been taken. However, his detractors claimed that Pompey had exaggerated the scale of the Cilician threat in order to look good; perhaps they were correct.

His popularity with the mob made Pompey a natural rival to Julius Caesar, especially after the latter's extraordinary success in conquering all of Gaul for the empire. Pompey's opposition to Caesar's political ambitions eventually led to civil war after Caesar crossed the Rubicon and wrested control of Rome from the senate. Pompey fled to Greece and raised an army, only to be defeated by Caesar at Pharsalus in 48 BC. The great man was assassinated later that year when attempting to land on the Egyptian coast. It remains one of history's ironies that the pirate hunter's son Sextus should become the Roman Republic's last serious pirate. After Julius Caesar's assassination in 44 BC, his adopted son Octavian (later Augustus, Rome's first emperor) was confronted head-on by Sextus Pompeius, whose avenging republican army had seized a fleet of warships, taken Sicily, and turned to a life of piracy from the large island's safety. It took Octavian's closest advisor and friend, Agrippa, to turn admiral and destroy the Sicilian pirates.

Gnaeus Pompeius Magnus (Pompey the Great) masterminded the Roman campaign to eradicate Cilician pirates from the Mediterranean. After Pompey's fall and eventual death, his sons Gaius and Sextus led the republican rebels against the Caesarians in Spain. Gaius was killed in battle, but Sextus (**his coin below**) escaped to Sicily, where he set up a rival state to Caesar's successor, Octavian. His actions were nothing less than those of a pirate.

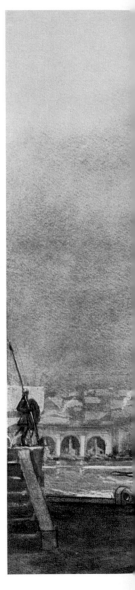

A Roman quinquereme leaves port, its heavily armored beak designed to ram enemy ships. Although Pompey's flagship would have been this type of vessel, most of his naval force consisted of far smaller craft, mainly biremes and *liburnians*. Each carried a complement of highly trained Roman legionaries, ready to board pirate ships using the *corvus*, seen here at the stern (*see also page 14*).

By the foundation of the Roman empire in about 27 BC under Augustus, the Mediterranean was a Roman sea, and shipping was immune from pirate attack for four centuries. The collapse of the Western Roman empire in the early fifth century AD plunged that part of the Mediterranean into anarchy, and again piracy spread rapidly. While the eastern portion of the Roman realm developed into the Byzantine empire, further to the east Arabic expansion threatened the stability of the eastern Mediterranean. The Byzantines placed a strong emphasis on the maintenance of a powerful navy, and while the region never reverted to the secure existence it had enjoyed during the Roman heyday, both pirates and invaders were largely held at bay for another half-millennium.

CHAPTER THREE

Into the Middle Ages

From barbarians to privateers

Almost exactly 70 years before the date widely accepted as the fall of the Western Roman empire (AD 476), a coalition of Germanic tribes crossed the frozen Rhine in the bitter winter of 406/7 and rapidly overran Gaul and Spain, effectively ending Roman administration in the region. In many respects the invading barbarians wanted the benefits of Roman culture and came to absorb, not to destroy. However, in the nature of things, much of Roman Classical civilization did collapse. Among the barbarian tribes, the Vandals were prolific in their migrations, quickly establishing a Spanish kingdom before moving on to Africa. Within only a few years, the Vandals had ejected Romans from the valuable provinces of North Africa

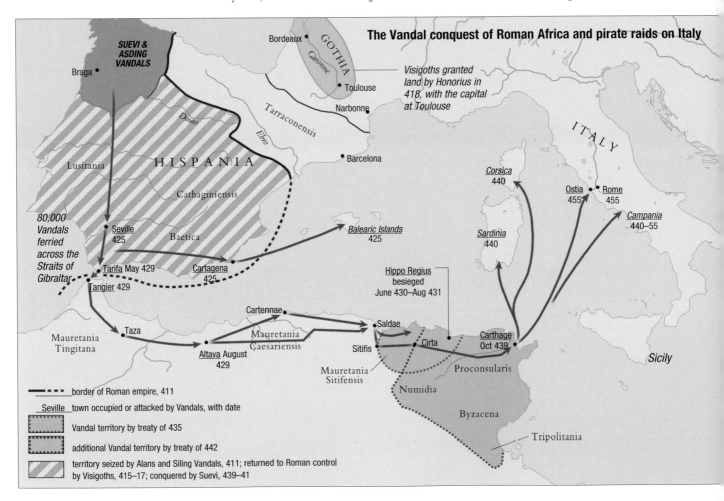

The Vandal conquest of Roman Africa and pirate raids on Italy

SUEVI & ASDING VANDALS

Braga

GOTHIA

Bordeaux

Garonne

Toulouse

Visigoths granted land by Honorius in 418, with the capital at Toulouse

Narbonne

Tarraconensis

Barcelona

ITALY

Douro

HISPANIA

Lusitania

Ebro

Corsica 440

Ostia 455   Rome 455

Cathaginiensis

Campania 440–55

80,000 Vandals ferried across the Straits of Gibraltar

Seville 425

Baetica

Balearic Islands 425

Sardinia 440

Tarifa May 429

Cartagena 425

Hippo Regius besieged June 430–Aug 431

Tangier 429

Cartennae

Saldae

Carthage Oct 439

Taza

Mauretania Caesariensis

Sitifis   Cirta

Sicily

Mauretania Tingitana

Altava August 429

Mauretania Sitifensis

Proconsularis

Numidia

Byzacena

Tripolitania

border of Roman empire, 411

Seville   town occupied or attacked by Vandals, with date

Vandal territory by treaty of 435

additional Vandal territory by treaty of 442

territory seized by Alans and Siling Vandals, 411; returned to Roman control by Visigoths, 415–17; conquered by Suevi, 439–41 and founded a barbarian kingdom in what is now modern Tunisia and eastern Algeria, with its capitals at Hippo Regius (Annaba) and Carthage (today a leafy suburb of Tunis).

Fatally weakened, the western Roman army and navy were unable to recapture the lost territories, and soon Italy came under piratical attacks from Vandal ships. It was the raid on the city of Rome itself in 455 that earned the Vandals a reputation for pillage that has since remained in the lexicon to describe wanton destruction. Although they never conquered Italy, the Vandals settled Africa in the region of modern Tunisia until their defeat in 533 at the hands of Belisarius, the great Byzantine general sent by the emperor Justinian.

While the collapse of the Western Roman empire plunged Europe and the western Mediterranean into the period known as the Dark Ages, the Eastern Roman empire—battered and often overrun—nevertheless weathered the initial barbarian storm. For the next thousand years the Byzantine empire, as it came to be known, exerted its influence over the eastern Mediterranean. The Byzantine empire was founded in AD 330 when the Roman emperor Constantine established his new capital on the site of Byzantium. The ancient Greek trading center had always held strategic importance; now it was given political significance as well. Renamed

Constantinople was a city of churches and palaces, the largest of which was the Great Palace, overlooking the confluence of the Sea of Marmara and the Bosporus. The city's massive land and sea walls made it virtually impregnable, but pirates and raiders were easily able to attack the soft underbelly of the empire.

Constantinople after its founder, the city sat at a nexus of vital land and sea trading routes, guarding communications between the Black Sea and the Mediterranean, and acting as the bridge between Europe and Asia across the narrow channel of the Bosporus.

Constantinople's fabled wealth and the astonishing value of mercantile trade arriving or leaving its many harbors were to prove eternally attractive to pirates, whether they came as freelances or acted in the name of Byzantium's numerous enemies—Sassanians, Arabs, Bulgars, Turks, steppes barbarians, and even fellow Christians. At first, this was of small importance, thanks to the powerful Byzantine navy. Warships patrolled the eastern Mediterranean, defending the empire's maritime trade, while her armies tried with mixed success to prevent the spread of Islam.

By the late 12th century the Byzantine empire had shrunk—her power only extended as far as Greece and most of modern Turkey. Although still fabulously wealthy, constant political turmoil had undermined the power of Byzantine military forces. In 1204 neither the navy nor the army were able to prevent the capture and sack of Constantinople by the Christian forces of the Fourth Crusade. One reason for the disaster was the collapse of the Byzantine navy. For years it had relied on recruiting Italian seamen, but conflict with Venice and other Italian states in the late 12th century

In perhaps the most disgraceful act of piracy of the entire crusading era, an unholy alliance of greedy Venetians and grasping Italian-Normans perverted the goal of the Fourth Crusade from attacking Egypt in 1204 to sacking Constantinople. The city's defense was brave and the massive walls kept the Europeans at bay for days, but Constantinople was betrayed and fell for the first time in its history.

led to the widespread arrest of many sailors. Those who were simply flung into the street to look after themselves took to piracy, further weakening the already crippled navy.

Pirate bases sprang up almost overnight in well chosen remote havens, away from the last bastions of Byzantine authority in the region. Crete and many of the smaller Aegean islands were favored, as were remote mainland harbors such as Anaia (now Kusadasi in southwest Turkey) and Monemvasía in southern Greece. The Ionian islands of the southern Adriatic were also home to many pirates, ruled by the Italian knight Margaritone of Brindisi. Although the Venetian navy attacked several of the pirate bases on their way to Constantinople in 1203, the pirates soon returned, and these Italian and Greek renegades used the islands of Corfu, Zante, Ithaca, and Cephalonia as bases until they were annexed by Venice in the late 14th century. The Republic of Venice was hardly above piracy. In fact the greatest act of piracy of the entire medieval period occurred when the Fourth Crusade was hijacked by the Venetians and, instead of attacking Egypt as intended by the pope, turned on Constantinople.

Islamic corsairs based on the North African coast and the islands of Sicily and Crete adversely affected Genoese trade in the Mediterranean and with Byzantium. By 1390 the Genoese ambassadors had persuaded the French and English to launch a joint campaign against the pirates.

For 56 years what was left of the Byzantine state operated from separate enclaves in Epirus and Bithynia in Asia Minor, while a Latin-Christian kingdom occupied the former Byzantine territories in Europe. And then a resurgence of Byzantine spirit resulted in the ascension of a provincial governor as the new emperor in 1259. During the early 1260s Michael III Palaeologus recaptured Constantinople and large tracts of Greece that had been occupied by feudal Italian-Norman overlords. While these petty nobles welcomed pirates to their waters, and saw them as an extra source of income, the Byzantine emperor used them as a political tool. He hired pirate captains to form a reconstituted Byzantine navy, and these corsairs were encouraged to attack Italian shipping in the Aegean. According to the early 14th-century Italian historian Torsello, most of the pirates were themselves Italians, many from

With Constantinople and much of the Byzantine empire in the hands of Norman adventurers, the other monarchs of Europe took advantage by seizing the last shreds of Byzantine control in the Mediterranean. This illumination shows the "saintly" Louis IX of France departing on the Sixth Crusade in 1248.

Genoa and Venice. A Venetian document of 1278 making a compensation claim against Constantinople supports Torsello's claim. In it, among the pirates listed, the names Michele Balbo, Manuel de Marino, and Bartolomeo Foscolo betray their north Italian origins. One pirate in the service of the emperor, Giovanni de lo Cavo, rose to prominence as a naval commander and became overlord of Rhodes in 1278. Not all of the pirates operating in the Aegean were Italian—Bulgarians and Greeks like Bulgarino d'Anaia, George de Malvasia, and George Makrycheris also preyed on shipping.

Of all the pirates who damaged the Byzantine empire, the most famous were the Catalan freebooters under the command of a merciless and grasping adventurer called Roger de Flor—and they came at the invitation of the emperor. The Grand Company of Catalans, formed at the command of Peter III of Aragon, served with distinction in several campaigns, but when the former Mediterranean pirate Roger de Flor became the company's captain, things went downhill fast. He sold their services to Byzantium, and they arrived in Constantinople in 1303. The price was high: four times the standard rate of pay and the emperor's daughter in marriage for Roger. At first, the Catalans did as they were supposed to do, recovering many former Byzantine strongholds in Anatolia from the Turks.

But Roger de Flor showed little concern for ownership, and his freebooters were as happy slaughtering Greeks and their allies the Alans as they were Turks. When a unit of Alan cavalry attacked and killed de Flor near Adrianople, the Catalans began to rampage throughout Thrace. The massacres were as severe as any perpetrated centuries earlier by the Goths and the Huns. By 1310, they had inflicted as much damage in less than a decade than the Turks had done in a century. Eventually, the band moved into Greece, capturing Athens, where they set up their own duchy. From here they eventually amalgamated with Islamic corsairs, pirates with a dual role. While they protected their own Turkish shipping along the coasts of Syria and Egypt, they also attacked vessels of their religious enemies. After the Catalan disaster Byzantium's enemies took advantage of her greater weakness. The northwestern mass of Anatolia fell to the local Turkish tribes of Karasi and Saruhan, whose piratical raids began to devastate first the Aegean islands and then threaten the European side of the Dardanelles.

After the Ottoman Turks annexed the region, they were able to use the Karasi pirate fleet to cross the Dardanelles in 1352 and establish a foothold in Europe. The respite from raiding this gave the Aegean islands allowed the Genoese to grab several for themselves by 1360: Lesbos, Chios, Samos, and Ikaria. From this point on, these were to change hands between the Genoese, Turks, and Byzantium several times until their final conquest by the Muslim Ottomans. Following the collapse of the Byzantine empire and the Ottoman sack of Constantinople in 1453, the stage was set for a religious conflict between Christians and Muslims that would engulf the whole Mediterranean and facilitate the rise of the Barbary corsairs, many of whom would be born on these Aegean islands.

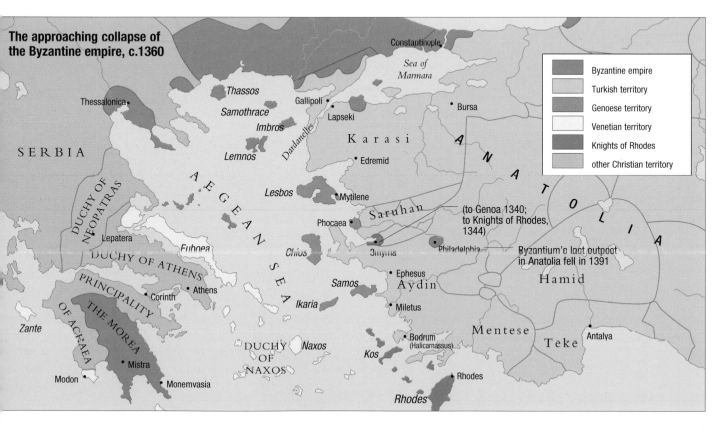

The approaching collapse of the Byzantine empire, c.1360

Legend:
- Byzantine empire
- Turkish territory
- Genoese territory
- Venetian territory
- Knights of Rhodes
- other Christian territory

Constantinople · Sea of Marmara · Thassos · Thessalonica · Gallipoli · Bursa · Samothrace · Lapseki · Imbros · Dardanelles · Karasi · ANATOLIA · SERBIA · Lemnos · Edremid · DUCHY OF NEOPATRAS · Lesbos · Mytilene · AEGEAN SEA · Saruhan · Phocaea · (to Genoa 1340; to Knights of Rhodes, 1344) · Lepatera · Euboea · Chios · Smyrna · Philadelphia · Byzantium's last outpost in Anatolia fell in 1391 · Hamid · DUCHY OF ATHENS · Ephesus · Aydin · PRINCIPALITY OF ACHAEA · THE MOREA · Corinth · Athens · Samos · Ikaria · Miletus · Zante · Mentese · Teke · Antalya · Mistra · DUCHY OF NAXOS · Naxos · Bodrum (Halicarnassus) · Kos · Modon · Monemvasia · Rhodes · Rhodes

Early European pirates

The barbarian invasions of the fifth and sixth centuries that had plunged Europe into the so-called Dark Ages brought maritime commerce to a virtual standstill and any resurgence of trade was ended by the Viking attacks of the late eighth century. For the next 300 years Scandinavian raiders in their fearsome longships dominated the waters of northern Europe, and in their wake came Norse and Danish settlers. During the early medieval period, piracy formed part of everyday life, as Norse raiders and merchant-adventurers reached as far afield as Russia and the Mediterranean. In the 13th century, the rise of new national identities and a greater centralization of authority prompted a tougher stance on piracy. The growing importance of towns and their tax revenues meant that piracy impeded political and national growth. The Angevin kings of England and parts of France, particularly, did their best to suppress it. The first English record of an execution for piracy dates to 1228, when William de Briggeho was convicted of the crime.

However, like their Mediterranean counterparts, the authorities often found it handy to encourage pirates, so long as they harried the enemy. One such menace—perhaps the first with a recognizably eccentric pirate-type name—was Eustace the Monk. He was a Fleming and a renegade cleric who found favor with England's King John (1199–1216). Placed in command of a large fleet of ships, Eustace attacked French shipping from bases in the Channel Islands. Unfortunately, whenever the opportunity arose he also struck at English vessels, and eventually his assaults angered his patron. Eustace was forced to flee to France, where he was promptly hired as a mercenary captain. The pirate monk led a French raiding force against the English coast in 1217, but was intercepted off Dover. In the ensuing battle, the English hurled lime to blind the enemy—a form of early chemical weapon—then captured the French raiders. Eustace the Monk was summarily executed.

Medieval feudalism established a political and economic system that resulted in dynastic wars that plagued Europe at different periods until the 19th century. To its benefit, it also

The clinker-built hulls of the Danes and Norsemen's longships flexed with the sea's movement and made them astonishingly seaworthy for their size. These ships allowed Viking raiders to sail the deepest oceans and—with their shallow draft— penetrate far up rivers to reach their prey.

imposed a degree of peace on the continent and enforced a generally agreed set of commercial principles and laws. Peace encouraged business, towns grew, and maritime trade flourished between the fledgling ports of the Baltic Sea, northern Europe, Spain, and Italy; and almost as a natural consequence, so did piracy. In the Classical age, maritime commerce was generally controlled by private individuals, but during the early medieval period it became increasingly a concern of the aristocracy, often acting in a consortium to spread the risks. For the first time since the Cilicians threatened Rome's patricians, pirates again challenged the power of the elite.

In 1241 the wealthy German cities of Lübeck and Hamburg, which bordered the Baltic Sea, joined forces under the banner of the Hanseatic League, a merchant guild that supervised maritime trade and the suppression of piracy. Other free cities (those not bound to a feudal overlord) joined, until by 1300 this trading fellowship incorporated 19 ports and was virtually an independent state. The Hanse had become a major force and took the lead in combating piracy in northern European waters. Similar, smaller organizations were to follow, such as England's League of the Cinque Ports, established in the early 14th century to protect the English Channel from pirates and to encourage trade from its five principal ports, which included Dover and Hastings. While the Hanseatic League remained true to its ideals, the Cinque Ports degenerated into a

Top: A 14th-century miniature shows a battle between two *cogs*. Archers were an important complement of a medieval ship of war, their arrows softening up the opposition before a boarding action. The addition of fighting castles at the fore and stern ends of a basic 13th-century craft, **center,** converted it into a warship. Within a hundred years, improved ship design produced the Hanseatic cog, **bottom,** a tasty target for pirates of the Baltic Sea and around the Danish shores.

Above: Stoertebeck and 70 accomplices are executed in Hamburg, 1402. A similar fate awaited the later Baltic pirate Henzlein, executed with 32 of his crew in 1573.

quasi-legal piratical outfit that protected its own shipping but attacked that of everybody else.

In the Baltic, several German seamen formed a band known as the Victual Brothers and waged war against the Hanse. They attacked the Norwegian Hanseatic port of Bergen in 1392, threatening the very survival of the league. In 1402 the pirates were trapped by a fleet of Hanse ships from Hamburg, and pirate leader Stoertebeck and his followers were beheaded in Hamburg.

Along with the expansion of urban wealth, the almost continuous warfare in the late 14th and early 15th centuries between England and France, but also involving Spain and Italy—the Hundred Years' War (c.1337–1453)—encouraged the growth of piracy in the waters of the English Channel. As the conflict progressed, the piracy began to take on a more national character. English seamen, such as John Hawley of Dartmouth in Devon and Henry Pay from Poole in Dorset, frequently attacked French and Spanish shipping, inviting reprisal attacks from foreign pirates such as Pero Niño of Castile and Frenchman Charles

de Savoisy. Since the early 13th century there had existed a royal policy known as the "right of reprisal," a permission to ship owners who had suffered losses to raid in return. The policy actively encouraged this form of national raiding, and the system eventually developed into the licenses known as letters of marque that allowed private vessels to plunder enemy ships, and which in its fully formed operation was to cause so much controversy in the 17th to 19th centuries.

Benefitting from improved ship designs, the introduction of shipborne artillery, and their letters of marque bearing the royal signature, privateers roamed the waters of the English Channel and the Bay of Biscay, sailing further from their home ports than ever before. They were the men who would develop into the Sea Rovers of the 16th century, combining warfare in the name of religion and the national interest with a ruthless quest for plunder.

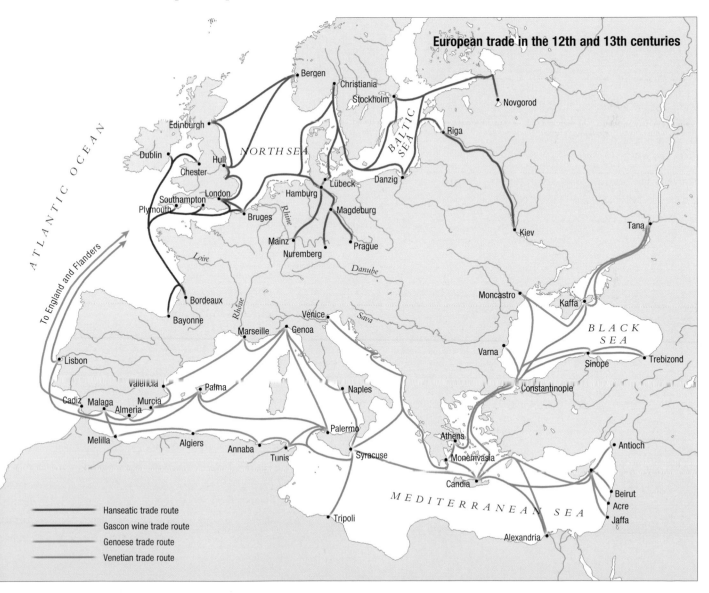

European trade in the 12th and 13th centuries

- Hanseatic trade route
- Gascon wine trade route
- Genoese trade route
- Venetian trade route

CHAPTER FOUR

Pirates of the Barbary Coast

A clash of faiths makes for lucrative trade

The semi-nomadic Berber tribes that lived on the fringes of the North African Roman provinces plagued the colonies in the later centuries of the Western Roman empire, and they continued to be an irritant to the invading Vandals and then the Byzantine exarchate of Carthage in the sixth century AD. The Berbers—from the

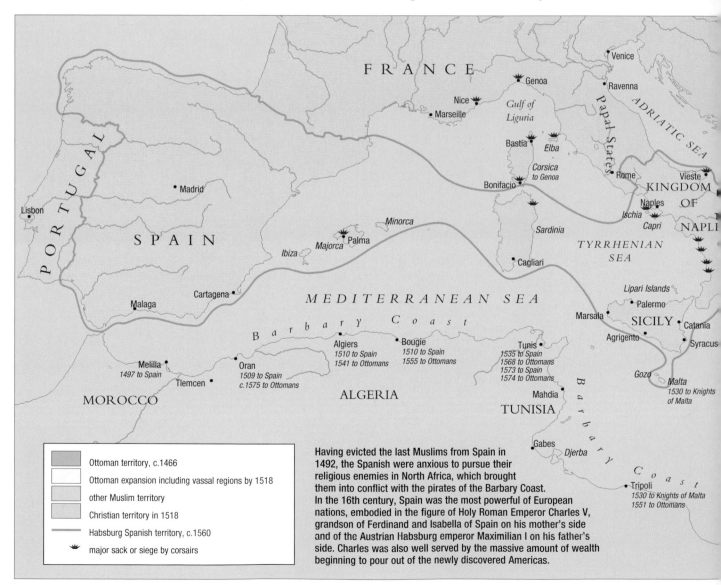

Ottoman territory, c.1466

Ottoman expansion including vassal regions by 1518

other Muslim territory

Christian territory in 1518

Habsburg Spanish territory, c.1560

major sack or siege by corsairs

Having evicted the last Muslims from Spain in 1492, the Spanish were anxious to pursue their religious enemies in North Africa, which brought them into conflict with the pirates of the Barbary Coast. In the 16th century, Spain was the most powerful of European nations, embodied in the figure of Holy Roman Emperor Charles V, grandson of Ferdinand and Isabella of Spain on his mother's side and of the Austrian Habsburg emperor Maximilian I on his father's side. Charles was also well served by the massive amount of wealth beginning to pour out of the newly discovered Americas.

Greek *barbaroi*, meaning "barbarian"—were eventually incorporated into the Arab Islamic state as Umayyad Arab forces swept unstoppably westward along the North African coast in the last half of the seventh century. The Mediterranean shore of North Africa is known as the Barbary Coast after the Berbers.

For more than 150 years, from the late 15th century onward, the string of city-states skirting the Mediterranean played host to a highly organized community of corsairs known as the Barbary pirates. They combined piracy with mercenary service on behalf of the Ottoman empire, and for much of the 16th century they were at the forefront of the bitter religious war fought for the domination of the Mediterranean basin. The Barbary pirates attacked European shipping and raided

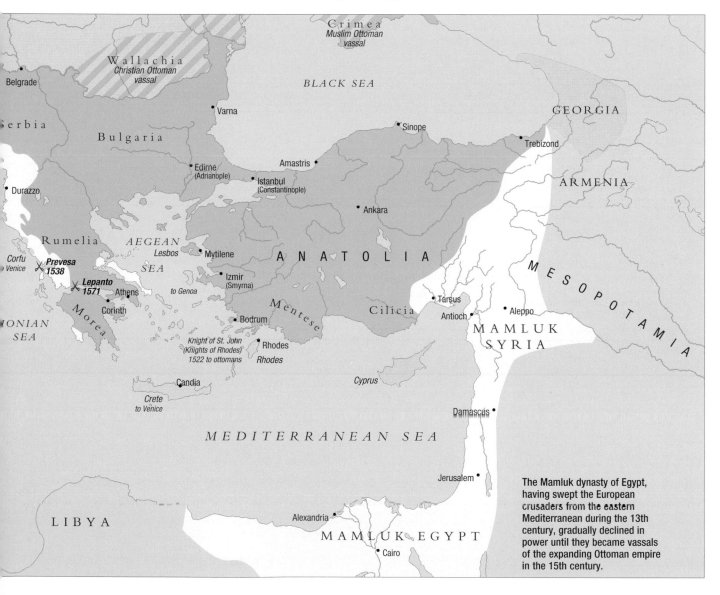

The Mamluk dynasty of Egypt, having swept the European crusaders from the eastern Mediterranean during the 13th century, gradually declined in power until they became vassals of the expanding Ottoman empire in the 15th century.

coastal settlements from the Strait of Gibraltar and the Atlantic to the Holy Land, and their reputation for ferocity was legendary. For centuries their long, sleek galleys and *galiots* (*see pages 19–20*) plundered shipping and turned the Barbary ports into busy markets for slaves and booty.

Strung out along the southern Mediterranean shore, the cities of Algiers, Tunis, and Tripoli, plus a score of smaller coastal towns in between, were ideally located bases from which to harass passing shipping. The pirates enjoyed a symbiotic relationship with the local *beys* or more senior *beylerbeys*, the ruling potentates who owed their position to the Ottoman Turkish sultan in Istanbul, before 1453 the Byzantine capital of Constantinople. The Barbary states sat on the edge of the Sahara Desert, and their sparsely populated hinterland of small African settlements produced the barest essentials required to support the coastal cities. Under Roman civilization, agriculture had spread deep into the Sahara in Tunisia, Algeria, and Morocco, but centuries of neglect had allowed the desert to encroach almost to the coast in many places.

Royal Navy marines board an Algerian corsair in the early 19th century. By the end of the 16th century, the conflict between Christians and Muslims over North Africa had more or less ended, with the Barbary Coast recognized as an integral part of the Ottoman empire. However, corsair activity continued until the Napoleonic Wars. European powers united with American forces in 1801 to pacify the region. One American naval officer who took part was David Porter (*see pages 198–200*).

Any wealth, therefore, had to come from the sea, so during the late 15th and early 16th centuries the local beys encouraged corsairs to use their ports as pirate havens. In return, they received a portion of the profits—and piracy proved to be a lucrative business. During the 16th century it became entirely normal to find a bey appointed from the ranks of the pirates themselves, making piratical activity an integral part of the economy, as well as the secular and religious policy of the Barbary Coast.

While a Barbary corsair *rais* (captain) owned his ship and had considerable autonomy over his operations, he enjoyed less freedom than a European pirate captain. The Barbary corsairs were all organized by a ruling captain's council, the *taife raisi*. This body supervised the running of the pirate havens and acted as a link between the corsairs, local potentates, and the Ottoman sultanate. At sea the rais was assisted by an *aga*, who commanded the boarding party, and a scribe appointed by the *taife raisi* who ensured that booty was shared between the rais and the local bey at the end of the cruise. Typically, the local ruler claimed ten percent, plus a fee for

Selim and Zuleika (1857) by the French painter Eugène Delacroix depicts a scene from Lord Byron's tale *The Bride of Abydos*, which relates the tragic fate of the lovers Zuleika, daughter of Giaffir Pasha, and the Barbary corsair Selim. Imprisoned in the harem by her father prior to her loveless arranged marriage, Selim helps Zuleika to escape. The lovers hide in a cave by the sea to wait for Selim's pirate crew to rescue them. But when the corsair fires his pistol to summon his comrades who wait offshore, his shots attract the attention of pursuing Giaffir and his men. Selim is shot dead by Giaffir, and Zuleika dies of grief. An extreme exponent of the romantic, Delacroix gives us a sympathetic view of the Muslim pirate that was at odds with the reality.

the use of his harbor. The general policy of the *taife raisi* was to confine attacks to non-Muslim shipping, but in keeping with a powerful economic polity the captains' council also made suitable treaties with some Christian states, when it was in the sultanate's interest to do so. As an example, the Republic of Venice remained at peace with the Ottoman Turks for much of the 16th century and so Barbary pirate attacks on Venetian ships were discouraged (though by no means eradicated).

Barbary pirates were portrayed by Christians at the time as fanatical Muslims, waging an undeclared war against their religious enemies. In fact, many corsairs were born Christians; some were captured as children and raised in the Islamic faith, while others embraced Islam in order to pursue a piratical career. Renegade Christians formed a substantial portion of corsair numbers.

The Barbarossa brothers

Two Christians were numbered among the first of the larger-than-life Barbary corsairs and became mentors to many who followed their bloody trail. The Greek brothers Aruj and Hizir were born during the 1470s at Mytilene, the main town on Lesbos. Their mother was the widow of a Christian priest who had remarried an ex-Janissary of the Ottoman army (many of this elite corps were Christians). Lesbos had remained under Byzantine or Genoese control almost up to the fall of Constantinople in 1453. Now under Ottoman sway, the Aegean island was a pirate haven for both Greeks and Muslims, and a bustling, cosmopolitan port where the cultures and religions of the Mediterranean mixed freely. So it would be hardly surprising that Aruj Barbarossa, the elder of the two youths, should enter service with a corsair galley operating out of Lesbos, attacking shipping in the Aegean. At some point the Knights of St. John captured his ship and took him prisoner.

Another version claims that Aruj was not a pirate at first but on a peaceful trading mission assisting his father, who had established a respectable career in pottery, their vessel fell foul of the Christian knight-sailors. Whichever story is the more correct, the fact remains that the Knights of St. John, also known as the Hospitalers or the Knights of Rhodes, were brigands clothed as crusaders. They occupied several of the southeasterly Aegean islands, including Rhodes, from which base this militant religious order combined a convenient piracy with religious fervor. Aruj was bound to the rowing benches as a galley slave for about a year until with others he was ransomed by the Mamluk emir of Egypt. Taken to Alexandria, Aruj sent for his brother

The Barbarossa brothers Aruj (**left**) and Hizir terrorized the Tyrrhenian and Ligurian seas from their bases in Djerba and Algiers.

Christian slaves in a Barbary town; slavery was one of the most profitable businesses on the Barbary Coast.

Spanish Men of War Engaging Barbary Corsairs by the Dutch painter Cornelis Vroom (1591–1661). The Spanish remained implacable foes of the Moors of North Africa and their Barbary protectors out—despite the implication of this painting—Spanish galleons usually came off the worst against the Barbarossa brothers.

Hizir, and together they fitted out corsair galleys, funded by the emir. The brothers proved to be skilled captains. By about 1505, they had moved their small *galiots* to the western Mediterranean where, with the consent of the bey of Tunis, they made their base on the island entrepôt of Djerba.

Aruj Rais now ranged as far north as the Gulf of Liguria, and in the course of one raid off the island of Elba the brothers captured two galleys belonging to Pope Julius II (1503–13). These were not merchantmen but fully manned and armed warships, and the implication of their capture terrified Christians everywhere. According to the 16th-century Spanish historian Diego Haedo, "The wonder and astonishment that this notable exploit caused in Tunis, and even in Christendom, is not to be expressed, nor how celebrated the name of Aruj Rais was to become." Haedo also tells us that due to the carroty red coloring of the brothers' beards, they were thereafter called Barbarossa, the Italian for "red beard."

The Barbarossa brothers' next exploit—the capture of a becalmed Spanish sailing warship seized off the Lipari Islands north of Sicily—showed the advantages of corsair galleys over sailing ships in the generally light Mediterranean winds. The base in Djerba swelled with prizes, and other corsairs flocked to serve under the brothers. Their success was due in no small part to the policy of manning the galleys' oars with free men in preference to slaves. This meant that everyone onboard a Barbarossa ship was a fighting man, eager for conquest and booty. In 1511 the brothers shifted their base of operations to Djidjelli near Algiers after a falling out with the bey of Tunis but also in response to a request from the rival bey of Algiers who sought their help to defend his territory against the Spanish.

Not everything went the brothers' way. In 1512 Aruj overestimated his abilities and lost an arm when his attack on a Spanish-held fort on the North African coast was repulsed. A second, vengeful, assault two years later also failed to dislodge the Spanish. From this point on the Barbarossa brothers increasingly singled out Spanish shipping and forts as their prime targets. In 1516, an even larger prize presented itself. Local unrest was running high against the apathetic bey's lack of response to the growing Spanish threat. Aruj fomented a popular uprising and took full advantage of the situation to lead a corsair force into Algiers, where he murdered the potentate and proclaimed himself bey.

Now the elder Barbarossa had to prove himself as a warrior-ruler. His corsair army—assisted by a severe storm—succeeded in repulsing a Spanish attack in 1518, launched from their toehold in Algiers bay. But Aruj knew that a defensive policy would not win Muslim hearts and so he turned on another Spanish stronghold at

59

Oran, west of Algiers. However, this was not a well-prepared amphibious assault. While he was securing the hinterland around Oran, a large Spanish force surprised the Barbary corsairs. Amid fierce fighting, the Spanish infantry drove the pirates inland, where they took refuge behind the walls of Tlemcen. After a six-month siege, the desperate corsairs attempted to break out of the town, but the Spanish countered and in the engagement Aruj Rais was defeated and slain.

Hizir Barbarossa, who had remained behind in Algiers, now took charge. Khair-ed-Din (the gift of God), as he had come to be called, continued to resist Spanish attacks around Algiers. In return for offering his fealty to the Ottoman sultan, Suleiman I the Magnificent (1520–66), he was officially recognized as the bey of Algiers, which meant that he could put in a claim for regular Ottoman troops and manned galleys to defend his territory. As an official Ottoman commander, Khair-ed-Din launched repeated raids on Spanish possessions in the Mediterranean. Although the Spanish captured Tunis in 1535, he sacked Majorca and Nice in return. He helped to defend Ottoman interests in the eastern Mediterranean by defeating the Christian galley fleet of the emperor Charles V at Prevesa (1538) at the entrance to the Gulf of Corinth, which was commanded by one of Christendom's great Barbary pirate hunters, the Genoese admiral Giovanni Andrea Doria.

Although Khair-ed-Din was increasingly based in the sultan's court at Istanbul, he maintained a tight grip on his extensive North African territory. By the time of his death in 1547, the younger Barbarossa brother had helped to establish Ottoman control throughout the Mediterranean.

The drawn sword of Islam

One of Khair-ed-Din's brightest pupils was a Turk. Born at some point between 1514–18 into a poor family from the Mentese region of Anatolia, Turgut probably took his name from his village of Turgat. This was situated close to Bodrum, formerly the Greek city of Halicarnassus. In his early 20s Turgut entered naval service and later became a protege of Khair-ed-Din Barbarossa, under whose tutelage he soon rose to become a chief lieutenant, commanding a wing of the Ottoman fleet at Prevesa. In the following year, 1539, he recaptured the Dalmatian town of Castelnuovo from the Venetians. Flushed with success, Turgut now accompanied Khair-ed-Din around the heel and toe of Italy to ravage the coasts of Spanish possessions Sicily and the Kingdom of Naples. The corsairs sacked the island of Ischia, off the coast near the city of Naples, and slighted the Spanish-held castle on the neighboring island of Capri. Thousands of captured prisoners were deported to the Barbary Coast slave markets.

Disaster struck in 1540, when Turgut was ambushed by the warships of a vengeful Andrea Doria while anchoring his vessels in an inlet on Corsica. Pressed himself into slavery, the Barbary corsair toiled for four long years at the oars of a galley commanded by the admiral's nephew, Gianettino Doria. Offers by Barbarossa to ransom Turgut were refused, so in 1544 he laid siege to Genoa with a fleet of 120 ships. These—provided by the sultan as aid to his temporary ally Francis I of France against his bitter enemies the Spanish—were on their way to Marseille, but when they appeared off Genoa, negotiations began. Turgut was finally released in exchange for a hefty ransom of gold ducats.

After the death of Khair-ed-Din, command of the Barbary fleet became Turgut's and in a career spanning the better part of two more decades the poor Turkish boy from Bodrum gained such a reputation that in the Islamic world he was hailed as "the drawn sword of Islam." With a fleet of 24 galleys, he returned to Naples and attacked the coasts of Calabria and Puglia. Early in 1550 he returned to North Africa and wrested control of the greater part of Tunisia from the Spanish. The allied Christian response was swift and in September a large fleet commanded by Andrea Doria drove the pirates out of Tunis, with great losses on both sides. Having forced them to sail south to Djerba, Doria thought he had his arch enemy trapped against the island, but Turgut evaded the Christians by dragging his galleys and *galiots* across the island on a greased track, and so escaped to sail away to Istanbul.

The sultan now placed Turgut in command of a powerful fleet of 114 galleys for a long-planned assault on Malta and its military order of knights—the former Hospitalers or the Knights of Rhodes. But Malta was too well defended and the campaign of 1551 failed. Turgut turned on the small Maltese island of Gozo, laying it to waste and enslaving the population. And he was more successful in the summer, attacking and capturing Tripoli, which had been a possession of the Maltese knights since 1530. The sultan rewarded Turgut with the title and powers of *sanjak bey* (provincial governor) of Tripoli. From his new capital, the drawn sword of Islam wreaked havoc on Christian shipping and possessions. He again defeated the Spanish fleet of Andrea Doria near Ponza in 1533, then raided the Calabrian coast, sacked the island of Elba, and captured the strongholds of Bonifacio and Bastia on Corsica. For his efforts, Turgut was made beylerbey of the Mediterranean Sea.

A 19th-century print portrays Turgut Rais in a suitably ferocious pose. By modern considerations, there is little to admire in the brilliant but cruel Barbary pirate. A typical example of his behavior may be found in the 1554 sacking of Vieste, a small Italian town. Unable to take the castle, all the wounded, infirm, and elderly or unfit for either ransom or slavery were decapitated on a rocky outcrop later called *chianca amara*, the "bitter stone." Illustration by Alexandre Debelle (1805–97).

Turgut Rais' end came at Malta, during the siege of 1565, when a cannon shot struck the ground close by and threw up shrapnel that mortally wounded him. The great Barbary corsair died of his injuries a few days later.

The corsair who saved an empire

Born Giovanni Dionigi in southern Italy in 1520, Uluj Ali was the son of a poor fisherman. He took to the sea in his father's boat almost as soon as he could walk and, until he was 16, followed his father's trade. But then in 1536 the notorious Algerine pirate Giafer Rais, who raided the Italian coast under the command of Khair-ed-Din Barbarossa, stormed the fishing vessel and captured Dionigi. The young Italian was made a galley slave, but when offered the chance to join the corsairs he willingly accepted, converted to Islam, and took the Muslim name of Uluj Ali. From this unpromising beginning, Uluj Ali went on to become a skilled pirate, a natural leader, and eventually commander of the Ottoman fleet.

By the time he was 40, Ali was running his own small *galiot* out of Tripoli, where he served under Turgut Rais. While acting as a fleet scout off Djerba in 1560, he earned the commendation of the supreme Ottoman admiral Piyale Pasha. The island, which changed hands continuously between the Spanish and the Muslims at this time, was under the governorship of Andrea Doria for the Holy League of Philip II of Spain. In a great battle of May 14, the Muslims severely defeated the Spanish fleet and took control of Djerba. Piyale did not forget Ali, who was given a prime command in the attack on Malta in 1565. In the end, the siege of the Maltese knights failed, but Uluj Ali distinguished himself sufficiently that he

Algiers, seen in about 1700, its crumbling walls belying what was still a formidable corsair stronghold. Christian prisoners, manacled together, are herded ashore from a Barbary *galiot*. The lucky ones were ransomed, the fit chained to a galley's oars, and the rest quickly worked to death.

was appointed as the bey of Tripoli to succeed the deceased Turgut Rais. From here he coordinated Barbary raids on Christian shipping and the coastal towns of Sicily and southern Italy, continuing the work of his former commander.

Within three years the sultan rewarded his efforts by naming Ali beylerbey of Algiers. The Spanish, who still held much of the region around Tunis, were evicted, and Ali raised Moorish revolts in Morocco against their mutual enemy. Avenging the failure of the attack on Malta, he captured a powerful Maltese squadron in 1570. In 1571 Ali was called to the east, where he was put in command of a squadron of the Ottoman fleet. Matters had come to a head as Ottoman armies swept across the Balkans into western Europe in the early 16th century, prompting deep unease in

Venice at possible future Turkish intentions. Consequently, Venice joined the Holy League (ironically formed as much to counter Venetian dominance of Mediterranean trade as to fight the Ottomans). The outcome was the naval battle of Lepanto (modern Nafpaktos), fought on October 7, 1571 in the mouth of the Gulf of Corinth. The allied Christian powers defeated the Turks, but Uluj Ali's tactics almost saved the day. His performance was widely praised and he became a national hero.

Defeats at Malta in 1565 and now at Lepanto led to an instant reorganization of the Ottoman navy, and Uluj Ali was named its supreme admiral. Over the next year, his skilled campaigning prevented the complete collapse of Ottoman power in the central Mediterranean, but left a vacuum in the west, where a resurgent Spain recaptured Tunis in 1573. Uluj Ali was sent to dislodge the Spanish again, taking a powerful Ottoman force with him. A combined naval blockade, amphibious attack, and land assault brought about the city's surrender in June 1574. Ali went on to consolidate Ottoman power along the North African coast from Oran to Tripoli, and he greatly improved the Barbary ports' defenses.

Spain in the later 16th century became increasingly embroiled in a struggle against the Protestant powers of northern Europe, and consequently needed to focus her resources. As a result, the emperor and the sultan signed a truce, ending the near-permanent warfare that had existed between Spain and the Barbary Coast for 50 years. While the Italian states and Habsburg Austria were not included in this peace, it guaranteed the continued Ottoman control of the North African coast. Uluj Ali now led raids further afield, in the Adriatic and the waters of the Black Sea, and back in the west against the pro-Spanish autonomous government of the port of Salee in Morocco. This failed to drive out the Moors after Ottoman in-fighting between some commanders and the campaign fall apart. Regardless of this disappointment, by the time of his death in 1587, Uluj Ali had secured the Barbary Coast for the Ottoman empire and had contained the power of the only Christian coalition that ever threatened the Ottoman territories.

The bold corsair Murat Rais

As Khair-ed-Din battled the Spanish, an Albanian fisherman's wife gave birth to a son who would become one of the most notorious of the Barbary pirates. His Christian name was unrecorded, but Murat Rais was probably born in 1535. At the time, Albania was a march fought over by Christian states and the expanding Muslim Ottoman empire. The rule of law barely existed, and while brigands ravaged the interior, pirates raided the coasts with impunity. In 1546 the Barbary pirate Kari Ali Rais captured the 12-year-old Albanian boy, who adopted the Muslim name Murat and joined the corsairs.

After Kari Ali's death in 1565, Murat Rais launched his own pirate career somewhat ignominiously—he was shipwrecked off the southern Italian coast. Undeterred, he and his small crew employed some kind of subterfuge to seize a

The Spanish army launches an amphibious assault on a Barbary Coast town in the mid-16th century.

A French resident of Algiers is fired from a cannon in reprisal for the French blockade of the town in the early 17th century. Many citizens suffered the same fate.

passing Christian sailing vessel. In this ship the Albanian attacked and boarded three Spanish trading vessels, which he sold in one of the North African Barbary ports. Basing himself on the North African coast, he specialized in attacks on Spanish and Italian shipping, and coastal raids around the Christian shores of the Mediterranean. These highly profitable expeditions soon earned Murat wealth and a reputation as an audacious corsair. However, his very boldness frequently made him flout the social codes of Barbary pirates as, for instance, when he boarded a Maltese war galley ahead of his superior, Uluj Ali, in 1570. This lack of courtesy no doubt contributed to the 20-year delay in his receiving an appointment as an official navy commander.

That he would gain the Ottoman sultan's approval can hardly have been in doubt. Murat Rais was among the slyest of Barbary tacticians and a favorite ploy encouraged opponents to underestimate his fighting strength. He lowered the masts of his smaller *galiots* and towed them behind his other galleys, out of the enemy's sight. Tricks like these made him a popular choice of captain and, as profits from his activities mounted, others joined his band to share in the booty and bask in his reflected glory. In 1574 the bey of Algiers nominated Murat "Captain of the Sea," but the appointment was not ratified by Suleiman the Magnificent until 1594. In addition to his new duties to defend the sultanate's shores, Murat continued to expand his list of piratical exploits. In 1578, his capture of two powerful Spanish war galleys, one carrying the viceroy of Sicily home to Spain, sent shockwaves throughout the Mediterranean. No less so, three years later, did his capture of three French ships and the fortune in silver and gold they were transporting to Toulon.

As though the Mediterranean held little further challenge for the Albanian, now well into his 50s, in 1586 Murat led an expedition out into the Atlantic to assault Lanzarote, in the Canary Islands. The Spanish town remained in Barbary hands for several weeks, while Murat ransomed its citizens. Returning to the inner sea, Murat Rais turned his guns on the Knights of St. John in Malta, taking a large war galley prize. And then in 1595 he celebrated his official recognition as Captain of the Sea by leading a large Algerian amphibious force against Sicily and southern Italy. The campaign produced a string of great prizes, including three Spanish-Sicilian warships.

From the early 17th century until his death in 1638, the Ottoman war fleet commanded by Murat Rais dominated the eastern Mediterranean and the waters of the Aegean and Adriatic seas. Despite his advanced years—he was more than 100 when he died—Murat also served as a successful land commander. And it was on land, during the Ottoman siege of the Albanian town of Vlorë, that he was killed.

As Christian authorities breathed a sigh of relief, their Ottoman enemies grieved over a tragic loss.

For much of his piratical career, Murat Rais used the Barbary Coast port of Algiers, seen here in the 17th century, as his main base of operations.

Wolves in monks' habits

Not all the Mediterranean corsairs were Muslims of the Barbary Coast. Among the Christian enemies of the Barbary pirates, few were more feared or hated than the Knights of Malta. This religious crusading order already had a long history. Founded in 1113 as an order of hospice monks in Jerusalem, offering shelter to pilgrims and caring for wounded and sick crusaders, the order was known as the Hospitalers of St. John of Jerusalem. In time the order became one of the military orders of crusader-monks, like the Templars, and were known as the Knights of St. John or the Knights Hospitalers.

After the final eviction of Christians from the Holy Lands with the fall of Acre in 1291, the order found refuge on the island of Cyprus and there modified the manner of their warfare from land-based to naval. Equipping war galleys to attack Muslims on the sea, the Knights of St. John became efficient sailors and seaborne warriors. In 1309 they captured the island of Rhodes, which became the center of a small empire of Aegean islands held by the knights. Until their eviction by Ottoman forces in 1522, they were more commonly known as the Knights of Rhodes. By this time, little was left of the Christian crusading order, and their attacks on the Muslim cities of mainland Asia Minor were happily combined with seizing what Christian-held strongholds were left along the shore. It was in such a pirate raid that the knights captured Aruj Barbarossa. Their habit of using captives as galley slaves made the Knights of Rhodes hated, since the Ottoman and other Muslim galleys of the time were usually manned by free men. Thereafter, any Christians taken captive by the Turks and without hope of ransom found themselves chained to the rowing benches of Ottoman war galleys in imitation of the Hospitalers.

Spanish Engagement with Barbary Corsairs by Andries van Eertefeldt.

The order fled to the western Mediterranean after the fall of Rhodes, and in 1530 Charles V, the Spanish-Habsburg emperor, granted them control of Malta. Then, as now, Malta's midway position between Sicily and the North African coast made it strategically important and Charles hoped the renamed Knights of Malta would provide a bulwark against Ottoman expansion into the western Mediterranean. The rent for this valuable possession was one live Maltese falcon, the bird presented annually to the emperor's viceroy in Sicily. The symbolism is apparent—the knights were birds of prey, protecting Christendom. The Knights of Malta also held Tripoli on the North African coast, but the severe disruption caused to Ottoman trade by Maltese galleys prompted the Turkish campaign of 1551 led by Turgut Rais, which failed to seize Malta but succeeded in taking the knights' secondary port of Tripoli.

The knights maintained a small fleet of war galleys—originally not more than seven ships—and participated in naval campaigns against the Ottoman empire during the mid-16th century, part of a large allied fleet of Christian maritime powers. When the Maltese war galleys were not engaged in officially sanctioned campaigns they cruised off the Barbary Coast, raiding settlements and capturing Muslim shipping. Those knights who could afford it were also permitted to equip their own private galleys to give chase to Turkish

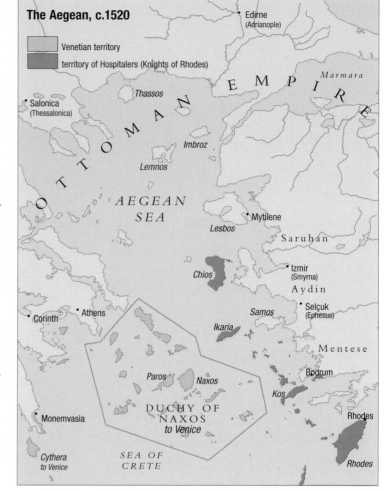

raiders. Sadly, the enthusiastic young captains did not always confine their attacks to Muslims; Jewish and on occasion Christian ships were also attacked. And with Venice at peace with the Ottomans for much of the 16th century until the battle of Lepanto in 1571, Venetian merchantmen were also singled out for attack, despite the opposition of Pope and Holy Roman Emperor.

In the early 1560s, Maltese raids into the eastern Mediterranean increased, some as far off as Egypt and others up into the order's old hunting ground of the Aegean. Clearly such far-ranging expeditions had little strategic value; they were really no more than pirate raids driven by the desire for plunder and casual slaughter. All the booty—and there was a great deal of it—filled the order's coffers on Malta. One of the most successful captains of this period, Brother Romegas, seized an Ottoman galleon in the Adriatic in 1564. It was a hugely valuable prize, but the act put the Maltese in the greatest peril of the order's recent history. Suleiman the Magnificent—supremely successful on land and still master of Mediterranean waters—was so enraged by this act of piracy that he ordered a full-scale assault on Malta to wipe out

Portrait of a Knight of Malta by the Dutch painter Anthonis Mor (c.1517–77).

Opposite: Detail from the massive fresco series painted in 1584 by Mattia Perez d'Aleccio (1547–1616) shows the east side of Malta as the Ottoman forces land from their galleys.

the Christian corsairs. A massive Ottoman force under Piyale Pasha, Turgut Rais, and Uluj Ali besieged Malta in 1565. The Turks managed to land a large force and take possession of part of the island, destroying nearly the whole of the old city, killing half the knights and almost 8000 soldiers as they did so. But a resolute defense led by Grand Master La Valette held the rest of the island, which was finally delivered by a Spanish army of relief. The Ottomans withdrew after four months of bitter fighting, leaving an estimated 30,000 dead behind them.

Despite this essential Spanish aid, continual raids on Venetian shipping had eroded Christian support for the Knights of Malta. But, with the island's defenses in tatters and a city to rebuild, money was needed. And so in direct contravention of papal decrees, La Valette and his council sanctioned further attacks on Venetian traders and even on Venetian-held strongholds in the Adriatic. In so doing, the Knights of Malta crossed the fine line between privateering and piracy, and certainly in Venice they were referred to with disgust as "corsairs parading crosses."

The knights continued to act as semi-legal corsairs throughout the 17th century, capturing huge numbers of slaves in the process. A thousand slaves were required to equip the order's galleys alone, but even so there was always an excess, which made Malta an important slave market until well into the 18th century. Nevertheless, the order's power was on the wane. A life of violence and brutality undermined the higher morals of the knights, discipline became lax and, in the later 16th century, revolts became frequent. The Knights of Malta came to resemble the pirates of the later Caribbean, whoring in disobedience of their vows of celibacy, hoarding wealth in contravention of their vows of poverty, drinking alcohol—even locking up their own grand master in 1581. With the advent of Protestantism, the order's widely held European possessions fell to confiscation. By the 1650s the Maltese had become an anachronistic relic, and although the knights retained Malta until the end of the 18th century, the island ceased to be regarded as a dangerous haven of Christian corsairs. On June 12, 1798, Grand Master Count von Hompesch cravenly surrendered Malta to the French general Napoleon Bonaparte as he made his way toward Egypt.

CHAPTER FIVE

War on the Spanish Main

Protestant pirates play the religious card

For two main reasons, the year 1492 proved to be a memorable one for Spain. The event least noticed by ordinary people of the day was certainly the most significant for the nation's future—the discovery of the islands of the Bahamas by Christopher Columbus. The most momentous was the final eviction of the last Moors from Granada by the forces of Ferdinand of Aragon and Isabella of Castile, the king and queen who had united all of Spain under a single crown. The Christian capture of Granada brought to a conclusion over five centuries of reconquest and almost eight centuries of Muslim occupation of the Iberian peninsula. It also sponsored a wide-ranging ambition to capture Moorish, Berber, and Ottoman North Africa, sparking the conflict that brought Barbary corsairs to the forefront of Islamic resistance in the Mediterranean, covered in the previous chapter.

When Ferdinand died in 1516, he was succeeded by his grandson Charles I, who became Charles V of the Holy Roman Empire in 1519 when his paternal Habsburg grandfather Maximilian I died. To the Spanish crown, which already included the kingdoms of Sicily and Naples, Charles added his Habsburg family's dominions in Austria, Styria, Carinthia, the Tyrol, in Flanders and the Low Countries, the Franche-Comté, and a number of German principalities. Even before he acquired the extensive Duchy of Milan in 1535, Charles had made Habsburg Spain by far the dominant European power. Running such a complex economy, as well as funding continual wars for control of the Holy Roman Empire with France, was a costly business, and in the way that solutions often spring up when the need arises, the "discovery of America" by Columbus provided the finance Charles needed.

Ruler of all he surveyed, king of Spain, commander of all Habsburg possessions, and Holy Roman Emperor, Charles V was Europe's most powerful monarch, but he needed the unimaginable wealth of Spain's New World empire to pay for his costly wars for ever greater possessions.

A spate of Spanish explorers following in Columbus's wake launched Spain on a course of rapid colonial expansion that soon led to her domination of the Caribbean basin, much of the continent of South America, and great chunks of North America bordering the Gulf of Mexico. The Treaty of Tordesillas is testament to the rate at which these discoveries were made, not to mention the recognition of how wealthy were the finds. Spain and her major trading rival Portugal signed the treaty in the presence of Pope Alexander VI in June 1494, only two years after Columbus's first voyage. Tordesilla drew an imaginary line down the Atlantic, giving Spain dominion over every yet undiscovered land to the west, while Portugal retained control of the east side, ensuring her eventual monopoly of trade into the Indian Ocean. The line's position was supposed to give Spain all of the New World, but at that early stage no one knew that the southern continent projected so far east into the southern Atlantic, which is why Portugal got Brazil when it was discovered a few years later.

The Spanish wasted little time in setting their new empire to rights. Barely had the tiny ships of discovery returned from each new expedition than brutal armies of conquistadors descended. First the islander Carib Indians, then the mainland Aztec fell to European swords. Soon the poor remnants of the once mighty Maya empire bowed under the yoke, and not long after a mere handful of Spaniards conquered the entire Inca nation of Peru. Within a few years, disease and cruelty had decimated the native populations and the survivors found themselves enslaved. When they began to die out, the Spanish bought African slaves from Portuguese slavers, even then making their way down the west coast of the continent. The Spanish conquerors came as rapacious pirates, and the wealth of the Americas began its long journey back across the Atlantic to swell the imperial coffers. Before long, relieving the Spanish of some of their New World riches would become a patriotic duty of both French and English privateers.

During the 16th century the Caribbean basin came to be known as the Spanish Main. The term—first used by other European interlopers to the region—was originally derived from a translation of the Spanish name for the territories of Venezuela, New Granada (Colombia), and Panama, which were called collectively Tierra Firme, or "mainland." But by the end of the century, when a pirate referred to the Spanish Main, he meant all Spain's possessions in the New World, including New Spain (Mexico) and the Viceroy of Peru (South America's Pacific coast and Ecuador), as well as the Gulf of Mexico and the outer Caribbean islands. The very words are evocative of buried treasure, tropical islands, the raids of Elizabethan Sea Dogs, and 17th-century buccaneers—the stuff of romantic fiction. However, before the pirates of the Caribbean appeared, the Spanish controlled the waters exclusively and their exploitation of the region was allowed to continue almost unimpeded.

The first hints that trouble might be brewing appeared when French, Dutch, and English settlers began establishing communities on the North American seaboard. Apart from a national antipathy for the Spanish, these newcomers were predominantly of the Protestant faith and disinclined to obey the dictates of the Treaty of Tordesillas—a deal struck by a Catholic Pope and two staunchly papist co-signatories. Although the Spanish were unable to prevent these unwelcome incursions into the fringes of their sphere, any advance into the Spanish Main itself was firmly quashed. But inevitably, the wealth of Spain's New World empire attracted harder men who came to the Caribbean to muscle in on the benefits the region offered, and in the early 17th century other European powers managed to secure tiny bridgeheads among the islands of the West Indies.

Successor to Charles V, Philip II pursued Spain's ambitions. Under his rule, the Spanish Main expanded as output from the American mines increased, making the annual treasure fleet the target of every pirate on the high seas.

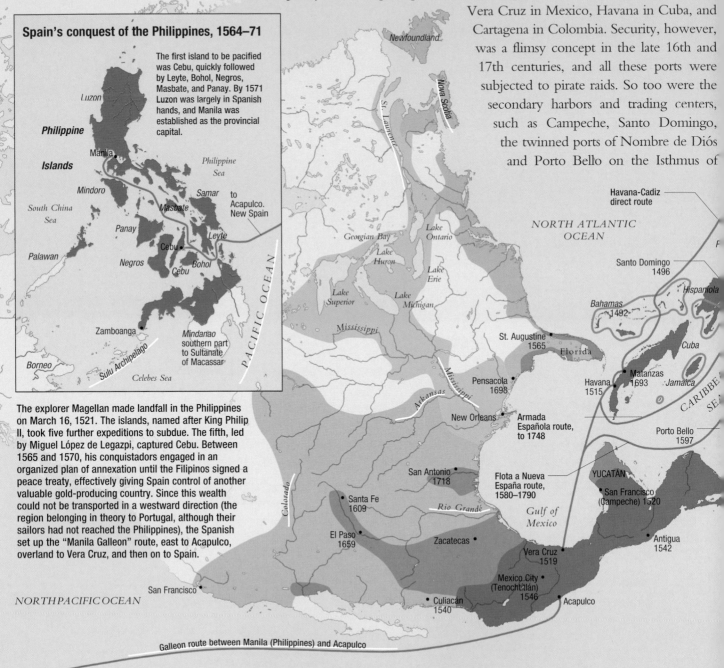

The Spanish Main, 1492–1750

In the early decades these precarious settlements suffered from a continuous stream of Spanish attacks as Castilian noblemen enforced the policy of "no peace beyond the [Tordesillas] line," but by the mid–17th century French and English colonies in the Caribbean were strong enough to repulse the enemy. The small ports that sprang up were soon playing host to pirates who came to prey on the rich Spanish shipping. And there was plenty of it. The principal secure anchorages were heavily fortified harbors like Vera Cruz in Mexico, Havana in Cuba, and Cartagena in Colombia. Security, however, was a flimsy concept in the late 16th and 17th centuries, and all these ports were subjected to pirate raids. So too were the secondary harbors and trading centers, such as Campeche, Santo Domingo, the twinned ports of Nombre de Diós and Porto Bello on the Isthmus of

Spain's conquest of the Philippines, 1564–71

The first island to be pacified was Cebu, quickly followed by Leyte, Bohol, Negros, Masbate, and Panay. By 1571 Luzon was largely in Spanish hands, and Manila was established as the provincial capital.

Luzon

Philippine Islands

Manila

Philippine Sea

Mindoro

Samar

to Acapulco. New Spain

South China Sea

Masbate

Panay

Leyte

Cebu

Negros

Cebu

Bohol

Palawan

Zamboanga

Mindanao southern part to Sultanate of Macassar

Borneo

Sulu Archipelago

Celebes Sea

PACIFIC OCEAN

The explorer Magellan made landfall in the Philippines on March 16, 1521. The islands, named after King Philip II, took five further expeditions to subdue. The fifth, led by Miguel López de Legazpi, captured Cebu. Between 1565 and 1570, his conquistadors engaged in an organized plan of annexation until the Filipinos signed a peace treaty, effectively giving Spain control of another valuable gold-producing country. Since this wealth could not be transported in a westward direction (the region belonging in theory to Portugal, although their sailors had not reached the Philippines), the Spanish set up the "Manila Galleon" route, east to Acapulco, overland to Vera Cruz, and then on to Spain.

NORTH PACIFIC OCEAN

Newfoundland

Nova Scotia

St. Lawrence

Havana-Cadiz direct route

NORTH ATLANTIC OCEAN

Santo Domingo 1496

Hispaniola

Georgian Bay

Lake Ontario

Lake Huron

Lake Erie

Bahamas 1492

Cuba

Lake Superior

Lake Michigan

Mississippi

St. Augustine 1565

Florida

Matanzas 1693

Jamaica

Pensacola 1698

Havana 1515

Arkansas

Mississippi

New Orleans

Armada Española route, to 1748

Porto Bello 1597

CARIBBE SEA

San Antonio 1718

Flota a Nueva España route, 1580–1790

YUCATÁN

San Francisco (Campeche) 1520

Santa Fe 1609

Rio Grande

Gulf of Mexico

Colorado

El Paso 1659

Zacatecas

Vera Cruz 1519

Antigua 1542

Mexico City (Tenochtitlán) 1546

Acapulco

San Francisco

Culiacan 1540

Galleon route between Manila (Philippines) and Acapulco

72

Panama, Panama City on the Pacific coast, and Caracas. The French and, later, the
Dutch pirates were successful raiders, but it was the English who undertook piracy
on the Spanish Main at a strategic level. When Spanish warships drove off the initial
exploratory trading voyages of English vessels, captains such as Francis Drake returned
to the Spanish Main seeking revenge. And what was the fuss all
about? Fabled Aztec gold was only a small part of the
overall wealth of Central and South America, and
looted treasures soon ran out. The earliest
permanent Spanish colony—Puerto
Real on Haiti, founded in 1503,
only 11 years after Columbus's
first visit—was sited to take
advantage of a good
natural harbor but

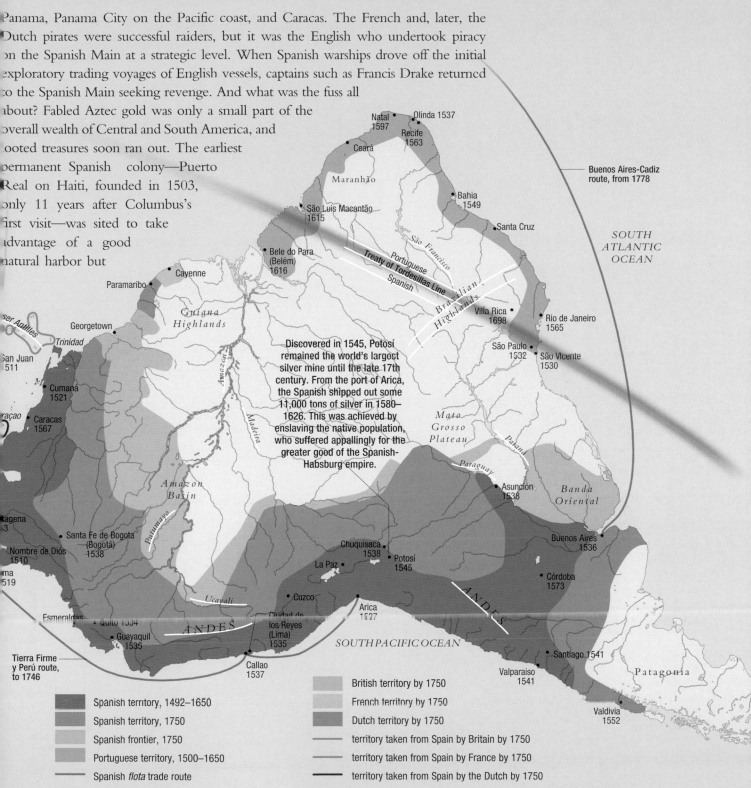

Buenos Aires-Cadiz
route, from 1778

SOUTH
ATLANTIC
OCEAN

Natal
1597
Olinda 1537
Recife
1563
Ceará
Maranhão
São Luis Macantão
1615
Bahia
1549
Santa Cruz
São Francisco
Bele do Para
(Belém)
1616
Portuguese
Treaty of Tordesillas Line
Spanish
Cayenne
Paramaribo
Guiana
Highlands
Brazilian
Highlands
Villa Rica
1698
Rio de Janeiro
1565
Georgetown
São Paulo
1532
São Vicente
1530
sser Antilles
Trinidad
San Juan
1511
Discovered in 1545, Potosí
remained the world's largest
silver mine until the late 17th
century. From the port of Arica,
the Spanish shipped out some
11,000 tons of silver in 1580–
1626. This was achieved by
enslaving the native population,
who suffered appallingly for the
greater good of the Spanish-
Habsburg empire.
Cumaná
1521
raçao
Caracas
1567
Amazon
Madeira
Mato
Grosso
Plateau
Paraná
Amazon
Basin
Paraguay
Asunción
1538
Banda
Oriental
tagena
Santa Fe de Bogota
(Bogotá)
1538
Patumayo
Chuquisaca
1538
Potosí
1545
Buenos Aires
1536
Nombre de Diós
1510
La Paz
Córdoba
1573
ma
519
Ucayali
Cuzco
Arica
1537
ANDES
Esmeraldas
Quito 1534
ANDES
Ciudad de
los Reyes
(Lima)
1535
SOUTH PACIFIC OCEAN
Guayaquil
1535
Santiago 1541
Tierra Firme
y Perú route,
to 1746
Callao
1537
Valparaiso
1541
Patagonia
Valdivia
1552

British territory by 1750

French territory by 1750

Dutch territory by 1750

territory taken from Spain by Britain by 1750

territory taken from Spain by France by 1750

territory taken from Spain by the Dutch by 1750

Spanish territory, 1492–1650

Spanish territory, 1750

Spanish frontier, 1750

Portuguese territory, 1500–1650

Spanish *flota* trade route

also to mine the silver nearby. Many of the larger Caribbean islands provided similar mineral deposits, but nothing compared to the vast wealth of South America. At Potosí in Peru the conquistadors were led to a mountain of silver, the richest mineral mine in the known world. Work began in 1545, the city first named Villa Imperial de Carlos V, in honor of the Holy Roman Emperor Charles V. Shipments home of refined silver began almost immediately and continued for over 200 years. In the mid–17th century, Potosí, with a population of almost 200,000 and more than 86 churches, was one of the largest cities—and certainly wealthiest—anywhere in the world.

Peruvian silver was the most visible tip of an iceberg; gold from Ecuador, emeralds from Colombia, and pearls from Venezuela all contributed to the riches pouring from numerous smaller silver and gold mines in Mexico and the Caribbean islands. In Spain, Seville acted as the center of administration for the Spanish Main, and its offices rapidly expanded to become one of the largest bureaucratic organizations of its time. Spanish galleons rarely sailed alone—the French Huguenot pirates had made this too serious a risk within only a few years (*see page 76*)—but formed part of a large convoy. From Seville, hundreds of clerks ensured the efficiency of operation for this annual treasure fleet, or *flota*.

Almost every year from 1530 to 1735 the *flota* sailed from Spain, bound for the Caribbean. Once past the West Indies the fleet split into three, one squadron sailed to Tierra Firme visiting first Porto Bello to collect Peruvian silver and then Cartagena for Ecuadorian gold, Colombian gems, and Venezuelan pearls. The New Spain fleet went to Vera Cruz in Mexico to collect the silver from Mexican mines and, after Spain's conquest of the Philippines in 1571, goods shipped across the Pacific in the "Manila galleon," mainly silks, porcelain, and spices from the Orient. The third, smaller Honduras fleet called at Trujillo in modern Honduras to load indigo dye and spices from Central America. Once the collections had been made, the three fleets met at Havana in Cuba and prepared to sail home in convoy. Additional fleets transported the goods of the empire to meet the *flota* galleons. The South Seas fleet shipped Peruvian silver to the Pacific port of Panama from where it was transported by pack-mules over the narrow isthmus on a road called the Camino Real to the Caribbean port of Nombre de Diós. This settlement later moved slightly along the coast to become

The "silver mountain" of Potosí was the richest silver mine in the world. Captive Inca slaves dug out the raw silver ore from shafts sunk into the mountain, and when the natives sickened and died, the Spanish imported slaves from Africa.

the more defensible Porto Bello, after attacks by Sir Francis Drake proved Nombre de Diós too vulnerable to pirates. The Manila galleon sailed from the Philippines to Acapulco in Mexico. From here, mules again made the long overland trek to the Spanish Main and the port of Vera Cruz.

By 1550 output from the Peruvian mines at Potosí alone exceeded the rest of the world's combined silver production. The sheer weight of this material made the Spanish transport galleons cumbersome to handle, since they wallowed in the water. While in a Spanish Main harbor they were well protected by substantial fortifications and much heavier cannon than any pirate ship could field, but once at sea, even in convoy, they were vulnerable to attack and needed the protection of well-armed galleons to guard the treasure. Nevertheless, attacking a large fleet was a hazardous undertaking, but pirates such as Sir Francis Drake constantly sought fleets laden with treasure. The South Seas fleet of ships felt safer, protected by the vast bulk of the South American continent from the predatory pirates of the Caribbean, and so were often not very well armed, if at all. Drake famously proved them wrong when he rounded the Horn and captured the treasure galleon *Cacafuego*—one of the most stirring pirate conquests of all time.

English sea raiders attacking Santo Domingo, Hispaniola. Founded in 1496, Santo Domingo was the earliest center of Spanish authority in the Caribbean, soon followed by San Francisco de Campeche on the Yucatán peninsula and Caracas in Venezuela. All three were subject to pirate attacks during the 16th and 17th centuries.

Huguenots—French religious pirates

Before the famous English pirates like Hawkins and Drake sailed the tropical seas of the Spanish Main, French privateers brought havoc to their bitter enemy, Spain, and were first to challenge her monopoly of the New World. It began in 1523 when Spain and France were at war. The first Spanish treasure ships made the Atlantic crossing on their own or in twos or threes, no threat having materialized to that point. And so it happened that Jean Fleury (also written as Florin), a French privateering captain, encountered three such ships off the Spanish coast returning home from the New World. In a quick engagement, Fleury took them as prizes and discovered to his astonishment that their holds were full of treasure. There were valuable Aztec souvenirs of enameled gold and jade, gold and silver ornaments, emeralds, pearls, and exotic wildlife. This stolen hoard was on its way to Spain and Charles V, sent by Mexico's conqueror Hernando Cortez. It was clear to the privateer—and soon after to the French crown—that Spain's American colonies were producing more wealth than could possibly be imagined by her European rivals.

The French had no part in 1494's Treaty of Tordesillas, and Francis I (1515–47) refused to recognize its edicts giving Spain dominion over the New World. A

The annual fleet convoy of Spanish treasure ships—the *flota*—represented the greatest plunder any privateer could wish for. Since this wealth was fueling the Spanish war chest for European conquests, French, Dutch, and English pirates could regard their attacks on the *flota* as a patriotic duty.

soon as the region's enormous wealth had been established, the French crown sanctioned attacks on Spanish ships and settlements in the Caribbean. Letters of marque were issued, which guaranteed the king a share of any profits the privateers made. French privateers began to attack Spanish shipping in European waters and in the New World itself, but also turned south along Africa's western seaboard, where they attacked Portuguese ships. Alarmed by the sudden losses encountered in a continuous string of single, vulnerable treasure ships, the Spanish authorities responded by instituting the system of annual convoys that became known as the *flota*—an organization unrivaled in maritime history. Despite this precaution, piratical French attacks continued, with the smaller and more maneuverable vessels acting in concert to cut out a single, lumbering Spanish galleon from the convoy's mutual protection. The French did not always have it their way—in 1527 Jean Fleury was captured and hanged as a pirate.

Before the *flota* system, a continuous stream of ships moved wealth across the Atlantic, but a vast convoy could only make the crossing approximately once in a year. In consequence, land-based treasure houses had to be built to hold the incoming goods ready for the annual *flota*. With less frequent shipping to attack, the French turned to raiding ports on the Spanish Main. Lack of fortifications at

this time made the treasure houses vulnerable, and French privateers began causing mayhem in the Caribbean. Puerto Rico was attacked, as were the pearl beds off the island of Margarita, near the Venezuelan coast. Spanish experts were soon called in to begin the design and construction of massive defenses for the major cities. The French upped the ante. The earlier pinprick raids escalated into ambitious assaults launched by French pirate fleets in the 1540s and 1550s. Havana was caught napping and raided. An attack on heavily fortified Cartagena in 1544 used information supplied by a Spanish traitor to find a hidden route into the city. It was plundered and razed to the ground, while the French raiders made off with a fortune in booty. A peace treaty between France and Spain in 1544 failed to end these raids, Charles V of Spain lost patience with Henry II (1547–59), and the two countries were back at war again by 1552.

Contemporary woodcuts depict the havoc French raids caused in the Spanish Main. A lightly armed convoy of Spanish ships (**top**) comes under fire from Huguenot guns off Havana, while (**bottom**) Huguenot pirates burn the city during an amphibious raid. The loot is loaded aboard small pinnaces (foreground) and rowed out to the waiting French galleons.

However, France was having its own problems in the form of the Protestant revolution sweeping through the country, led by religious reformers collectively known as the Huguenots. The adherence of many leading French nobles to the Protestant cause further soured relations between the French and Spanish crowns, despite the obvious fact that the Catholic French monarchy was equally under Huguenot threat. In the course of the last half of the 16th century, Huguenots came in and out of power, and later still were evicted from France. As a result, they traveled, making pioneering trips across the oceans to various destinations, including the Americas. The first Huguenots came as pirates, adding their fury to the first French pirates' and venting it against the hated Catholic Spanish. One of the first actions took place in the Canary Islands, Spain's launching pad for voyages to the New World, when François le Clerk, a French Huguenot pirate known as "Jambe de Bois" (Pegleg), caused mayhem. In 1553 raids along the coast of Hispaniola were followed in the next year by a devastating attack on the Cuban city of Santiago.

In 1555 it was the turn of Havana again, as Huguenot pirates captured the city for the second time and held it to ransom. The assault was led by one of le Clerk's deputies, Jacques de Sores, who demonstrated a startling ruthlessness as the French devastated Havana and the surrounding countryside. By the late 1550s French privateers appeared able to rampage through the Caribbean with impunity, but in the 1560s the civil wars of religion wracked France and interrupted further French raids in the Caribbean. In the respite, recently crowned Spanish monarch Philip II bowed to pressure to spend precious financial resources on strengthening the ports of the Spanish Main.

Huguenot pressure mounted again in the following decade, led by the power and influence of Gaspard de Coligny, the most senior French admiral, ardent Protestant, and friend of a French king with reformist leanings, Charles IX (1560–74). De Coligny financed an expedition to found a settlement in the Americas, and Protestant exiles established a foothold on the Atlantic coast of northern Florida on the south bank of the St. Johns river at Fort Caroline (near present-day St. Augustine) in 1564. The admiral was under no illusions as to what his intrepid settlers really were—certainly not authentic colonists—and de Coligny said of them: "There were no tillers of the soil, only adventurous gentlemen, reckless soldiers, discontented tradesmen, all keen for novelty and heated by dreams of wealth." The settlement was clearly designed to provide a pirate base for Huguenot attacks on Spanish ports and shipping. Sadly, for the Huguenot cause, the gentlemen were not soldiers enough and they were no match for the new Spanish force in the region— Pedro de Menéndez de Avilles.

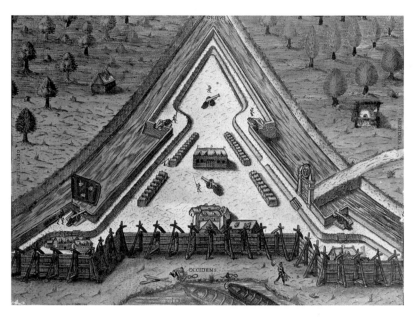

The Spanish explorer Juan Ponce de León was the first Spaniard to set foot on the continent of North America when he made landfall on April 2, 1513, somewhere between the future sites of Fort Caroline and St. Augustine. He named his discovery Tierra de Florida (Land of Flowers) and claimed the peninsula for Spain. The arrival of French Protestant Huguenots and their construction of Fort Caroline (**above**) was an insult Spain could never swallow.

An empire's merciless defender

The encroachment by Huguenot pirates gave Philip II grave concerns over the security of his New World possessions, their wealth so central to Spain's political ambitions in northern Europe and the Mediterranean basin, where the depredations of Barbary corsairs required a strong counter. The king needed a strong man to handle the situation, and settled on the nobleman Pedro de Menéndez de Avilles. Together with his brother Bartolomé, he was owner of several vessels plying their trade between the Old and New Worlds, so he was no stranger to the West Indies and the Caribbean. In April 1562 de Menendez left Spain as captain general (admiral) of the combined annual treasure fleet. With him, he carried a commission from the king to conduct a study of the defenses of the Spanish Main and submit his findings on his return.

His orders also carried this warning: "In the Indies sailing routes go some French, English and Scotch corsair ships, seeking to steal what comes." The ruthless treatment of any pirates captured was recommended. Unfortunately, the captain general found himself at the center of a controversy on his return to Spain in June 1563. Detractors raised questions about the truthfulness of the cargo manifests relating to those of his ships that had sailed back with the *flota*, and he was accused of smuggling contraband. Philip, who had high hopes of his protege, wrote to officers at Seville ordering that the matter be found in the admiral's favor.

Meanwhile, de Menéndez delivered his security report to the king, which revealed serious problems at many of the major treasure ports, particularly Havana and Cartagena. He suggested that squadrons of nimbler galleons be maintained in the region to patrol likely avenues of pirate attack. But perhaps his most perceptive recommendation was that Spain should establish a fortified settlement on Florida's Atlantic coast, where it would be best sited to protect the homeward-bound *flota*.

Philip's interference in the smuggling matter was deeply resented in Seville and de Menéndez' prosecutors continued to press charges. To cut matters short, he confessed and was arrested, tried, and in January 1564 found guilty. With ruffled tempers somewhat assuaged, his inquisitors imposed a fine and de Menéndez was released. During the course of the trial, tragic news reached Seville—his son had been lost in a shipwreck off Hispaniola, along with several of his own ships. Apart from the personal loss, his finances had been damaged both by the storm and the fine, but the king threw him another lifeline. Information had arrived suggesting that the French had founded a colony on the Atlantic coast of Florida, almost exactly as de Menéndez had suggested the Spanish should do. Philip wanted this disturbing intelligence confirmed and something done about it; he was prepared to refinance his captain general, contributing ships, troops, and money. The expedition's aim was to establish a fortified settlement in Florida and use it as a base from which to attack the French. Soldiers and marines numbering 2000 joined some 600 colonists at Cadiz, and in June 1565 boarded a force of 30 ships to set sail for Florida. A storm scattered the fleet, but de Menéndez continued with five ships and 600 men.

Philip's worst fears were proved true when, in September, the Spanish arrived off the French settlement at Fort Caroline. De Menéndez quickly realized that the defenses were too powerful for his depleted force to attack and so he sailed a short distance to the south and there landed in "a good harbor," where he founded the colony he named St. Augustine. As the initial fortifications were erected, French ships out looking for the Spanish sailed past, unable to turn because of a freshening wind. As the terrible storm swelled, de Menéndez seized the initiative, marching 500 men north into the Florida swamps to attack the now poorly defended French fort from the landward side. Taken by surprise and unable to resist, except for a few who managed to escape, the Huguenots were slaughtered to a man. Leaving a

Huguenots in the Americas

Georgia

Fort Caroline

St. Augustine

The French fleet was wrecked off present–day Daytona Beach

ATLANTIC OCEAN

St. John's

Peace

Florida

Lake Okeechobee

GULF OF MEXICO

Grand Bahama

Freeport

Abaco

New Providence

Andros

Key West

Florida Keys

Straits of Florida

Havanna

CUBA

By attacking Fort Caroline from the landward side of the fort instead of sailing up the river, merchant-adventurer, engineer, and able pirate hunter Pedro de Menéndez de Avilles (**below**) took the depleted French garrison by surprise. This illustration shows Indian fighters at the left. De Menéndez was later successful in forging friendly relations with several local tribes, but it is doubtful that any joined him in this battle.

garrison behind at Fort Caroline (renamed Fort Mateo), de Menéndez force-marched south beyond St. Augustine, searching for any French survivors of the storm. In the area near to present-day Daytona, he caught up with about 200 beached French sailors. No mercy was shown and every prisoner was executed.

Two weeks later the Spanish captain general caught those Huguenots who had escaped from Fort Caroline, including de Coligny's newly arrived settlement leader, Jean de Ribault. De Menéndez marked their mass grave with a sign which read, "I do this not to Frenchmen but to heretics." De Menéndez was rewarded for his actions by an appointment to the position of governor of Havana and enjoyed further royal favors. His brutal tactics ensured that organized French resistance to Spain's monopoly of the New World was broken, and it was left to the English Sea Rovers to continue disruption of the Spanish Main's commerce.

In the war with Philip II of Spain, the virgin queen, Elizabeth I, was prepared to use any weapon, including the sanction—albeit often secretly—of piracy.

Queen Elizabeth's Sea Rovers

For a period of 30 years starting in the mid–1550s, the New World became the target for a series of attacks that devastated Spanish shipping and coastal settlements. Nicknamed the Sea Rovers or the Sea Dogs, Elizabethan captains like Sir Francis Drake and Sir John Hawkins became national heroes for their harrying of Spanish shipping in the name of Queen Elizabeth of England (1558–1603). To the Spanish these sea raiders were nothing more than pirates, and any caught were more likely to face the hangman's noose as common criminals than meet a nobleman's honorable end by the sword.

Intermittently over the two decades following the 1570s, English expeditions ventured into the Caribbean in ever-increasing numbers, intent on attacking Spanish shipping and plundering her towns. The political justification was that the flow of treasure from the New World to Spain had to be disrupted in order to hinder Spanish ambitions in Europe—1588, after all, was the year Philip II's armada attempted to conquer England and English feelings for anything Spanish were hardly warm. However, Drake's initial attacks in particular were conducted without the knowledge or approval of the queen. It seems likely that Elizabeth I came to secretly condone his piracy and, after 1577, probably financed ventures conducted in her name, without openly published letters of marque; deniability remained her watchword when it came to dealing with Spain until after the failed armada.

The legal status of the Elizabethan Sea Rovers varied from time to time; Hawkins and Drake both sailed as legal privateers one moment and as pirates the next. On his capture of the *Cacafuego* in 1579, Drake told her captain that he was "to rob by command of the Queen of England." Meanwhile, Elizabeth delighted in referring to Drake as her "pirate." Against the Spanish Armada, Drake and his colleagues

The war in the Caribbean (Francis Drake's attack on Cartagena in 1586, **far left**) was part of a larger picture. Spain's desire to bring England to her knees culminated in Philip II's Armada of 1588 (**left**). Despite the terror the massive invasion fleet caused throughout the British Isles, its defeat by England's navy was only the most dramatic incident in the long-running war. Most of the action was fought in the Caribbean by Queen Elizabeth's Sea Dogs. In the attack on Cartagena, several stages of the action are depicted. The English fleet is seen entering the inner bay, while the landed troops storm the city walls.

The gold and silver of Mexico, Peru, and Bolivia were minted into coins before shipment to Spain. The two main coins were the gold doubloon (**above**) and the silver piece of eight (**below**), from which was later derived the Spanish *peso*. Huge quantities of doubloons crossed the Atlantic in the holds of treasure galleons—many also found their way into pirate hands.

Frobisher and Hawkins represented nothing less than England's navy, and indeed were the forerunners of that very successful institution, which had yet to take on the definitive form it would in the 17th century. However, it was John Hawkins, a man who combined commerce, warfare, and piracy with national defense—at various times slave trader, pirate, naval administrator, and national hero—who was the first Elizabethan Sea Dog. In his attempts to break the monopoly of the Spanish Main, his piratical attacks set the tone for later English raids against Spain's overseas empire.

Sir John Hawkins—trader, pirate, hero

John Hawkins was a most interesting character, a fine example of Elizabethan mixed morality. He was knighted for his efforts in reorganizing the English navy that would later destroy the Spanish Armada, but the expeditions of his earlier years were openly piratical and a negative inspiration to many who followed in his wake. His own inspiration was also close enough to hand—his father. John Hawkins was born in 1532 in the port of Plymouth in the county of Devon, a region of southwest England renowned for maritime activity. His father William was one of the richest merchants in Plymouth, boasting an annual income of some 150 pounds at a time when the wealthy port's revenues amounted to a mere 63 pounds. William seems to have benefited financially as Plymouth's Lord Mayor when, at King Henry VIII's command, the fabulously wealthy Roman Catholic monasteries were dissolved.

In the services to his king from which he did so well, William received the King's Commission to "annoy the King's enemies," letters of marque that gave him freedom to tread the fine line between legality and piracy. William organized a fleet of privateers and his repeated voyages to Portuguese-held Africa and the Spanish Main were more than peaceful trading missions. Trade with Spain's provinces was not forbidden, but any dealings had to be approved by the Seville authorities, which strove to maintain a monopoly of trade to the New World. The young Hawkins soon learned from his father that bypassing official channels was the sensible way to trade in the Spanish Main, and by the time he came to command his own ships he knew that the profits produced by illicit trade would greatly outweigh the risk.

In preparation for his future career, John journeyed to London soon after 1560. There, he married Catherine, daughter of Benjamin Gonson, the navy treasurer. His father-in-law opened doors for the young man, who soon fronted a powerful syndicate of officials and wealthy merchants that included Gonson, William Winter (later knighted), chief surveyor of the navy and master of ordnance, and Sir Thomas Lodge and Sir Lionel Duckett, both of whom were "Guinea merchant-adventurers" engaged in the gold trade off the Gold Coast of Africa, a stretch of the Guinea Coast. In addition to his metalurgical interests, Duckett was also a cloth manufacturer, owner of a waterworks company, and Lord Mayor of London. William Winter was another licensed privateer who harried French shipping on his way to West Africa in ships sponsored by the monarch. Within only a few more years Hawkins could also count among his regular backers political shakers like Robert Dudley, Earl of Leicester and Henry Herbert, Earl of Pembroke.

No doubt due to information provided by Lodge, Duckett, and Winter, Hawkins departed on his first voyage with four vessels in October 1562 for West Africa and the Guinea Coast. The plan was to capture natives in the region of modern Sierra Leone and transport them across the Atlantic to the Caribbean to sell as slaves. In so doing, he fell foul of both Portuguese and Spanish authorities. Hawkins had already established links with Pedro de Ponte, a member of an important family of Genoese descent living in the Canary Islands. De Ponte was something of a pirate himself, preying on Portuguese interests in defiance of the Treaty of Tordesillas and selling his gains in Hispaniola and Jamaica. With de Ponte's help Hawkins secured the services of a pilot who knew the African coast intimately, a renegade Spaniard from Seville named Juan Martinez. Between them, they gathered about 400 slaves from the coast, as well as by boarding two Portuguese slave ships and stealing their

84

human cargoes. As mentioned above, the Spanish settlers in the Caribbean were desperate for labor to replace the natives who had died out and so when Hawkins arrived off Hispaniola, he was easily able to sell his cargo illegally in the small towns, well away from the Spanish authorities in the main settlement of Santo Domingo. Bartering the slaves for pearls, some gold and silver, hides, sugar, and other luxury goods, the enterprise produced a huge profit and proved that piracy—stealing slaves from the Portuguese—could increase his margin. Hawkins was encouraged to repeat the venture in the following year, taking his young cousin, one Francis Drake, along with him.

The following year, relations between England and Spain deteriorated, and the Spanish crown forbade any trade with English merchants. Undeterred, Hawkins planned another slaving voyage to the Caribbean via West Africa. Elizabeth I was one of his backers and lent him the warship *Jesus of Lübeck*. Hawkins left Plymouth in 1564, arriving a few months later in the Spanish Main off the coast of Venezuela and sold the slaves in the small port of Rio de la Hacha, despite the hindrance of local Spanish officials. He reaped a further healthy profit from the slaves, and the expedition returned safely to Plymouth in September 1565. The Spanish were furious and pressured Elizabeth to forbid further interloping voyages. She agreed but secretly continued to back Hawkins, who planned a new voyage in 1566. He was unable to take part and it was a failure.

Hawkins led the next trading voyage, accompanied by Drake, sailing in October 1567 with five ships, including the *Jesus of Lübeck*. As usual he attacked Portuguese slaving ships, stole their human cargoes, and then crossed the Atlantic. Back in Rio de la Hacha, the governor refused to deal with the Englishman —until Hawkins burned part of the town and captured hostages. In September 1568, a storm forced Hawkins up against the "floating" fortress of San Juan de Ulúa (*see map, page 94*), which guarded Vera Cruz. Since more silver, gold, gems, and precious stuffs were stored in and shipped from Vera Cruz than almost any other place on earth, it was an attractive target. As a result, it was also heavily defended. Of a string of offshore forts constructed on low-lying sandbars, the newest, only commissioned the year before Hawkins' attack, was San Juan de Ulúa. The English were forced to fight their way out, and only Hawkins' and Drake's ships got away, barely escaping with

The formidable walls of the fort of San Juan de Ulúa, which protected Vera Cruz from pirate attack. Against these stones, the crews of John Hawkins (**opposite**) and his cousin Francis Drake met a grim fate in 1568, although the two pirate-captains made good their escape.

85

Sir Francis Drake damaged the Spanish treasury more than any other privateer. It has been estimated that the haul from his capture of the *Cacafuego* was worth more than 100,000 million pounds in today's values.

Largely due to Arabic learning, European navigators' instruments for determining a vessel's position at sea were improving. Made by the leading Elizabethan instrument-maker Humphrey Cole, this object, said to belong to Drake, provided the sailor with many cities' latitudes, as well as lunar and solar dials to calculate latitude; measuring a ship's longitude was still beyond anyone.

their lives. Hawkins left behind the queen's flagship, most of his crew, and all of his profits. This disaster signaled the end of his trading expeditions; Drake would take up where his cousin left off.

Hawkins became treasurer of the navy in 1577 and began the reorganization that reaped rewards during the battle against the Spanish Armada a decade later. In 1588 he was knighted and appointed chief administrator of the navy, leading a squadron against the Armada in the same year. In 1590 Hawkins tried to attack the returning Spanish treasure fleet off the Azores but failed. It appeared he was losing his touch, and in his last expedition in 1595, the 63-year-old commander fell out with Drake during a joint raid on the Spanish Main. He died onboard his flagship while the English ships lay off San Juan in Puerto Rico.

El Dragón—scourge of the Spanish Main

Pirate or national hero, Sir Francis Drake is probably the best-known English seaman of the Elizabethan era. He certainly earned his sobriquet of the "scourge of the Spanish Main" and, with the capture of the galleon *Cacafuego*, brought back the greatest ever treasure stolen from the Spanish. Drake, born the son of a puritan preacher in Plymouth in 1540, sailed in the ships of his older cousin John Hawkins in 1566 and 1567. In the second expedition, Hawkins gave Drake the command of a captured prize, but his ship was trapped in the following year with the rest of Hawkins' small fleet at San Juan de Ulúa. Although this expedition was a financial disaster, it showed Drake the Spanish Main's potential, and engendered in the young man a lifelong hatred of Spaniards. The 27-year-old seaman swore he would

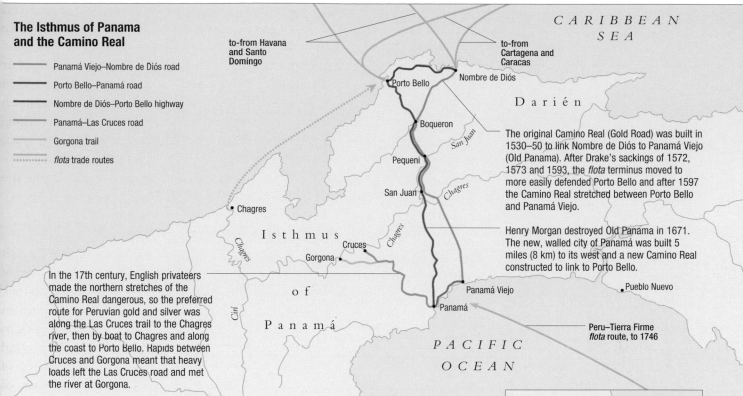

The Isthmus of Panama and the Camino Real

— Panamá Viejo–Nombre de Diós road
— Porto Bello–Panamá road
— Nombre de Diós–Porto Bello highway
— Panamá–Las Cruces road
— Gorgona trail
····· *flota* trade routes

The original Camino Real (Gold Road) was built in 1530–50 to link Nombre de Diós to Panamá Viejo (Old Panama). After Drake's sackings of 1572, 1573 and 1593, the *flota* terminus moved to more easily defended Porto Bello and after 1597 the Camino Real stretched between Porto Bello and Panamá Viejo.

Henry Morgan destroyed Old Panama in 1671. The new, walled city of Panamá was built 5 miles (8 km) to its west and a new Camino Real constructed to link to Porto Bello.

In the 17th century, English privateers made the northern stretches of the Camino Real dangerous, so the preferred route for Peruvian gold and silver was along the Las Cruces trail to the Chagres river, then by boat to Chagres and along the coast to Porto Bello. Rapids between Cruces and Gorgona meant that heavy loads left the Las Cruces road and met the river at Gorgona.

launch a one-man war against the Spanish, and his endeavors eventually earned him the nickname El Dragón.

Drake's first expedition to the Spanish Main in his own name came in 1570, and twice more in succeeding years. Hawkins combined raiding in the Caribbean with trading, but unlike his cousin Drake refused to engage in ordinary commerce, preferring to hit Spanish ports and capture prizes in a quasi-legal privateering war he claimed was fought in the name of his queen. The expedition of 1572 started promisingly enough when Drake's small force of two ships and 73 men captured Nombre de Diós on the Darién peninsula on July 29. Shortly after, and before the Englishmen could reach the king's treasure house, reinforcements arrived from Panama. The fight was fierce, with blood spilled on both sides, including Drake's. His wound was not severe and he managed to lead a retreat to their beached pinnaces, taking little in the way of plunder and leaving behind silver bars and other treasures. Undeterred by this setback, Drake sailed a little way up the coast, anchored in a bay and led his men ashore to reach the Camino Real. There, he tried to ambush the annual mule convoy carrying Peruvian silver across the isthmus from Panama City. But the Spanish authorities had been alerted to the attempt and set a trap in the surrounding swamps to ambush the ambushers.

Driven off again, the intrepid captain sailed away to lick his wounds and regroup. In the course of the rest of the year he formed an alliance with a French Huguenot pirate, with whom he laid plans for the following year. On April 1, 1573 Drake attacked Nombre de Diós again and the superior numbers of his joint Anglo-French force won the day. A mule train loaded with treasure was captured just outside the port. This time, they took every thing they could carry. Drake returned to England with his loot, but discovered that he was out of favor. England and Spain were technically at peace at the time, and the king of Spain's ambassadors had condemned his 1572 attacks as acts of piracy. Caught in a dilemma, Queen Elizabeth refused to condone her subject's activities and Drake went into hiding for a little over two years.

There was greater approval for Drake's successful raid among Elizabeth's courtiers, however, and doubtless the queen harbored secret affection for her "pirate." In any event, he was welcomed back to court again in 1577, as the queen secretly backed a new expedition. Drake set out again at the end of the year, in command of five ships, two supply vessels, and three men-of-war including his flagship, the three-masted *Golden Hind*. The ambitious plan was to enter the Pacific Ocean and take the Spanish by surprise where they were at their most vulnerable. After sailing down the African coast, the squadron crossed the Atlantic to South America and turned south along the continent's east shore. Disaster struck off Cape Horn when a storm sank some ships and forced others to return home. On her own, *Golden Hind* sailed north up the Pacific coast of South America, sacking Valparaiso in Chile.

A contemporary woodcut shows Drake's *Golden Hind* attacking the *Cacafuego*. When Drake returned to England in 1580, news of his exploit increased his popular admiration, and a great many pamphlet illustrations—of more verve than accuracy —soon appeared to satisfy public demand.

Between the Horn and Valparaiso, Drake encountered further severe storms, although these ill winds blew the privateer some good. After makeshift repairs to the devastation wrought to the ship's sails and rigging, Spaniards he encountered failed to identify the *Golden Hind* as a pirate ship and fell easy victim to El Dragón's attacks. When he had slipped through the strait of Magellan in the spring of 1578, Drake was the first privateer to do so and he took the Spanish authorities completely by surprise. In addition, the extremely long, convoluted coastline, hemmed in by the Andes, made communications very slow for the Spanish authorities. Over the course of the year, Drake sailed ahead of news of his approach. He plundered a Spanish warship and in early 1579 pillaged Peru's main port of Callao (near Lima). While there was some loot to be seized, the real treasure turned out to be information. Drake learned that the 120-ton treasure ship *Nuestra Señora de la Concepción* (*Our Lady of Conception*) had just left Callao headed for Panama City, where her cargo and important passengers would cross the isthmus on the way to Nombre de Diós and thence to Spain.

The taking of the *Cacafuego*

Loaded down with plunder, the *Golden Hind* continues sailing northwest along the North American coast to the vicinity of San Francisco before turning due west for Drake to complete his circumnavigation of the globe.

Drake catches up with the slow *Cacafuego* off Esmeraldas in March and takes her prize with only a few shots fired.

Spanish territory by 1570

route of the *Golden Hind*

major Spanish road

Callao sacked early in 1579. Drake hears of the rich treasure ship *Cacafuego*, sailing for Panama and goes in pursuit.

Drake's small fleet of five ships crosses the Atlantic from the African to the South American coast late in 1577.

Drake sacks Valparaiso, 1578.

A severe storm sinks two ships and forces the rest except Drake's *Golden Hind* to return to England. Drake sails through the Strait of Magellan in spring of 1578.

Falkland Islands

Nombre de Diós · Cartagena · Panamá Viejo · New Granada · TERRE FIRME · NORTH ATLANTIC OCEAN · Buenaventura · Esmeraldas · Quito · Manta · Guayaquil · Tumbes · VICEROY OF PERU · Amazon · Trujillo · Callao · Ciudad de los Reyes (Lima) · Cuzco · La Paz · Arica · Potosí · Asunción · Córdoba · Valparaiso · Santiago · Buenos Aires · SOUTH ATLANTIC OCEAN · SOUTH PACIFIC OCEAN · Strait of Magellan

Despite her properly Catholic name, the sailors of *Nuestra Señora de la Concepción* called her something far more vulgar—*Cagafuego* (it was later inaccurately rendered in records as *Cacafuego*, which spelling has endured). Literally translated, it means "she shits fire." The nickname was probably barely appropriate because although pirates had been raiding the Spanish Main for decades, at that time Spanish captains thought the Pacific was safe, and since they did not expect to encounter marauders, most ships went at best lightly armed. After a fevered pursuit of some days, the *Golden Hind*'s topman sighted their prey on the first day of March near Esmeraldas, Ecuador. Drake's intent was to attack after nightfall, and since it was barely after midday he needed to slow down. But how to do it? Lowering sail would surely arouse the suspicions of the *Cacafuego*'s captain and Drake did not want to lose his advantage of surprise. He ordered his men to lower tethered wine caskets over the side to act as weather anchors, their drag slowing the ship without altering the sails.

Some nine hours later, the *Golden Hind* came alongside her target. Expecting to meet only Spanish ships, the *Cacafuego*'s captain took no precautions and when Drake's men swarmed aboard, the Spanish crew surrendered quickly. The English privateer then took both ships out to sea. Beyond sight of the coast he treated his captives with great generosity, dining with the officers and noble passengers. On the following day he offloaded his captives in the vicinity of Esmeraldas, some even with presents appropriate to their rank.

Transferring the plunder to the *Golden Hind* took three days, so rich was the Spanish cargo. On his release, one youthful Spaniard had joked that the *Golden Hind* should now be named *Cacafuego* while the former of that name should now be known as the *Cacaplata*, for indeed she did "shit silver." The ships separated on March 6 and the *Golden Hind* began the long, perilous voyage home. Unwilling to return the way he came, Drake sailed on up the Pacific coast of America to California, then west across the ocean in July. After a mammoth voyage of circumnavigation, he arrived back in Plymouth on September 26, 1580.

The value of the astonishing haul he brought back is uncertain. Only Drake knew the amount of his booty and Queen Elizabeth forbade him to reveal it to anyone else. The *Cacafuego*'s holds appear to have carried an amount of valuable items that were not listed on her manifest, and it is likely that the queen appropriated a substantial portion of this in excess of her investor's share. For their part, Drake claimed that each of his backers received 47 pounds for every pound invested, a handsome return for their faith, even after Elizabeth's unlawful appropriation. The true worth will never be known; the Seville bureaucrats put their loss at 360,000 pounds, but that did not account for the unlisted treasure, nor the valuables taken from the *Cacafuego*'s wealthy passengers. The voyage had brought Drake fame, wealth, and the queen's admiration; he was knighted in 1581.

Five years later, Drake proposed and won royal sanction for another campaign against the Spanish Main. The degree to which the elite of the kingdom flocked to Drake's banner to invest in his venture is indicated by some of the leading names found on the consortium rolls. Among the peers of the realm, the earls Leicester, Shrewsbury, Rutland, and Bedford backed the expedition, while Shrewsbury contributed the *Talbot* and Leicester offered Drake the galleons *Speedwell* and *Leicester*, captained by another great English Sea Dog, his brother-in-law Francis Knollys. Lord Admiral Charles Howard provided the *White Lion* and John Hawkins' navy backer Sir William Winter gave the *Sea Dragon*. Hawkins himself, by this time holding the important post of treasurer of the navy, was earnest in supporting his cousin's preparations. In all, as 1586 dawned, Drake led a fleet of more than 25 ships to the Spanish Main. Once in the Caribbean he caused mayhem, capturing the ports of St. Augustine in Florida, Santo Domingo in Hispaniola, and Cartagena in Colombia. However, the voyage was not a great financial success, and the growing threat of a Spanish invasion of England prevented another expedition for a decade.

Raids on the Spanish coast in 1587 failed to prevent the sailing of the Spanish Armada in 1588, but the English fleet comprehensively defeated the massive Spanish force. Drake took a leading part and received national renown for his actions. He returned to the Spanish Main in 1595 in joint-command with Hawkins of a fleet of 27 ships. The expedition's aim was to capture Panama, but Drake was sidetracked by other opportunities and attacked Las Palmas in the Canary Islands and then Puerto Rico—to be thwarted at both locations. After several assaults on

The first English sea atlas, the Mariner's Mirrour, appeared in 1588, the same year that Elizabeth knighted Sir John Hawkins and the Spanish Armada sailed against the British Isles. The atlas was hardly original, most of its information had been "borrowed" from Dutch charts.

the port of San Juan were repelled, he was forced to withdraw, having fallen out with Hawkins, who died shortly afterward.

Drake cruised off the coast of Venezuela, capturing a number of small towns without finding much booty. Eventually, in August, he took the Caribbean port of Nombre de Diós and set off across the isthmus towards the Pacific coast and Panama on the Camino Real. But once again the Spanish were ready for him and stopped the English advance in its tracks. Forced to retire, Drake had Nombre de Diós burned to the ground before boarding his force. As the fleet sailed toward Porto Bello, Drake caught a fever and became mortally ill. Fearing his end was near, he drew up his will on January 27, 1596, bequeathing the greater part of his huge estate, comprising several manors and other holdings in Devon and around Plymouth, to his brother. He died at sea on the following day and was buried at sea off the harbor of Porto Bello on January 29. Sir Francis Drake died a national hero, and is remembered as one of England's greatest sea captains. To the Spanish, he would always remain the murdering El Dragón.

An accurate, full-scale replica of Drake's flagship, the *Golden Hind*.

CHAPTER SIX

A Piece of the Action

Buccaneers from all over Europe rip apart the Spanish Main

From modest beginnings on the northwestern edges of Hispaniola (modern Haiti and Dominican Republic) in the late 16th century, a scattering of initially French outlaws grew to become a dire threat to Spain's monopoly of the Spanish Main. The lives and colorful exploits of so many of these buccaneers, as they came to be called, are known to us through the writing of Alexander Olivier Exquemelin (c.1645–1707, also spelled Esquemeling). He brought them to vivid life in his *History of the Bucaniers of America*, and was himself one of their number.

Born in either Harfleur or Honfleur, both close to Le Havre, France, to probably Huguenot parents, Exquemelin was indentured by the French West India Company and sailed to the Spanish Main in 1666. Having suffered the typical brutality of an indentured laborer's life in the colonies, he gained his freedom after some three years and became a privateer, enlisting with the buccaneers on Tortuga. According to his own account, he was present at the raids led by Sir Henry Morgan that plundered Maracaibo in 1669 and Panama in 1671. In the following year Exquemelin turned merchant, and sailed on several expeditions to the Americas with both Spanish and Dutch fleets, serving as a barber-surgeon. His return to Europe took him to Amsterdam—Holland was notably tolerant of Huguenots, now virtually banished from France—where in 1678 his book was published under its original Dutch title, *De Americaensche Zee-Roovers*.

It was an instant bestseller, probably because its publisher, Jan ten Hoorn, freely edited the text, adding anecdotes and even whole sections to make it more exciting. The probable intent of the original was further lost when the book went into French, German, Spanish, and—in 1684—English editions, each time being edited to suit the local market's taste for adventure and infamy. For ten years after the Dutch publication the events of Exquemelin's life are unknown until we find him in Paris, 1686, writing an intelligence account for the French navy about his experience of the Chagres river in Panama. At the close of the century the former buccaneer emigrated to a French colony in North America. With so many rewrites by different hands, it remains a matter of opinion as to how much of Exquemelin's book is reliable; certainly he was the first of a tradition of romantic writing about pirates, imitated ever since—as fact or fiction.

Opposite: *Buccaneer attack on a Spanish Galleon*, oil painting by Howard Pyle. The early buccaneers rarely had their hands on large vessels, but used small sailing boats or sloops to attack Spanish shipping off Hispaniola.

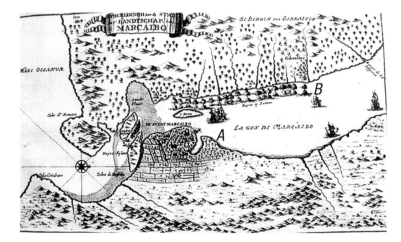

A map of Lake Maracaibo in Venezuela, showing the towns of Maracaibo (**A**) and Gibraltar (**B**) from the 1678 Dutch edition of Exquemelin's pirate book. The French author witnessed first-hand the mayhem caused here by Sir Henry Morgan during the buccaneer's raid of 1668.

Louisiana

Biloxi •
• New Orleans

St. Aug

FLORIDA

San Antonio •

Florida key

Straits of

HAVANA • Mata

G u l f   o f
M e x i c o

Monterrey •

Zacatecas •

Isla de Pino

N
E
W

• Mérida

San Blas •

Cayman Isl
to England a
1

Bay of
Campeche

• Campeche
(San Francisco)

Mexico •

• Vera Cruz

YUCATÁN
PENINSULA

Gulf of
Honduras

MEXICO

S
P
A
I
N

• Villhermosa

Isla Cozumel

Puerto Cortés •
• San Pedro

Mosquito Coast

HONDURAS

• Guatemala

P A C I F I C
O C E A N

Lake
Nicaragua

Managua •

Granada •

NICARAGUA

Turrialba •   • Pu
Li

Cartago •

COSTA RICA

Vera Cruz

Sandbank
at low
tide

North Channel

North Fortress

Bridge

Sandbanks at low
tide

Fortress of
San Juan de Ulúa

Customs House

South Channel

Vera Cruz

Mexico
Road

"De Stad Vera Cruz in Nieuw Spanje"
—from a late 17th-century Dutch
map of the fortified town.

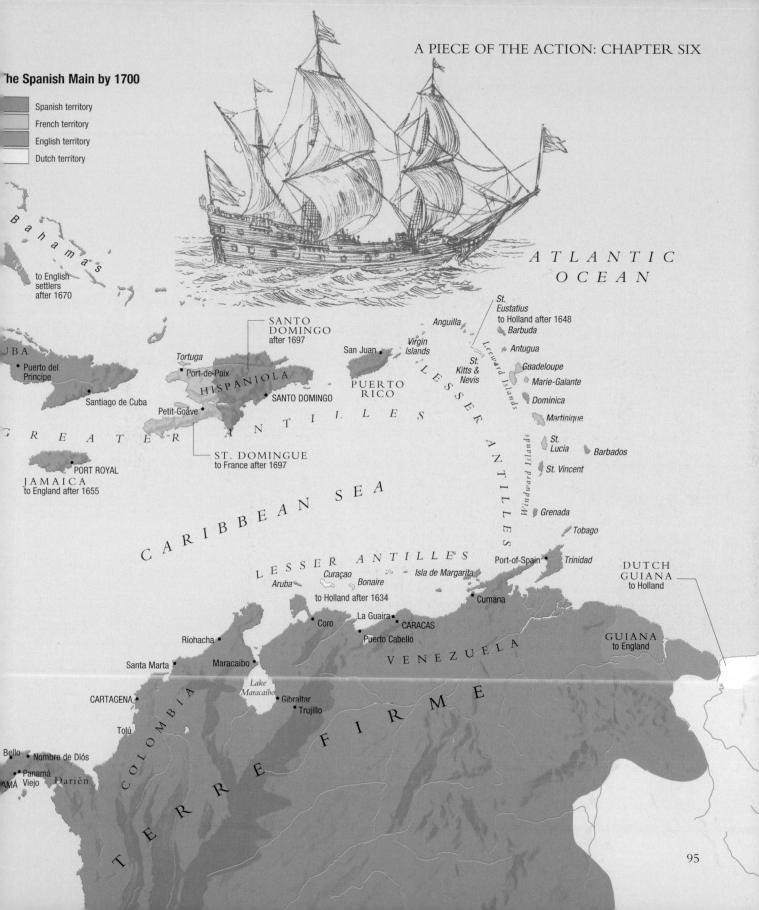

The Spanish Main by 1700

Spanish territory
French territory
English territory
Dutch territory

ATLANTIC OCEAN

B a h a m a s

to English
settlers
after 1670

CUBA

• Puerto del
Principe

• Santiago de Cuba

G R E A T E R   A N T I L L E S

• PORT ROYAL

JAMAICA
to England after 1655

Tortuga

Port-de-Paix •

HISPANIOLA

Petit-Goâve •

SANTO
DOMINGO
after 1697

SANTO DOMINGO •

ST. DOMINGUE
to France after 1697

San Juan •

PUERTO
RICO

Virgin
Islands

Anguilla

St.
Eustatius
to Holland after 1648

Barbuda

Antugua

St.
Kitts &
Nevis

Guadeloupe

Marie-Galante

Dominica

Martinique

St.
Lucia

Barbados

St. Vincent

L E S S E R   A N T I L L E S

Leeward Islands

Windward Islands

Grenada

Tobago

CARIBBEAN SEA

L E S S E R   A N T I L L E S

Curaçao

Aruba

Bonaire

Isla de Margarita

Port-of-Spain •

Trinidad

to Holland after 1634

Cumana •

DUTCH
GUIANA
to Holland

Coro •

La Guaira •

CARACAS •

Puerto Cabello •

Ríohacha •

Santa Marta •

Maracaibo •

V E N E Z U E L A

GUIANA
to England

CARTAGENA •

COLOMBIA

Lake
Maracaibo

Gibraltar •

Trujillo •

Tolú •

Bello •

• Nombre de Diós

• Panamá
Viejo

PANAMÁ

Darién

T E R R E   F I R M E

95

A buccaneering start

Well before Exquemelin's time, the seeds of buccaneering were sown by Pedro de Menéndez de Aville's destruction of the French Huguenot settlement on the Florida coast at Fort Caroline in 1565, recorded in the previous chapter. Driven from Florida, a few Huguenots moved to Hispaniola, where they lived wild, out of Spanish sight, mostly on the small island of Tortuga. The Florida massacre had served to worsen relations in France between the growing numbers of Protestant and Roman Catholics. More Huguenots opted for voluntary exile in the New World than face an uncertain future in a France controlled by powerful Catholic ministers, but many of these immigrants found piracy preferable to a life of husbandry in the raw territories of America. Inevitably, they followed rumors and

Port-au-Prince, the modern capital of Haiti, did not exist in the buccaneering era, although when Tortuga became crowded the region was quickly inhabited because it was rich in wild game. The French government moved from Petit-Goâve to Cap-Français at the start of the 18th century, and then to Port-au-Prince in 1770.

Spain officially ceded the western third of Hispaniola to France in 1697, but already by 1650 Spain's remit failed to run across the boundary and the unofficial French colony of St. Domingue was effectively under the control of a "governor" appointed by French authorities in the Lesser Antilles, and later from Paris. In the one serious attempt to remove the Huguenot pirates and French buccaneers, the Spanish troops were outnumbered and soundly beaten. A brief "English" period was also overthrown and the colony returned to local French rule.

migrated to join those Frenchmen who had fled from Spanish authority to the heavily forested outreaches of Hispaniola and Tortuga.

Before the 17th century these were not pirates but outlaws, ragged men generally operating in pairs who roamed the island hunting wild game, not unlike the few remaining indigenes. And the name of "buccaneer" comes from the Arawak Indian word *buccan* (or *boucan*)—a fire specially banked to smoke meat in order to preserve it. The early buccaneers were tough frontiersmen, who dressed in rough rawhide and skin clothing. Knives were the commonest weapons; as many as could owned hunting muskets and few boasted a sword. In time, as their numbers grew and they looked for an easier life, the buccaneers began rustling cattle from Spanish estates. They soon became a serious threat to the peace. The authorities in Santo Domingo determined to rid Hispaniola of the pests in the early 1600s. While the campaign succeeded in respect of its principal aim, it failed in another and more important way; the buccaneers stole small boats and—many concentrating on more easily defended Tortuga—turned from hunting game to attacking ships.

Hispaniola's rugged and convoluted northern coastline made it difficult for the Spanish to root out the French buccaneers, and by the 1620s the pirates were venting their hatred on passing Spanish ships with great success. Now dressed in the garb that was to characterize the ordinary buccaneer—coarse shirts, woolen breeches, and hats or headscarves to ward off the fierce sun—they slunk out from the mangrove creeks in flotillas of small sailing or rowing boats known as *flibotes* (flyboats) or pinnaces, to creep up astern of larger Spanish ships, preferably under cover of darkness, and board them before the alarm could be raised. While marksmen shot the helmsman and officers, other buccaneers wedged the ship's rudder to prevent its escape, then swarmed up the vessel's side. The French buccaneers rarely spared their prisoners if there was the least hint of resistance, and their reputation for cruelty when opposed was usually enough to encourage Spanish crews to surrender without a shot being fired. In one particularly gruesome example, the French buccaneer L'Ollonais is colorfully described in Exquemelin's book as growing "outrageously passionate" as he interrogates his captives. We are told that L'Ollonais "drew his cutlass, and with it cut open the breast of one of those poor Spaniards, and pulling out his heart with his sacrilegious hands, began to bite and gnaw it with his teeth like a ravenous dog." Terror was a weapon, and a record of cruelty discouraged resistance and made a pirate's life simpler.

The buccaneers' success soon became bruited abroad, and runaway slaves as well as the exiled, dispossessed, wretched, and the outlawed of most European nations (but particularly of England) swelled their numbers. By the 1640s, the buccaneers were sufficiently strong to kick out the remaining Spanish settlers from the island of Tortuga, which was fortified and became a haven for fugitives of any nation. And their numbers continued to climb. When the English drove the Spanish out of Jamaica in 1655, a place entirely free of the hated enemy was an attractive lure to those English buccaneers who now found

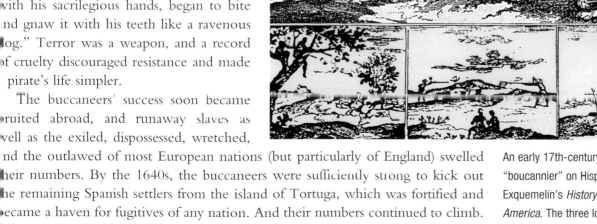

An early 17th-century Huguenot "boucannier" on Hispaniola, from Exquemelin's *History of the Bucaniers of America*. The three lower scenes show him hunting and smoking the game over a smoldering *buccan* fire.

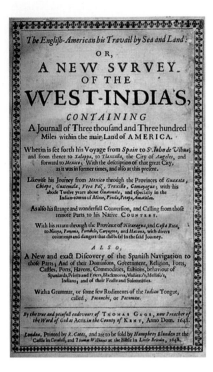

The Engliſh-American his Travail by Sea and Land:

OR,

A NEW SVRVEY.
OF THE
WEST-INDIA'S,

CONTAINING

A Journall of Three thouſand and Three hundred
Miles within the main Land of AMERICA.

Wherein is ſet forth his Voyage from *Spain* to S*t. Iohn de Ulhua*;
and from thence to *Xalappa*, to *Tlaxcalla*, the City of *Angeles*, and
forward to *Mexico*; With the deſcription of that great City,
as it was in former times, and alſo at this preſent.

Likewiſe his Iourney from *Mexico* through the Provinces of *Guaxaca*,
Chiapa, *Guatemala*, *Vera Paz*, *Truxillo*, *Comayagua*; with his
abode Twelve years about *Guatemala*, and eſpecially in the
Indian-towns of *Mixco*, *Pinola*, *Petapa*, *Amatitlan*.

As alſo his ſtrange and wonderfull Converſion, and Calling from thoſe
remote Parts to his Native COUNTREY.

With his return through the Province of *Nicaragua*, and *Coſta Rica*,
to *Nicoya*, *Panama*, *Portobelo*, *Cartagena*, and *Havana*, with divers
occurrents and dangers that did befal in the ſaid Journey.

A L S O,

A New and exact Diſcovery of the Spaniſh Navigation to
thoſe Parts; And of their Dominions, Government, Religion, Forts,
Caſtles, Ports, Havens, Commodities, faſhions, behaviour of
Spaniards, Prieſts and Friers, Blackmores, Mulata's, Meſtiſo's,
Indians; and of their Feaſts and Solemnities.

With a Grammar, or ſome few Rudiments of the *Indian* Tongue,
called, *Poconchi*, or *Pocoman*.

By the true and painfull endevours of THOMAS GAGE, now Preacher of
the Word of God at Acris in the County of KENT, Anno Dom. 1648.

London, Printed by R. Cotes, and are to be ſold by Humphrey Blunden at the
Caſtle in *Cornhil*, and Thomas Williams at the Bible in Little Britain, 1648.

The spirit of exploration that characterized the 16th century was not entirely lost to the drive for material gain in the 17th, as proved by the adventures of Thomas Gage (c.1603–56), as recounted in his journal *A New Survey of the West-India's*, published in 1648. Gage's journey took him 3300 miles from "Spain to St. Iohn de Ulhua; and from thence to Xalappa, to Tlaxcalla, the City of Angeles, and forward to Mexico." Having described "that great City, as it was in former times, and also at this present," he traveled through the provinces of New Spain, visiting Guatemala, then on to Nicaragua, Costa Rica, Panama, and Cartagena. His return trip took in many Caribbean islands and a stop at Havana. His close observation of Spanish provincial customs, the militia, castles, fortifications, and harbors provided the French and English buccaneers with valuable intelligence about their mutual enemy.

themselves packed in like sardines on Tortuga, and many moved to the Jamaican capital, Port Royal. The buccaneers of Tortuga and Jamaica, calling themselves the "Brethren of the Coast," developed a highly organized society and a form of almost military administration, and in many cases they were commanded by officers sent from England. In spite of their obvious lawlessness, the buccaneers evolved a code of conduct based on their earliest experiences as woodsmen needing each other's support in the cruel wilderness; and so they continued to pair off, foraging and fighting together and for each other. This partnership continued when they were in Port Royal, where it was quite usual for a common-law wife to be shared between a pair of comrades. The intimate buccaneer partnerships were especially useful in battle, with one looking out for the other. The buccaneers in Jamaica were generally well equipped on the proceeds of piracy but also found favor with successive governors, who encouraged and sometimes even sponsored them to attack Spanish interests. In the 1660s the Brethren began raiding Spanish towns, inspired by the example of government-appointed naval Commodore Christopher Myngs, who led a number of attacks, including a raid on the city of Santiago de Cuba.

Buccaneer raids were hard-hitting and usually followed a commando-style pattern in which a force of men was put ashore further down the coast from the target, so that when the ships opened fire from seaward, the enemy was surprised by a second attack from the landward side. Henry Morgan perfected this style of raid during the 1660s and 70s (*see pages 103–4*), of which 1668's sack of Porto Bello is a typical example. Considering their traditional background as hunters and woodsmen, it is no surprise that buccaneers were unusually skilled in the use of knives and musketry, but in combination with their rudimentary organization they often achieved a result similar to that of trained troops. In the stand-up land battle outside Panama in 1671, they outfought the regular Spanish troops, including the cavalry, having been trained to fire in volleys, like regular soldiers. The prime influence in military matters on Morgan was Myngs, one of those professional officers seconded to the irregulars of the Caribbean. His use of buccaneers as an "offensive" defense was a brilliant strategy that safeguarded the English foothold in the Spanish Main.

The Commonwealth's pirate

An English naval officer, Christopher Myngs combined his orders from Oliver Cromwell to protect the unanticipated gain of Jamaica as an English colony with the opportunity to harass the Spanish. He used buccaneers to raid Spanish settlements and blurred the line between piracy and actions performed on behalf of the state. Born in Norfolk in eastern England in 1625, the young Myngs joined the Royal Navy as a cabin boy a year or two before the English Civil War (1641–52) between King Charles I and Parliament. He sided with parliamentarians—the winning side—

and rapidly rose through the ranks, rewarded for his loyalty to Oliver Cromwell with promotion to flag officer rank. And then in 1656, Myngs was ordered to the Caribbean to clear up a mess left by General Venables in the previous year.

As Lord Protector of England and Her Commonwealth, Cromwell's puritan rule made any Roman Catholics natural enemies to be pursued with vehemence. The Irish soon discovered what that meant, and neither were the Spanish left out. In 1655 Cromwell dispatched an amphibious army under the command of Venables to attack the Spanish empire in the Americas, specifically to capture and hold some important stronghold like Santo Domingo, Havana, Vera Cruz, or Cartagena. Venables opted for the closest target, Hispaniola, but the first action aimed at its capital of Santo Domingo was a catastrophe. Aware of Cromwell's plans, the Spanish were too well prepared for Venables, and the English troops were driven back into the sea with heavy losses.

The tattered remnant of the English force sailed in a westerly direction until it reached Jamaica. Although Spain held the island, Seville considered Jamaica of less importance in comparison to the rest of her Caribbean holdings, and so its defenses were weak. Venables' 7000–8000 men easily took Santiago de la Vega, the island's only town, later renamed Port Royal. Despite the ease of conquest, the English troops suffered dreadfully from disease, fitful Spanish retaliation, and the depredations of Maroons, slaves who had seized the conflict as opportunity for escape. The Maroons had little reason to trust the white newcomers any more than their Spanish masters, although several later enlisted with pirate crews and with the buccaneers. Venables, having been recalled and thrown into the Tower of London for having taken such an insignificant prize instead of something like Havana, left the command of Jamaica to lesser men.

This, then, was the situation Christopher Myngs inherited when, in January 1656, he arrived in Port Royal aboard the 44-gun navy frigate *Marston Moor*, a vessel whose mutinous crew he had previously subdued with a firm hand. He quickly recognized that the best defense of Jamaica—surrounded by Spaniards on all sides—would be to take the offensive. He also concluded that the depleted and demoralized military force left behind by Venables would be of scarce use in any forthcoming amphibious

Sir Christopher Myngs, as painted by Sir Peter Leley. By the time he became an admiral of the English navy, Myngs was an experienced leader of buccaneers.

attack, and so turned to Port Royal's natural resource—the buccaneers. In May he led a raid on Santa Marta in Venezuela that demonstrated how buccaneers could help in his overall strategy as a commerce raider. By January 1657 he was given command of the Jamaican squadron of Commonwealth navy ships and buccaneer vessels, of which the *Marston Moor* became his flagship.

In October 1658, Myngs' squadron lay in wait off the coast near Porto Bello but narrowly missed taking ships from a treasure fleet. When the Spanish galleons arrived, most of the English ships had left to obtain fresh water. The *Marston Moor* and another vessel passed through the 29 Spanish ships, hung on their rear, and tried without success to scatter them. Perhaps more in revenge than compensation, the English fleet later burned Tolú (today in Colombia), captured two large ships in the harbor, and once again devastated Santa Marta. However, the profits here were slim because the fleet's sheer size had forewarned the inhabitants, who then fled inland with their possessions. Myngs changed his tactics. He split up the fleet, hoping to achieve surprise with less visible, smaller forces. The *Marston Moor* and two other ships attacked Cumana, Puerto Cabello (Caballos), and Coro on the Venezuelan coast, and achieved total surprise. Myngs also taught his men to press the attack well inland, pursuing any who escaped, a tactic which paid off handsomely at Coro, where they seized a large silver shipment belonging to the Spanish crown. The entire haul from the raid was valued at over a quarter of a million English pounds, exceeding all expectations.

The English naval officer now slid across that fine dividing line between privateering and piracy. By general consent, the booty belonged to Parliament and the Commonwealth, but Myngs put forward an argument that would later sustain Henry Morgan, that his commission was a naval one and the plunder had been taken in a land-based action. Maintaining that the provisions of his orders were therefore irrelevant, he split the haul with his men, rather than keep a share for the Jamaican governor and the English treasury.

On his return to Port Royal, a warrant for his arrest waited and he was sent back to England to be tried by the Admiralty on charges of embezzlement, but in the event he was fortunate. It was 1660 and back home the only matter on anyone's mind was the restoration of the monarchy. In the confusion that accompanied King Charles II taking over the reins of constitutional power, the case against Myngs was forgotten. So too was his parliamentarian stance of earlier years and by 1662 he was back in Jamaica as a captain in the new Royal Navy, commanding the 12-year-old, 34-gun HMS *Centurion*. Although by then Spain and England were at peace, the Jamaican authorities continued to harass Spanish possessions.

In October 1662 Myngs and his joint naval-buccaneer command stormed Santiago de Cuba, the large island's second city. The buccaneers captured several ships and treasure, then slighted the port's defenses before leaving. Since he had apparently avoided English censure over this theoretically unlawful action, Myngs pushed into the Gulf of Mexico in February 1663, leading a force of 1500 buccaneers, including French and Dutch pirates in over a dozen ships. The buccaneers captured San Francisco de Campeche, in the Bay of Campeche, after a bitter fight. The town produced 150,000 pieces of eight in booty, and Myngs captured 14 Spanish ships at anchor in the harbor.

The Spanish crown reacted with predictable fury against the raids on Santiago and Campeche, and laid such strong evidence of atrocities committed by Myngs and his "pirates" that the English crown was obliged to take notice. Charles II forbade any further naval action against Spain. The furore, however, had no detrimental effect on Myngs' career. He returned to England in 1665 to be promoted to the rank of vice-admiral. He saw action in the Second Anglo-Dutch War (1665–67), when he was knighted following his performance in the Battle of Lowestoft (1665), in which the Dutch were soundly defeated. In the Four Days Battle (June 11–14, 1666), which remains one of the longest naval engagements in history, Sir Christopher Myngs took two musket balls, first through the cheek then in the left shoulder, fired by a sniper from the rigging of the Dutch flagship. The vice-admiral was rushed to land and back to London, but succumbed to his wounds at the start of August.

Myngs died a distinguished naval officer and hero, but during his time in Jamaica demonstrated that he was also a skilled buccaneer and, by helping to defend

Opposite: A rusty cannon looks out over the harbor entrance at Santiago de Cuba and reminds visitors of the port's violent past. Despite its formidable defenses, Cuba's second city suffered many buccaneer and outright pirate attacks during the 17th century. This fort—the notorious Castillo del Morro—was destroyed by naval artillery in the attack of 1662 by Christopher Myngs, accompanied by the young Henry Morgan.

Henry Morgan, as seen on the English edition's frontispiece of Exquemelin's *History of the Bucaniers of America*. In it, we are told that Captain Morgan, exhorting his men, said he intended in that expedition *"to plunder Porto Bello…being resolved to put the whole city to the sack, not the least corner escaping his diligence. Moreover, to encourage* [his captains], *he added: This enterprise could not fail to succeed well, seeing he had kept it secret in his mind without revealing it to anybody; whereby they could not have notice of his coming. To this proposition some made answer: They had not a sufficient number of men wherewith to assault so strong and great a city. But Captain Morgan replied: If our number is small, our hearts are great. And the fewer persons we are, the more union and better shares we shall have in the spoil. Hereupon, being stimulated with the ambition of those vast riches they promised themselves from their good success, they unanimously concluded to venture upon that design."*

Jamaica, made Port Royal a haven for the next generation of pirates. Above all, he encouraged Henry Morgan, who continued Myngs' policy of defending Jamaica by devastating the Spanish Main at every level.

Morgan, a most successful buccaneer

Sir Henry Morgan's career as a privateer lasted for about a decade, and yet in that relatively short space of time he came to epitomize the successful buccaneer. Unlike many, he also survived to live off his ill-gotten gains. There are those who would claim that Morgan was no pirate—his raids were carried out in his capacity as a privateer and he was licensed to act as an agent of the English government in a region where it was difficult to supply official naval or military forces. Unfortunately, this comfortable argument takes no account of the several occasions when Morgan's actions exceeded those of his mentor Christopher Myngs and definitely represented those of a pirate, not a privateer.

Thanks to Alexander Exquemelin, Morgan is perhaps the best-known buccaneer. The author, who accompanied Morgan on two expeditions, vividly described his first-hand experience of these raids. Nevertheless, Exquemelin disliked Morgan, although he respected his accomplishments; and it is fair to say that Morgan had no liking for Exquemelin. When the English edition of *History of the Bucaniers of America* appeared in 1684, its publisher had failed to remove or ameliorate the "Unparalledl'd Exploits of Sir Henry Morgan" in a manner to please the English knight and Exquemelin accused Morgan of committing atrocities against Spanish communities. Morgan sued, winning damages and apologetic prefaces in subsequent editions. But what seems to have upset Morgan more than accusations of cruelty— hardly a stranger to conflicts of the 17th century—was Exquemelin's description of how Morgan came to be in the West Indies in the first place. The claim that Morgan arrived in Barbados as an indentured laborer, little more than a press-ganged slave, was an insult he could not accept. This is supported by the rewritten prefaces to Exquemelin's bestseller, which were at pains to point out that Morgan was "a gentleman's son of good quality in the county of Monmouth, and never was servant to anybody in his life, save unto his Majestie."

Morgan never spoke much of his early life. He was born into a Welsh farming family in about 1635. The Morgans appear to have been reasonably well founded; two of Henry's uncles were army officers, on either side of the English Civil War. Royalist Thomas rose to the rank of colonel, while his Parliamentarian brother Edward was made a major-general by Oliver Cromwell. The 20-year-old Henry Morgan was a junior officer on General Venables' staff in 1655, when Cromwell dispatched Venables to attack the Spanish in the Caribbean. This, at least, is the version he insisted on in contradiction of Exquemelin's alleged calumny. As we have seen, the assault on Santo Domingo was a disaster that Venables was unable to ameliorate by his unexpected capture of "paltry" Jamaica. As effects of the tropical diseases amoebic dysentery, yellow fever, and malaria further depleted the remaining English troops, Henry Morgan endured.

The arrival of Christopher Myngs marked an improvement in conditions on Jamaica and, though unrecorded, it is likely that Morgan served in some capacity under the commodore in the

Now much reconstructed, a bastion juts out from the walls of Castillo del Morro, guarding the bay of Santiago de Cuba.

Sunset silhouettes a corner tower on the Fort of San Miguel, part of the defenses that protected the port of Campeche on the west coast of the Yucatán peninsula.

Opposite: The French pirate Jean L'Olonnais, as he appeared in Exquemelin's *History of the Bucaniers of America.*

raids of 1558–60. He must have impressed sufficiently that, on his return to the Caribbean, Myngs made Morgan captain of a vessel in the attack on Santiago de Cuba in 1662, in which the notorious Castillo del Morro guarding the entrance to the bay of Santiago de Cuba was destroyed by buccaneer artillery. Morgan also followed Myngs into San Francisco de Campeche in 1663, captaining his own buccaneer ship, before setting up in his own right when Myngs returned to England. In early 1664 Morgan sailed for central America in command of a small squadron. During an epic two-year voyage, the buccaneers plundered three major cities in a campaign that surpassed anything the Spanish had yet suffered, and brought about another anguished outcry from Spain against Morgan's brutal tactics.

Returning to Port Royal an extremely wealthy man, Morgan remained in Jamaica, investing in the first of several plantations he would come to own and cultivating a friendship with the governor, Thomas Modyford. He also married Mary Elizabeth, daughter of his uncle, the now-knighted Colonel Sir Edward Morgan, who had recently arrived in Jamaica. Edward's sojourn was to be short, however: called to arms in the Second Anglo-Dutch War, he died during an assault on the tiny Dutch-held island of St. Eustatius (Statia) in the Lesser Antilles. 1666 was also the year that Henry Morgan became colonel of the Port Royal militia, in which defense force he had served for many years, and the buccaneers of Tortuga and Port Royal voted to make Morgan their "admiral" after the death of their former leader, the Dutch pirate Edward Mansvelt.

The experienced sailor Mansfield, as his name was Anglicized, had first arrived at Port Royal in 1659, taking a privateering commission from Thomas Modyford. Mansfield commanded several buccaneer vessels in raids on Spanish ports and small islands and rose to such prominence that he was elected "admiral" by his men in January 1666. Commanding a fleet of ten ships and a force of 500 men, Mansfield planned to take Cartago, one of the major inland towns in the area of Central America today called Costa Rica. A stout defense by the Spanish blocked his way at the smaller settlement of Turrialba and his force was repulsed. At this failure some of his captains left him and returned to Tortuga. Mansfield died shortly after, according to one source of an illness; another claims he was executed by the Spanish for his crimes; whichever, Morgan became his beneficiary.

The cruellest man on the Spanish Main

Morgan was not the only buccaneer commander with a harsh streak that was directed toward Spaniards. In this he was handsomely outdone by a contemporary menace: Jean L'Olonnais, the "Man from Olonne." This French buccaneer was widely regarded as the cruellest man of his time. A torturer, driven by an insatiable bloodlust, his attack on Maracaibo was to become an inspiration for others, including Henry Morgan.

Born Jean David Nau in western France at Les Sables d'Olonne, he was also called Fléau des Espagnols—the Flail of the Spaniards—because of his inhumanity to anyone of that nation. In 1650, like many Europeans at the time, L'Olonnais was taken to Hispaniola as an indentured servant. After about three years of unremittingly harsh labor, he escaped and joined the cattle hunters on Hispaniola, then turned to piracy, moving to the pirate haven of Tortuga. His first attacks on Spanish shipping were profitable, although it quickly became harder to take prizes once news of his psychopathic mistreatment of prisoners became common knowledge. As Exquemelin explained, instead of surrendering, the crews of merchant ships "fought until they could fight no more, for he granted Spaniards little mercy." During one voyage, L'Olonnais was wrecked on the Campeche coast, where the Spanish killed most of his men. He escaped certain death by covering himself with the blood of the slain and hiding under the corpses. He stole a canoe and, after many trials, eventually regained Tortuga. When L'Olonnais attacked a small port in northern Cuba shortly after this event, his band took a warship in the harbor and L'Olonnais executed the entire crew except for one man. This fortunate was given a written message for the governor of Havana. It stated, with surely unnecessary emphasis, that L'Olonnais would henceforward spare no Spaniard he captured.

These brutal acts took place during peacetime, but when a year-long war broke out between Spain and France in 1667, it gave L'Olonnais an even better excuse to commit atrocities. He planned to take the largest ever expedition against Spanish towns in Venezuela, particularly Maracaibo, and so in July set sail from Tortuga with eight small ships and 660 men. It must have seemed a good omen indeed when, a little to the east of Hispaniola, the rovers crossed the wake of a Spanish treasure ship, unusually sailing on its own. It was taken and yielded a rich cargo of gemstones, cacao (which was fetching high prices in Europe's chocolate markets), and 40,000 pieces of eight.

The buccaneers headed for Lake Maracaibo, on the entrance of which sat the town of the same name. The narrows were guarded by a fort, but the buccaneers landed out of sight and assaulted its reputedly impregnable walls from the undefended landward side—its 16 guns all faced out to sea. The prosperous town of Maracaibo was easily occupied because most of the inhabitants had fled into the forest with their possessions. The raiders caught a score of Spaniards guarding some 20,000 pieces of eight and tortured them to discover where the rest was hidden. L'Olonnais hacked one to death with his cutlass.

Any Spaniard unfortunate enough to fall into the bloodstained hands of L'Olonnais was assured of a painful death. In this illustration he is shown feeding to one prisoner the heart he has just hacked out of the other; L'Olonnais was also said to devour the heart in front of the dying man from whom he had freshly ripped it.

After two weeks, L'Olonnais moved on to Gibraltar, a small town across the lake garrisoned by 500 soldiers, since it was a vital center of the cacao trade. Most were slaughtered in the bloody fight and the town's fabric so badly damaged that it was abandoned within two years. L'Olonnais stayed for a month, collecting gems, gold, and silverware, as well as slaves, then returned to Maracaibo to extort a ransom of 20,000 pieces of eight. Altogether, the pirates divided up coins and jewels worth 260,000 pieces of eight. Typically, once the buccaneers were back in Tortuga, their spoils soon vanished, for as Exquemelin put it, "the tavern keepers got part of their money and the whores the rest."

The following year proved less successful. L'Olonnais took about six ships and 700 men and sailed for Nicaragua, but his fleet was becalmed and drifted into the Gulf of

Honduras. The pirates were reduced to pillaging the poor Indian villages along the way until they reached the impoverished port of Puerto Caballos. The sack was desultory, for most of the inhabitants had escaped and there was little left behind to steal. As usual, prisoners were tortured to obtain information. Exquemelin wrote: "When L'Olonnais had a victim on the rack, if the wretch did not instantly answer his questions he would hack the man to pieces with his cutlass and lick the blood from the blade with his tongue, wishing it might have been the last Spaniard in the world he had thus killed."

Two captives were thus persuaded to act as guides and take the buccaneers to the nearby town of San Pedro, which was close to an important gold mine and where it was hoped there would be better pickings, but on the way Spanish troops ambushed them and the pirates narrowly escaped with their lives. After defeating the Spaniards, L'Olonnais turned to his two prisoners and "ripped open one of [them] with his cutlass, tore the living heart out of his body, gnawed at it, and then hurled it in the face of the other." The remaining captive quickly suggested a route that would not be protected by troops.

San Pedro turned out to be little better than Puerto Caballos for loot, so they burned the town to the ground. The well of L'Olonnais' luck had run dry and, disappointed with their spoils, his captains deserted with the smaller boats. The Frenchman sailed with only his own ship's crew toward Nicaragua, but they ran aground and many of

SOUTH AMERICA

PACIFIC OCEAN

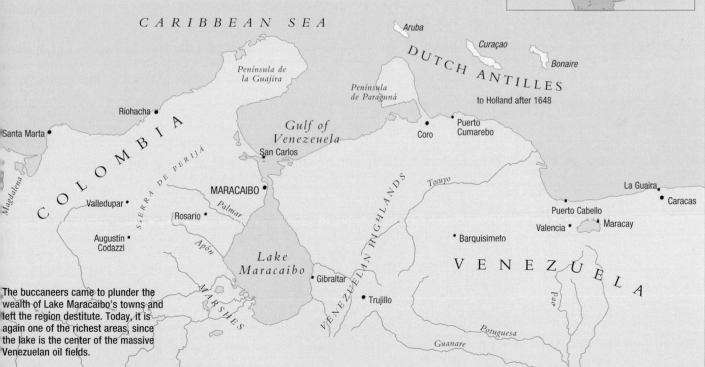

Lake Maracaibo

CARIBBEAN SEA

Aruba

Curaçao

Bonaire

DUTCH ANTILLES

to Holland after 1648

Península de la Guajira

Península de Paraguná

Ríohacha

Santa Marta

Gulf of Venezeuela

San Carlos

Puerto Cumarebo

Coro

COLOMBIA

SIERRA DE PERIJÁ

Valledupar

Palmar

Rosario

MARACAIBO

Magdalena

Augustín Codazzi

Apón

Lake Maracaibo

Gibraltar

MARSHES

Trujillo

VENEZUELAN HIGHLANDS

Tocuyo

La Guaira

Caracas

Puerto Cabello

Valencia

Maracay

Barquisimeto

VENEZUELA

Pao

Potuguesa

Guanare

The buccaneers came to plunder the wealth of Lake Maracaibo's towns and left the region destitute. Today, it is again one of the richest areas, since the lake is the center of the massive Venezuelan oil fields.

the now-demoralized buccaneers sailed home in the ship's boat. L'Olonnais marched to the Gulf of Darién, but on the way cannibalistic Indians attacked the remnants of his small band. The Indians grabbed L'Olonnais "tore him in pieces alive, throwing his body limb by limb into the fire and his ashes into the air." The murderous pirate was probably eaten; an appropriate end for such a vicious man.

Morgan attacks Porto Bello

The example set by L'Olonnais was not lost on others. Despite the 1667 non-aggression pact between Spain and England, Governor Modyford was insistent that the Spaniards were planning an invasion of Jamaica, and in January 1668 he ordered Henry Morgan "to draw together the English privateers and take prisoners of the Spanish nation, whereby you may gain information of that enemy." Morgan's commission permitted the capture of Spanish ships but not the use of his ships to take Spanish cities. This explains Morgan's increasing preference for landing his men to attack instead of using naval bombardment: under English rules, if he took booty at sea, half went to the English crown. In an oversight—though more likely on purpose—Modyford avoided mention of land actions in Morgan's commission, which meant that he and his men could split hairs and follow Myngs' example in dividing up the

Ruins of the Spanish fort at Porto Bello, Panama. Despite the French contingent deserting after the failure of the raid on Puerto del Principe, Morgan's reduced force of English buccaneers overcame the garrison by a surprise night assault.

entire haul between them. As Morgan's friend and sponsor, Modyford was doubtless to be well paid when it came to the final share-out. Attacks on cities may have been strictly speaking illegal piracy, but they certainly were most profitable.

Morgan assembled his ships and 500 men and sailed to the southern coast of Cuba, where he was joined by French buccaneers from Tortuga. The group decided that their force was too small to attack Havana, so instead they marched on Puerto del Principe, despite its name a town 30 miles inland. The Spaniards learned of the raid and laid various ambushes, but the buccaneers overcame the attacks. According to Exquemelin, prosperous Puerto del Principe's inhabitants were locked in a church and the wretched prisoners "were pained and plagued by unspeakable tortures." Despite their misery, the good people of Puerto Principe yielded spoils of only 50,000 pieces of eight. The capture of some "beeves" (cattle) did little to assuage the men's resentment at such poor booty, so Morgan proposed an assault on Porto Bello, the port from which treasure ships left for Spain but thought to be an easier target than Havana. Three massive forts guarded the harbor, but Morgan's agents reported that their garrisons were undermanned and badly equipped. Some of his captains argued against the venture, but Morgan ignored their fears and laid his plans.

Anchoring in a sheltered bay a few miles from the city, the buccaneers paddled in canoes to the outskirts of Porto Bello, landed and regrouped, and then attacked. In a series of savage assaults, the buccaneers took Porto Bello and its forts on July 11–12, 1668. In an unattractive but typically piratical tactic, women, nuns, and old men were forced at sword point to carry scaling ladders and at the same time act as a human shield in the assault on the city's San Geronimo castle.

Had this campaign really been conducted in the name of the king as a legitimate act of war, some provision for holding onto the seized property would have been evident. But Morgan and his buccaneers were only after loot—as much as they could carry off. Days of drunken celebration followed Porto Bello's capture, accompanied by the screams of citizens under torture to reveal the hiding places of their personal possessions. Panama's governor sent a militia force of some 3000 men to recapture the port after Morgan demanded 350,000 pieces of eight in ransom. It was an outrageous sum and the Spanish began firing their guns. After a short skirmish and further negotiation, 100,000 changed hands and the buccaneers returned to their ships and sailed off. Morgan's return to Jamaica in mid-August, with a total of 250,000 pieces of eight in plunder to be shared out, was greeted with universal glee.

In theory, the Porto Bello raid exceeded the terms of Morgan's commission and violated the treaty with Spain, but many at home agreed with the expedition, and in the end Morgan and Modyford avoided the Admiralty's censure. Indeed, in March 1669 the Admiralty court decreed the Porto Bello booty a legal prize, which was just as well because at Port Royal the buccaneers had already run through their share of the money in a non-stop drunken spree the year before; with his cut, Morgan purchased some more plantation land.

Trapped in the narrow mouth of Lake Maracaibo, Morgan used fireships to attack the Spanish galleons of Admiral Espinosa.

Maracaibo suffers again

In October 1668, Morgan arranged a rendezvous off Hispaniola with French buccaneers from Tortuga for a joint attack on Cartagena. Governor Modyford lent him an English man-of-war, HMS *Oxford*, but an accidental magazine explosion destroyed the ship, killing 200 of the crew and Morgan's chances of taking the large, heavily defended Spanish city with a force reduced by about a third. A sailor who had just enlisted with Morgan after serving for a while with L'Olonnais suggested they repeat the Frenchman's raid of the previous year on the easier targets of Maracaibo and Gibraltar. Once again, the dispirited citizens of both towns fled as Morgan's men chased them into the jungle. Those caught were tortured. After sailing around the lake's shore and ascertaining that L'Olonnais had left nothing for him at Gibraltar, Morgan sailed for the lake's exit in late April 1669, to be met by three blockading Spanish warships under the command of Vice-Admiral Alonso de Campo y Espinosa. Twelve of Morgan's men ran a fireship into the admiral's 48-gun flagship *Magdalen* and blew up both vessels. The pirates then captured the second galleon and the third was scuttled or, according to some accounts, fled the scene.

Espinosa and several of his crew managed to escape their burning ship and made it safely to shore, where they promptly occupied the fort that had proved unable to keep out L'Olonnais. But this put Morgan in a difficult position, since the fort's guns commanded the narrows through which he had to escape. He now resorted to a cunning trick, rowing troops to the shore behind the fort in broad daylight. After landing out of sight of the fort, two oarsmen rowed the boat back, but with the other men now lying flat. This to and fro continued for some time, giving Espinosa the impression that a powerful force was being gathered behind his position. Recalling that this was exactly how L'Olonnais had captured Maracaibo, the admiral had his men haul the sea guns around to face inland and so thwart Morgan's landward attack. As soon as the guns had been moved, Morgan gave the signal and the buccaneers sailed out with the ebb tide through the unguarded channel.

Cleverness had extracted Morgan from a tight spot, but in truth there was little to celebrate. L'Olonnais had already removed much of Maracaibo's wealth, so there was less for Morgan and his merry men. But the riches of the hinterland never entirely dried up and an amount exceeding 20,000 silver pieces of eight was captured from the Spanish squadron, plus a further 10,000 from the land attack. The raiders reached Port Royal in May 1669, where, yet again, most wasted their money in taverns and Morgan invested his into yet another plantation.

While Morgan was raiding Maracaibo, England had yet again agreed peace terms with Spain, and on June 14, 1669, Governor Modyford formally announced the news with ill-concealed bad grace. However, several small Spanish reprisal raids soon cheered him up. He gave Morgan ambiguous orders in August the following year, allowing him "to doe and performe all matter of Exployts which may tend to the Preservation and Quiett of Jamayca." The buccaneer was permitted to commission captains, and the raiders could split the spoils "according to their usual rules," although exactly whose usual rules was not entirely clear. To Modyford's credit, he also suggested that Morgan stop

An illustration from Exquemelin's *History of the Bucaniers of America* depicts Morgan and his men interrogating Spanish prisoners, a horror the author witnessed both at Maracaibo and after the land battle for the city of Panama in 1670.

torturing prisoners, which was giving his governorship a bad name. Morgan called for volunteers, and nearly every buccaneer in the Caribbean—and some from further afield when the news leaked out—responded. The spoils were to be massive in scale and the damage to Spain enormous. Morgan intended to take the richest prize of the Spanish Main—Panama.

The great raid on Panama

In December 1670, Morgan and 2000 buccaneers of almost every nationality sailed in 33 ships for the isthmus of Panama. An advance party of 500 men under the leadership of Morgan's second-in-command, Joseph Bradley, was sent to capture the fortress of San Lorenzo at the mouth of the Chagres river. The river represented half the route to the target, but Bradley's mission was also partly decoy, to deceive the Spanish about Morgan's real intention and to disguise the real size of his forces.

Remains of the Camino de Cruces, the old Spanish trail that linked the Chagres river with Panama Viejo and later new Panama.

In mid-January, the buccaneers paddled up the Chagres by canoe, then headed toward the city on the Cruces trail of the Camino Real. They attacked and routed Panama's defenders: 1200 militia infantry and 400 cavalry. When the buccaneer musket fire cut down Spanish cavalry and infantry assaults, the defenders gave up and fell back on the city. The pirates pursued and killed around 500 Spanish troops. As Morgan's men entered Panama, the defending militiamen started fires that destroyed most of the buildings, then fled into the jungle. The buccaneers spent four weeks picking through the city's smoking ruins, but much of its wealth had been taken south by sea to the safety of Ecuador—the surprise had been far from complete after all. Frustrated by their poor haul, the buccaneers razed to the

112

ground every building left standing, and tortured and raped their prisoners while seeking hidden treasure caches.

Leaving Panama in February 1671, the buccaneers returned to San Lorenzo and divided the small pile of booty. Seeing how little each was to receive, many of the angry buccaneers accused Morgan of cheating them. Turning his back on them, he sailed off alone with his ship and crew to raid the coast of Central America. The Spaniards abandoned the ruined city, Panama Viejo, building a new Panama (now Panama City) at a better and more defensible harbor 6 miles away.

Unknown to Morgan, even before he had left Jamaica, England and Spain had signed the Treaty of Madrid in July 1670, by which Spain recognized English holdings in the Caribbean, and both nations agreed to prohibit piracy against the other. In an irony of timing, Morgan had set out on his raid as a licensed privateer, but destroyed Panama as a pirate. The same bad timing had made a criminal of Governor Modyford,

The title of this contemporary engraving makes it clear that the illustrator was unsure of the precise legal status of Henry Morgan's force: *The battel Between the Spaniards and the pyrates or Buccaneers before the citty of PANAMA*. The largest battle fought in the Americas before the 18th century, Morgan's buccaneers (or pyrates) defeated the Spanish defenders in front of Panama, aided by "alarmed beeves"—the stampeding cattle can be seen to the left foreground of the picture.

and in launching Morgan's raid and appointing him as admiral, he had exceeded his authority. A new governor, Sir Thomas Lynch, arrested Modyford in August 1671 and returned him to England, where he spent two years in the Tower of London. As for Morgan, he was also arrested in order to appease Spanish outrage. He sailed to England under a cloud in April 1672, but was never imprisoned and—with all his enormous personal wealth—soon gained influential political friends.

Lynch was ousted in 1674, while Morgan was knighted and returned to Jamaica as lieutenant governor, where his old comrade Modyford soon joined him in the position of chief justice. By 1675, Morgan was 40, immensely rich, and the owner of several Jamaican plantations, which continued to increase his wealth. In 1682, his last year of office, Morgan the poacher turned gamekeeper when he dispatched the pirate-hunter Peter Haywood in the frigate HMS *Norwich* in pursuit of Laurens de Graaf. This Dutch pirate had by that time become one of the most feared names on the Spanish Main and also one of the cleverest; he escaped English hands with ease. In another political reversal, Lynch returned as governor in 1682 and removed Morgan from office. Morgan died six years later, the most successful buccaneer of the late 17th century. And if he had been an often cruel man, his actions did much to ensure the expansion of English interests in the Caribbean.

The cruel and unlucky buccaneers

Not every buccaneer in the Caribbean was as successful as Sir Henry Morgan. The Portuguese seaman Bartolomeo el Portugues and the Dutchman Rock Braziliano had two things in common: they operated in the same waters at the same time and they suffered from poor luck. While Rock was partially successful, Bartolomeo's career was remarkable only in that it appeared to be a catalog of disasters. He arrived in Port Royal soon after the English captured Jamaica in 1655. Bartolomeo served on expeditions raiding the Mexican coast off Campeche, but he started his independent career by cruising between Jamaica and the southern coast of Cuba in a small vessel with 30 men and four guns. He attacked a larger Spanish ship but was repelled, although he captured it in a second attempt, losing half his crew in the fighting. The prize contained coin chests filled with about 70,000 pieces of eight and sacks of valuable cacao beans. He abandoned the smaller vessel, but contrary winds prevented him from sailing back to Jamaica, so he headed west along the southern Cuban coast.

Off Cuba's western tip he sighted three powerful Spanish men-of-war making for Havana. The galleons gave chase and soon overhauled Bartolomeo's

Bartolomeo el Portugues, **below**, and the Dutch pirate Rock Braziliano, as depicted in Exquemelin's *History of the Bucaniers of America*. Bartolomeo's career was a chapter of disasters, while Braziliano— who fared a little better—was reckoned to match L'Olonnais in psychotic cruelty toward his victims.

vessel, capturing both it and the booty. Carried to Campeche in chains, Bartolomeo and his crewmen were held onboard while gallows were erected at the high tide mark, but they escaped and swam ashore. The fugitives cut across the Yucatán peninsula, heading for the eastern coast, and found a buccaneering ship that took them back to Port Royal. Bent on revenge, Bartolomeo returned to Campeche with 20 men and a seagoing canoe. Arriving there, he "cut out" the ship that had captured him, still laden with goods, and stole it. He escaped the harbor and made his way right across the Gulf of Mexico, only for bad luck to plague him again. The ship ran aground on Isla de Pinos (the Isle of Pines), off southern Cuba, and the pirates were forced to abandon ship and cargo, escaping to Jamaica in small boat. Bartolomeo was indeed one of the worst pirates anyone had ever seen. Apparently, he continued his attacks on the Spanish, since Exquemelin reported he made "many violent attacks on the Spaniards without gaining much profit from marauding, for I saw him dying in the greatest wretchedness in the world."

Rock Braziliano was a Dutchman who came to the Americas in the brief period when Bahia in Brazil was held by Holland. When the Portuguese drove off the Dutch in 1654, Braziliano moved to Port Royal and worked as a seaman. In the course of a violent quarrel with the captain of one vessel, he and others made off in the ship's pinnace and started a new buccaneering life. They succeeded in capturing a Spanish ship carrying gold and silver, and brought it to Port Royal in triumph.

The number of voyages Braziliano made as a captain is unclear, but at some stage the Spanish caught him and he was incarcerated in Campeche's gaol. He contrived to fake a letter to the Spanish governor that claimed to come from his friends outside, threatening that if Braziliano were to be executed, his fellow buccaneers would sack the town and kill every Spaniard they came across, adding that it would be best to set him free. The empty threat may have been taken seriously, but it did not have the desired effect, since they shipped Braziliano to Spain in chains shortly after. Detail is thin on the ground, but evidently he escaped and eventually returned to Port Royal.

In 1669 he sailed with a small vessel and crew for Campeche, but they ran aground. Forced to abandon the ship, the crew made their way through the jungle of the Yucatán peninsula to a known buccaneer rendezvous on the eastern coast. Nearing their destination, a unit of Spanish cavalry sighted the pirates, but the riders were held at bay by musket fire, and Braziliano and his crew managed an escape in canoes. They next captured a small local craft and used it to take a Spanish merchant ship laden with valuable cargo. Braziliano took his prizes on to Port Royal, if not exactly lucky, at least a little luckier than Bartolomeo el Portugues. His ultimate fate is unrecorded, but he probably died in Port Royal, where he was notorious for his cruel and intemperate behavior. As Exquemelin wrote: "He would roam the town like a madman. The first person he came across, he would chop off his arm or leg and anyone daring to intervene, for he was like a maniac. He perpetrated the greatest atrocities possible against the Spaniards. Some of them he tied or spitted on wooden stakes and roasted them alive between two fires; like killing a pig."

The Chevalier devastates Spanish settlements

During the 1670s a Frenchmen rose to prominence among the buccaneer communities of Tortuga and Hispaniola. Michel de Grammont's origins are obscure. Born in Paris, he had served in the French navy. At some point he was given command of a privateering vessel and sailed into the Caribbean, where he found Hispaniola in a state of flux. In the mid-17th century so many Frenchmen had arrived that the western end of the island had become in effect a French colony owing no allegiance to the Spanish authorities. The French buccaneers referred to their end of the island as St. Domingue (now Haiti).

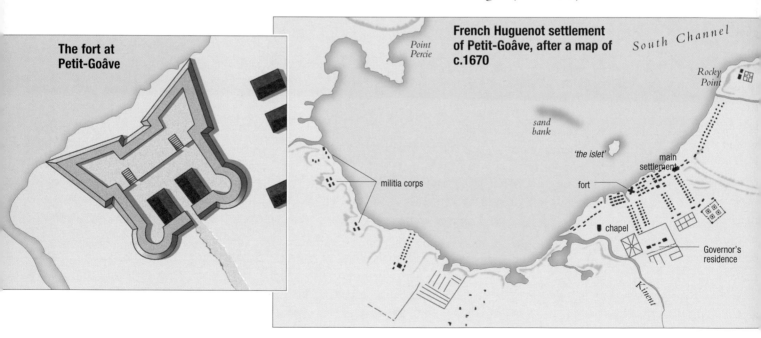

The fort at Petit-Goâve

French Huguenot settlement of Petit-Goâve, after a map of c.1670

Point Percie

South Channel

Rocky Point

sand bank

'the islet'

main settlement

militia corps

fort

chapel

Governor's residence

Kinent

Despite this *de facto* French state, Spain refused to accept the reality and was only to cede the western third of Hispaniola to France in 1697 with the Treaty of Ryswick, which ended the nine-year conflict known as the War of the League of Augsburg (*see page 120*). Spanish-controlled Hispaniola became Santo Domingo, today's Dominican Republic. But when de Grammont first came to Hispaniola, there was already a functionary who could call himself the governor of St. Domingue and who managed French affairs from the settlement of Petit-Goâve. De Grammont's arrival was marked by violence; he had seized a Dutch vessel off the coast. With this illegal action he fell foul of the authorities, and unable to return to France chose to remain in St. Domingue. There must have been something powerful in his character and bearing that made men look up to him because in a short space of time the buccaneers of Petit-Goâve and Tortuga elected de Grammont to be their "admiral," although he preferred his misappropriated title of "knight," or *chevalier* in French.

So much of the history of buccaneering revolves around good or bad timing. Had de Grammont taken his Dutch prize just a year or two later, it would have been lawful, for in 1678 France and Holland declared war. Suddenly, any Dutch possession was fair game, and de Grammont readily joined other buccaneers in a raid on the Dutch island of Curaçao off the coast of Venezuela. The buccaneers sailed from Petit-Goâve in May 1678 in company with a French naval squadron, which gave a combined raiding force of over 1200 men. However, the unpredictable Caribbean Sea scattered the ships in a fierce storm and several ships were dashed against the reefs of the Aves islands, west of the Lesser Antilles, and wrecked. As soon as the weather cleared, the navy ships returned to St. Domingue, leaving the buccaneers to salvage what they could from the wreckage. This was a lucrative opportunity and, as Exquemelin tells us, the salvors "were never without two or three hogsheads of wine and brandy in their tents, and barrels of beef and pork."

Probably the first of the "gentlemen" pirates of the Caribbean, the Chevalier Michel de Grammont was noted for the finery of his apparel, but an elegant appearance belied a ferocious temperament.

It was rumored that Curaçao's defenses were too strong for the remaining force to make an assault, so the buccaneers sailed for the Venezuelan coast and easier pickings. In June 1678 de Grammont's 700 men aboard six ships entered Lake Maracaibo. This expedition records the presence of another buccaneer of substance, the Dutchmen Laurens de Graaf, with whom the Chevalier was to associate on further occasions. The lake's shores still showed the devastation left by the plundering raids of L'Olonnais and Henry Morgan in the 1660s—indeed, the once vibrant cacao-trading center of Gibraltar was a ghost town. It all added up to a poor haul of booty. However, not all was lost. The previous buccaneer attacks never penetrated very far inland and local information dragged from the terrified inhabitants confirmed that thriving Trujillo remained untouched. Using captured horses, de Grammont led his men inland and up into the Venezuelan coastal range to assault Trujillo in September 1678. By late December the buccaneers were back in St. Domingue with a good haul of plunder.

The Chevalier's next expedition, although nowhere near as financially viable as his Trujillo raid, was one of the most spectacular since Morgan took Panama. He returned to Venezuela in May 1680 at the head of a large buccaneer force to attack La Guaira, the harbor that served Caracas, the region's Spanish capital. The buccaneers invested the port in a daring night attack, spearheaded by a small assault force that captured the two forts guarding the harbor's entrance and then threw open the town gates. But the Spanish authorities in Caracas counterattacked later the next morning, throwing 2000 regular troops against the town's walls, and the buccaneers found themselves besieged. Repeated Spanish assaults were repulsed in the bitter fighting that ensued, during which de Grammont took a musket ball in the throat. This proved to be little more than a scratch, however, and he was able to organize a fighting retreat. The buccaneers escaped to sea, but lacking the time to load more than a minimum of booty into their ships, they returned to St. Domingue almost empty-handed. The only saving grace to an otherwise desultory result came from ransoms raised from a few prominent Spanish hostages who had fallen into the raiders' hands during the campaign.

Dutch pirates join forces with the French

Three years later, in May 1683, de Grammont again joined forces with Laurens de Graaf for a combined assault on Vera Cruz. Born Laurens Baldran in the Netherlands, de Graaf was probably shipped to the Spanish Main as a captive, taken during the long Dutch war of independence against the hated Spanish sovereignty. In the early 1670s, de Graaf was a free man, probably a runaway, and a pirate in command of his own small vessel. A successful raid on Campeche in March 1672 yielded much silver and other valuable loot and kicked off a career that included the raid on Maracaibo led by Michel de Grammont. In 1679 he captured a 24-gun Spanish man-of-war, which he named the *Tigre*. The firepower now at his hands made de Graaf one of the most feared buccaneers off the Central American coast, sufficient to come to Sir Henry Morgan's ears in 1682, who—pot calling kettle black—referred to him as "a great and mischievous pyrate." De Graaf eluded the pirate-hunter Peter Haywood, sent to capture him, and instead ran into the Spanish man-of-war *Princesa*, a ship of comparable firepower to the *Tigre*, but bristling with troops. In the running gun battle that ensued, de Graaf out-maneuvered and out-gunned the enemy. Eventually, the *Princesa* struck her colors and surrendered. Honorably, de Graaf put the Spaniards ashore before sailing off with his prize and a booty of 120,000 pieces of eight—the annual payroll for Santo Domingo's garrison.

In the same year he attacked shipping in the vicinity of Cartagena, while avoiding the powerfully defended city itself, but found himself in competition with another notorious Dutch pirate. While hunting two potential prizes, de Graaf was beaten to the line by the sudden appearance of Nickolaas van Hoorn's ship. In their haste van Hoorn's men failed to spot how high in the water the Spanish galleons rode—the

A pirate ship at anchor in the Caribbean; watercolor by Alice B. Woodward from the *Peter Pan Picture Book*.

ships were unladen and worth little. Van Hoorn, who had preyed in European and African waters before venturing into the Caribbean, suggested joining forces with Laurens de Graaf, who not surprisingly rebuffed him. However, in the following year de Graaf relented and the two Dutchmen signed up with Chevalier Michel de Grammont, who was to lead the French contingent for the attack on Vera Cruz.

The pirate fleet arrived off the Mexican coast just before dawn on May 17, 1683. Those sentries who were awake were fooled into thinking that the ships hoving into view were Spanish because the pirates placed two captured galleons in the vanguard. The deception worked long enough to land a force of Dutch pirates. Led by Laurens de Graaf and a fellow Dutchman, Jan "Yankey" Willems, they caught most of the Spanish soldiers napping, and soon cleared the defenses. The combined French and Dutch forces then plundered the town. On the third or fourth day, the large New Spain fleet appeared on the horizon and hurried preparations for retreat were made. With valuable plunder, almost a thousand slaves, and scores of notable citizens held for ransom, the pirates retreated to defensible positions on a nearby island— appropriately called Los Sacrificios—and waited to negotiate. At this time Laurens de Graaf and Nickolaas van Hoon argued over how to divide the potentially immense spoils; a contemporary account claims that each common pirate's booty would have enabled him to purchase and fit out his own ship. The two Dutchmen fought a duel and van Hoorn received a wound to his arm, which became gangrenous and killed him a few days later. After the ransoms were agreed and paid, the pirates departed past the Spanish ships without hindrance. On his return to St. Domingue, Michel de Grammont faced charges of piracy because France was at peace with Spain at the time of the attack, but the French authorities in Petit-Goâve chose to turn a blind eye and the preoccupied French Admiralty never brought a prosecution against him.

Two years later, de Grammont and de Graaf linked up again for an attack on Campeche. After a protracted battle they succeeded in driving off the Spanish force and held the city and its surrounding countryside for three months during that summer. But the long-winded fight had bought time for the inhabitants to get most of their possessions safely away, and there was little left for the invaders to steal. Fortunately, the pirates had managed to round up at least some worthy captives to hold for ransom. But when the viceroy of New Spain refused to negotiate a payment for the town or to offer ransoms for its citizens, the pirates set the buildings alight and began a slaughter of those prisoners they held. De Grammont and de Graaf stepped in to stop the violence, pointing out to their men that the captives were worth more alive than dead and that the Spanish would in the end ransom them. And so the worthies of Campeche were spared and departed the blazing city with the buccaneers in September 1685.

In the following year, de Grammont planned another raid on Mexico, despite promises of respectability and a French colonial position if he gave up his embarrassing and illegal attacks on the Spanish. By April 1686 he was operating off the Yucatán

Undated pen-and-ink drawing of pirates in the Caribbean boarding a Spanish galleon from their small sloop.

peninsula, but stormy weather forced him to withdraw to the northeast. He later led an attack on Spanish Florida but became separated from the rest of his fleet. The Chevalier Michel de Grammont and his ship were never seen again.

Laurens de Graaf continued his career as privateer one moment, a pirate the next, attacking the Spanish on Cuba and the English on Jamaica by turn. In May 1695, the English navy attacked his Hispaniola base of Port-de-Paix, opposite Tortuga, sacked the town, and took hostage de Graaf's wife and two daughters. De Graaf was never captured by any authority, and was last heard of leading an expedition to found a French colony on the northern shore of the Gulf of Mexico near Biloxi, Mississippi, where it is supposed he died in due course.

Piracy as a national weapon—the sack of Cartagena

The later buccaneers of the era always eyed Cartagena with misty eyes and a deep sigh. What a prize! Reputed to be the Spanish Main's richest city since the destruction of old Panama, it had last suffered attack a century earlier by Sir Francis Drake, and since then its formidable defenses—designed and constructed by some of Spain's finest military architects and engineers—had scared off most buccaneers. To take Cartagena, it was thought, would require a full-scale assault by navy and army—and that was just about to happen. France was at war with the combined

The siege of Cartagena, 1689. A combined force of buccaneers and French regular troops brought the great Spanish city to its knees with heavy bombardment. After the walls were breached, the plunder began.

nations of England, the Netherlands, and Spain in a conflict known as either the War of the League of Augsburg (1688–97) or the Nine Years War. During its course, French Caribbean colonists helped their country by raiding enemy colonies, and Jean du Casse, the French governor of St. Domingue, issued numerous letters of marque to buccaneers from his office in Petit-Goâve. As the war in Europe drew to a close, French strategists looked for the opportunity to launch a last lucrative raid on some Spanish city and turned their eyes on Cartagena as an attractive target.

The offensive was organized as a government-sponsored business venture, complete with investors and hired buccaneers. In March 1689 the French admiral, Baron Jean de Pointis, arrived in St. Domingue to lead the expedition, and brought with him a squadron of ten French men-of-war. Buccaneers supplied a further seven ships, while Governor du Casse commanded his own squadron in the pay of the colony. The expedition was, therefore, composed of over 30 ships, 6500 men, and plenty of artillery. De Pointis quickly fell out with the tough buccaneers and du Casse had to persuade them to continue their involvement with the arrogant nobleman. Written contracts were drawn up detailing how the booty would be divided, and the expedition sailed by the end of the month. The large fleet arrived off Cartagena on April 13, 1689 and anchored while army surveyors studied the defenses.

Situated at the base of a narrow peninsula between the sea and an inshore bay,

Jean Bernard Desjean Baron de Pointis, as portrayed by Henri Bonnart, was a court functionary of Louis XIV, France's "Sun King," so nicknamed for the brilliance of his court. Sent out to lead the combined attack on Cartagena, de Pointis agitated the rough and tumble buccaneers with his dandified airs and know-it-all attitude. And after the campaign they felt he had swindled them of their fair share of the booty.

121

reefs and the city's gun batteries prevented any direct assault. Forts guarded the Boca Chica passage that gave access to the bay, and land fortifications extended north of the city and east along the peninsula. An inlet of the bay, which could only be crossed via the fortified island of Imanie, acted as a moat to Cartagena's north. While impressed by the scale and extent of the fortifications, the French military experts considered that they had been designed for an outmoded style of assault and whole sections were poorly designed to support each other. The other weakness was not immediately apparent—the garrison was well under strength.

The French fleet upped anchors, stormed and invested the forts guarding the inner bay's entrance, then anchored in its sheltered waters. The artillery pieces were then landed and a fierce bombardment commenced until, on April 30, a breach was made in Cartagena's walls. The defenders repulsed an attack led by du Casse in command of the buccaneers, and so the bombardment resumed, but it was clear that time was on the side of the attackers. Since there seemed to be no hope for a continued defense, on May 6, 1689 the Spanish governor surrendered. The French forces entered the city jubilantly, expecting a full-scale sacking, but de Pointis refused the men. In formal discussion with Cartagena's civil authorities, he agreed to sack only half the wealth of the city and its inhabitants. Representing to some degree the buccaneers' interests, du Casse cautioned against this civilized mercifulness, but de Pointis remained adamant. It was at least a partial blessing to Cartagena's citizens but

The walls (*las Murallas*) of old Cartagena meet at the Castillo de San Felipe de Barajas. The walls were begun in 1536 and continually enlarged and modernized up until 1657. However, they proved unequal to the task of keeping out the rapacious French invading army in 1689.

the buccaneers were angered and claimed the baron was swindling them. When the buccaneers made ready to leave on May 29, de Pointis handed over only a fraction of the share that they had anticipated from the enterprise.

As the French navy set sail, the buccaneers hung back, determined to help themselves to their fair share. They returned to Cartagena on the first day of June, imprisoned and tortured the population, and grabbed all the available booty. This was divided equally between the buccaneers, and then the raiders began to sail back to St. Domingue. While the buccaneer ships were on their way, a flotilla of English warships caught sight of the French fleet and went in pursuit. The French were fortunate in the weather and a gale allowed their escape. Turning back, the English then encountered the returning buccaneers, immediately pounced, and captured several of their ships and most of the Cartagena plunder. Accused quite properly of piracy, many buccaneers were hanged for their crimes. Baron de Pointis returned to France with an immense haul for the French king, but kept a substantial share for himself. King Louis XIV sent a cash award to the surviving buccaneers to thank them for their efforts, which made up for some of the loss, but the only real winners from the operation were the "Sun King," the admiral, and the French investors.

The Cartagena raid was one of the last conducted by buccaneers in the Caribbean. In 1697, the Treaty of Ryswick brought peace to the warring nations of Europe and settled a number of territorial disputes, especially those in the Caribbean. As a brief moment of quiet fell on the New World, many buccaneers turned their blood-stained hands to farming, but others—particularly the English—made for the Lesser Antilles or settled in the almost uninhabited Bahamas and turned to full-scale piracy. Theirs was to be called, euphemistically and with a good deal of irony, the "Golden Age" of piracy.

The Sack of Cartagena by Howard Pyle shows a moment after the official French contingent had departed. The buccaneers, furious at being cheated by de Pointis of what they considered to be their fair share, returned to extract even more plunder from the unfortunate inhabitants who had escaped the first sack.

CHAPTER SEVEN

The Most Notorious Pyrates

The "Golden Age" of piracy in the Indian Ocean

The mythology created by Hollywood in cowboy movies gives the impression that the stirring epoch known as the Wild West lasted for a long time, when in fact it was only a period of about 40 years. This is true, too, of another of Tinseltown's favorite genres, the swashbuckling pirate epic. Both were iconic periods not because of their longevity but because of their intensity—the simple piling up of human activity, the outpouring of adventure, the nature of doing and be damned. Defying centralized and often baleful authority, the freebooting sailors who operated between 1690 and 1730 made the period the "Golden Age" of piracy. During these short 40 years, there took place the greatest outburst of piracy in the history of seafaring.

The worst affected areas were the West Indies and the Atlantic seaboard of America, but pirates ranged further afield, particularly off the West African coast and in the Indian Ocean. Merchant ships that plied from Europe to the American colonies were the prey; or those that carried slaves from West Africa to the Caribbean, then returned to Europe carrying rum and sugar, and the East Indiamen, laden with the fabulous riches of India and the Far East. In fiction and on the silver screen, these pirates are shown, like their buccaneer forebears, carrying off gold and silver cargoes, but the real maritime criminals never expected to plunder treasure—they preyed on the everyday commerce of the colonial Americas.

While not strictly accurate, it is certainly convenient to split up the Golden Age into two geographical halves, the first comprised of the Indian Ocean and Arabian Sea, the second the North Atlantic and the West Indies. European piracy in the Indian Ocean lasted from the 1690s until 1721–2, while that along the American seaboard was mostly concentrated into the eight-year period between 1714 and 1722, the time portrayed by novelists such as Robert Louis Stevenson and J. M. Barrie, and by painters like Howard Pyle. This convenience, however, overlooks those who attacked in both spheres and those pirates who centered most of their operations along West Africa's Guinea Coast—the stretch between the Gambia and Gabon.

How did all this come about? Most pirates throughout history became so by circumstance rather than as a career choice, and it was no different in the second decade of the 18th century. The huge and, at first sight, seemingly spontaneous outbreak of piracy developed from a number of social factors. First, the end of the buccaneering era in the Caribbean—where, during the 1680s, England and

Blackbeard, suitably demonized here in Captain Charles Johnson's bestselling book about "pyrates," is the man who most epitomizes the Golden Age of piracy. Blackbeard was by no means the worst freebooter of the period, although he was certainly the most colorful.

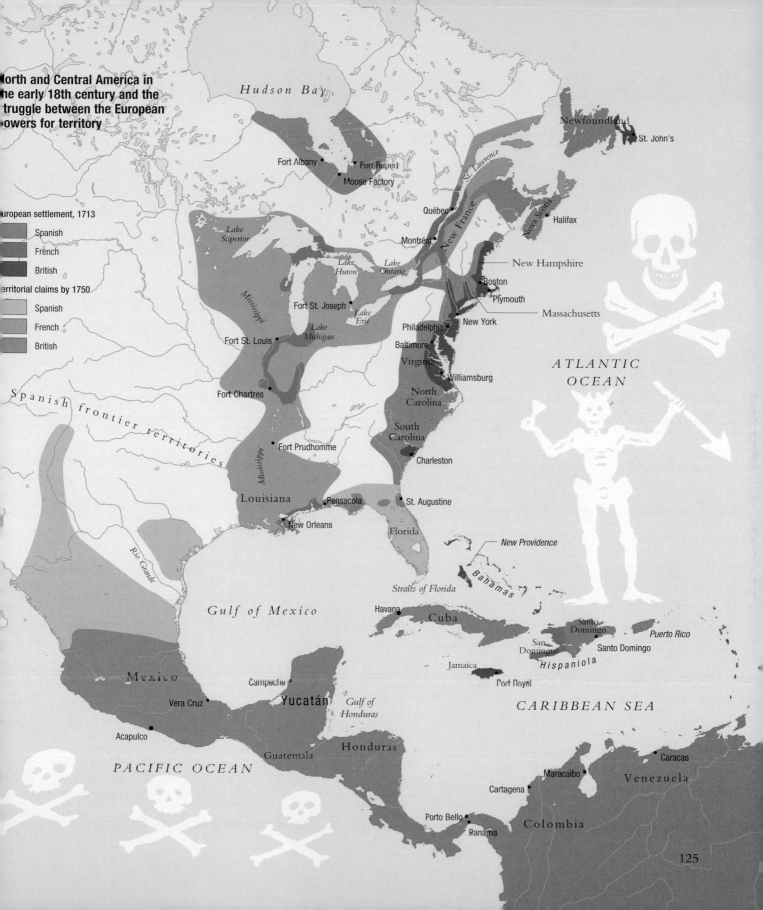

North and Central America in
the early 18th century and the
struggle between the European
powers for territory

European settlement, 1713

Spanish
French
British

Territorial claims by 1750

Spanish
French
British

Hudson Bay

Fort Albany
Fort Rupert
Moose Factory

Lake Superior

Lake Huron

Lake Ontario

Fort St. Joseph

Lake Erie

Lake Michigan

Fort St. Louis

Mississippi

Fort Chartres

Mississippi

Fort Prudhomme

Louisiana

New Orleans
Pensacola

Rio Grande

Spanish frontier territories

Newfoundland
St. John's

St. Lawrence

Québec

New France

Nova Scotia
Halifax

Montréal

New Hampshire

Boston
Plymouth

Massachusetts

Philadelphia
New York

Baltimore

Virginia

Williamsburg

North Carolina

South Carolina

Charleston

St. Augustine

Florida

New Providence

Bahamas

Straits of Florida

ATLANTIC OCEAN

Gulf of Mexico

Havana

Cuba

Santo Domingo

San Domingue

Puerto Rico

Santo Domingo

Jamaica

Port Royal

Hispaniola

CARIBBEAN SEA

Mexico

Vera Cruz

Acapulco

Campeche

Yucatán

Gulf of Honduras

Guatemala

Honduras

PACIFIC OCEAN

Caracas

Maracaibo

Venezuela

Cartagena

Porto Bello

Panamá

Colombia

125

The man who would be king of Spain and France—grandson of the French king, he inherited the Spanish throne as Philip V and became the cause of two European wars, and indirectly the employer of thousands of privateers as a result. Engraving after a painting by Hyacinthe Rigaud.

France had encouraged lucrative attacks on the Spanish Main—forced ex-privateers to look elsewhere. In Jamaica and later in the Bahamas a new mood of colonial optimism came to prevail, and with colonial governors adopting a more responsible attitude, an increasingly anti-piratical policy drove many former buccaneers toward piracy on the American Atlantic coast and on the outer edges of the Caribbean, the West Indies. The first to depart the Spanish Main crossed the Atlantic to prey on shipping along the slave shores of West Africa and, soon after, in the Indian Ocean. Within only months, others found the convoluted islets and inlets of the American coast ideal havens. For a while as the 17th century drew to a close, piratical activity in the Caribbean declined, but Europe was about to explode again into all-out conflict.

The War of the Spanish Succession (1701–13) sprang from the death of Charles II, who left no legitimate children. This placed the Austrian Habsburg and the French Bourbon houses—both having dynastic claims on Spain's crown—at loggerheads. Charles left all of his dominions to his closest link by marriage, Louis XIV of France's grandson, which made him Philip V of Spain and brought the huge Spanish empire into the French domain. The Habsburg Holy Roman Emperor Leopold I declared war on Louis to protect his own claim to the Spanish succession against the Bourbons. England (which in the course of the war became the United Kingdom of Great Britain by the Act of Union that joined England, Scotland, and Wales in 1707) sided with Leopold. So did the Dutch Republic, like England fearing French expansionist ambition; both nations also wanted a Protestant succession to the Spanish throne. The war was fought in Europe but also in North America and the Caribbean. British colonists later called the conflict Queen Anne's War, although it began under her predecessor, William III of Orange. It was ended through two treaties, Utrecht and Rastatt (signed in 1714), with Philip V retaining the Spanish crown but renouncing

ny claim to the French succession, while the Austrian Habsburgs received most of
pain's territories in the Low Countries and Italy.

Peace brings unemployment

During its course the war provided many opportunities for privateers hired in
Europe and the Americas to gain lucrative contracts from the various nations
involved. However, the most significant outcome of the peace for the British
privateers was that, as part of the treaty, Spain granted to Great Britain the exclusive
right to slave trading in Spanish America for a period of 30 years, a deal known as
the *asiento*. But in every other respect the war's end brought ruin to America's
seafaring community. The peace of 1714 left thousands of former privateersmen
with the options of unemployment on a shore awash with cheap slave labor, poorly
paid service in naval or merchant ships, or a career in piracy. It was not much of
an option—most chose the latter course, but many captains still balked at crossing
the lines of their old privateering contracts to attack ships of their own nationality.

In the wake of the war, an uncertain political situation in the North American
colonies aided the growth in piracy. The lack of strong government made the
Atlantic seaboard a natural hunting ground for pirates and, as had happened before
in Jamaica and St. Domingue, colonial governors welcomed the contraband that
pirates brought to their ports to sell. The obvious disruption of mercantile shipping
and the increasing price of insurance were balanced against the benefits to the local
economies of illicit trade. This was the case for at least a decade, but as peacetime
gradually brought about an increase in maritime trade, so colonial authorities began
to clamp down on piracy in American waters. A combination of judicial and
military force eventually ended the outbreak of violence and theft.

By 1730 the most rampant pirate activity had ceased. Although later outbreaks
of piracy did occur, this short period would remain lodged in popular and romantic
culture as the Golden Age of piracy. Contemporary writers such as Captain Charles
Johnson coined the romantic epithet. Johnson's *A General History of the Robberies and
Murders of the Most Notorious Pyrates* was published in 1724, and went on to be an
even bigger bestseller than Exquemelin's buccaneer history. Johnson's real identity
was never revealed, although he has been identified in the recent past so firmly as
Daniel Defoe that many libraries still list Defoe as the book's author; however, this
assertion remains quite unproved and is vigorously denied by other luminaries.

Familiarly known as *A General History of Pyrates* or by the even shorter
General History, the shocking tales Johnson narrated of characters like Blackbeard,
Bartholomew Roberts, and Henry Every (or Avery) caused a sensation and made them
legends in their own time. He also scandalized society by revealing the existence of the
female pirates Bonny and Read. Pirates became a popular early 18th-century source
of escapism, with their activities fully and often completely inaccurately reported in
news-sheets of the period. This popular image played vicariously on the notorious

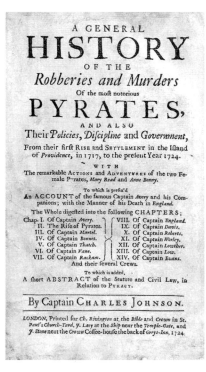

The title page of Johnson's *General History*,
which promises to cover the pirates'
"policies, discipline, and government from
their first rise and settlement in the island
of Providence, in 1717, to the present year
1724" as well as "The remarkable Actions
and Adventures of the two Female Pyrates,
Mary Read and Anne Bonny."

The first recorded black Jolly Roger, the skull, crossed bones, and hourglass of Emanuel Wynne.

Classic skull and crossed bones on the flag of Edward England.

Christopher Condent's triple jawless skulls and crossed bones image on a banner flag would have been easily identified by his victims around the Cape Verde Islands and off the coast of Brazil.

cruelty of many pirates, but failed to describe the misery and brutality of their lives and the inevitability that they faced an early death through battle or execution. And to the victims of pirate attacks, there was nothing "golden" about the age at all.

Flying the Jolly Roger

Many myths surround pirates of the Golden Age, but the Jolly Roger was real enough. It was said that the very sight of Blackbeard was sufficient to strike such terror into the hearts of seamen that they would surrender without a fight. However, at first sight out at sea it would not be possible, even through a telescope, to identify the captain of an approaching ship by his personal appearance. The real cause for terror in the Golden Age was the pirate flag flying from the main mast, which clearly identified its owner. The Jolly Roger, as this type of banner became known, was derived from the French for "pretty red" or *jolie rouge*, an ironic reference to the flags flown by the previous generation of buccaneers.

During the 17th century it had been common practice for privateers to fight under their national flag as part of a lawfully licensed navy, but also to hoist a red flag. The origin for red flags is unclear, but the color is identified with danger and it seems reasonable to assume that a red flag was intended as a warning to the enemy that no quarter would be given and that battle would be a fight to the death. As described in the previous chapter, a buccaneer frequently crossed the legal line and became a pirate, so his *jolie rouge* evolved to act as identification by the addition of a graphic device designed to intimidate victims by conjuring up images of dread. The flag effectively proclaimed, "Surrender is the only alternative to slaughter."

Quite why black became the preferred field color for the Jolly Rogers of the early 18th century is also unknown, although black's association with dread and death is probably as good an answer as any. Some have argued that black as opposed to red was flown to show that the ship was no longer a privateer but a pirate, however this seems unlikely because privateers were known to have displayed black flags as well as red ones and Golden Age pirates also flew both colors. The first recorded reference to a black Jolly Roger was in 1700, when the French privateer turned pirate Emanuel Wynne flew a black flag decorated with a skull, crossed bones, and an hourglass, and by 1714 the black flag was a clearly recognized symbol. The ill-prepared freebooter sometimes had to improvise, such as when Howell Davis first took to piracy and ordered his men to raise "a dirty tarpaulin, by way of black flag, they having no other." His French victim certainly understood the makeshift flag's meaning and attempted to make a run for it.

As the buccaneers had also done, 18th-century pirates sometimes flew a national flag as well as their Jolly Roger. Charles Vane flew the British Union flag from one mast and a black pirate flag from another, and Edward England flew a black flag from his mainmast, a red flag from his foremast, and the Union flag from his ensign staff while he was attacking a British East Indiaman vessel. There were still times when letters of marque were issued, and legal privateers might fly a national flag, but deception was a more pressing reason for pirates to display national flags. Since privateers were supposed only to attack ships of their own nation's enemies, by appearing as a privateer, a pirate could sneak up on a fellow national and pounce on the unsuspecting vessel. This ruse certainly provided an advantage to the small pirate sloop when planning to take a larger or better-armed ship; both Edward England and Howell Davis became masters of this deception.

Since flags meant little until the intent of an unknown sail was determined, it soon became general practice to hold a variety of national banners to help avoid attack in hostile waters, or to confuse or deceive an enemy until it was too late for them to escape. Even naval men-of-war flew foreign flags and signal banners in order to entice an enemy within range of their guns. The unwritten current rules of honorable conduct claimed it to be a legitimate *ruse de guerre* as long as any "lying" flags were replaced with the appropriate national emblem before opening fire. Pirates obeyed no such rules of conduct, of course, and would fly whatever flag they pleased. A natural consequence of these policies was—during times of war or when sailing in pirate-infested waters—to assume all shipping to be hostile until proved otherwise and flee as quickly as possible on sighting any sail on the horizon.

Ever after Emanuel Wynne unfurled his white skull, crossed bones, and an hourglass on its black field, the particular design of a flag helped to identify a specific pirate, so his victims would know who they were up against. The main function of the Jolly Roger was entirely practical: by intimidating victims into surrender without fighting, not only were pirate lives saved, but ships could be captured intact—far more valuable prizes than those badly damaged by gunfire. The merchantman unfortunate enough to see the unfurled flag associated with the likes of Bartholomew Roberts or Blackbeard was well advised to surrender immediately. Of course, there were pirates with such a vicious reputation that the sight of their

Walter Kennedy, Bartholomew Roberts's second in command, used mixed images, including a sword and hourglass.

A strange kind of pirate, Stede Bonnet combines elements that are harder to read —dagger for battle, heart for life….

Christopher Moody's Jolly Roger (**left**) and Henry Every's (**right**): Moody may have been with Bartholomew Roberts at some point—he was hanged at Cape Coast Castle at the same time as others of Roberts's crew. His was the most colorful of all pirate flags, retaining the buccaneers' red field. The hourglass is winged (your time flying away…). Henry Every's nicely detailed skull is unusual in being in profile. He used this same device on either black or red fields.

"Calico" Jack Rackham favored over-large crossed cutlasses to bones.

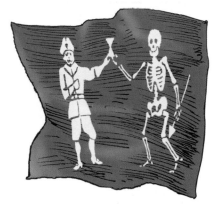

Dicing with Death; Bartholomew's first flag was later replaced by one advertising his hatred of Barbados and Martinique, **right**.

Richard Worley's simple skull and crossed bones suited a rather second-rate burglar turned pirate; hanged February 17, 1719.

flag inspired the crew to fight to the death, knowing they would see no mercy even by surrendering, as had been the case with L'Olonnais in the previous century.

The graphic devices on flags varied from pirate to pirate, although common themes predominated. The drawing had to be bold, simple, and easily recognized from a distance, and so we find imagery drawn from a shared pool of everyday experience: images seen on gravestones and mausoleums, allegorical paintings, church carvings… even tradesmen's signs. By far and away the most popular device was the grinning skull or a skeleton, an obvious symbol of death to all enemies. A skull with crossed bones beneath might be altered by swapping the bones for crossed swords—clearly representing the threat of a deadly fight ahead. Both symbols were popular images on 17th- and 18th-century cemetery headstones. The least obvious icon, an hourglass, would have been clear enough to anyone living in a time before the advent of handy chronometers: your time is running out….

Text messages were also included on the flags of some pirates, usually in the form of a specific threat aimed at a particular group of people. Bartholomew Roberts held a powerful grudge against the islands of Barbados and Martinique (*see page 174*), so as he cruised their waters during the late summer of 1720, he created flags designed to intimidate the islanders. One showed a pirate figure representing Roberts standing on two skulls. Under one skull the letters ABH meant "A Barbadian's Head," and the second was inscribed AMH, meaning "A Martiniquan's Head." The threat was clear, and sailors from these two islands could expect no mercy if they were captured.

While the skull was obviously associated with imminent death, the use of skeletons on flags appears more complex. Some records of pirate flags show skeletons dancing with each other or even with a human figure; this symbolized the pirate dancing a jig with death or dicing with death; in other words playing with the grim reaper, uncaring about fate—clearly not a man with whom to cross swords. Occasionally several symbols were combined, such as a raised hourglass toasting a skeleton wielding a spear on the flag of Bartholomew Roberts, or Blackbeard's showing a skeleton holding an hourglass in one hand and a spear in the other, with which he is stabbing a bleeding heart. These were all grim images and every version of the Jolly Roger shouted aloud that not only was resistance futile, it would result in death.

Dutch and British traders divide the East

Even before the short period of peace between 1697 and 1701, some of the more adventurous buccaneers took their field of operations across the Atlantic to the

Guinea Coast of Africa, and then further afield around the Cape of Good Hope and into the Indian Ocean. According to the Treaty of Tordesillas, this was Portugal's sphere, the routes down the western coast of Africa mapped out by her intrepid navigators from a time shortly before Columbus. As the Spanish were conquering, colonizing, and robbing the Americas, the Portuguese were opening up a new sea route between Indonesia and Europe following the return of the navigator Vasco da Gama from India in the late 15th century. In the 16th century, the Arab monopoly of land caravans was challenged by faster and more cost-effective maritime trade routes as Europeans expanded their commercial influence into the Indian Ocean.

During the late 16th and early 17th centuries the Portuguese dominated these sea routes, but by the mid-17th century Dutch, French, and English merchants also made regular voyages. This coincided with the shift of economic and mercantile power from the Mediterranean basin to northern Europe, its traders exporting cloth, manufactured goods, and precious metals to exchange for silk, spices, tea, porcelain, and opium. The Portuguese lost their monopoly and soon found themselves restricted to a minor role in Africa and the East, while English and Dutch trading companies flourished. By the last quarter of the 17th century the East India Company—also known as "John" Company—had established itself in India, and their Dutch rivals, V.O.C. (Vereenigde Oostindische Compagnie) or the Dutch East India Company, controlled Far Eastern business through trading settlements in Indonesia. Some ten years after the restoration of the English monarchy in 1660, Charles II awarded the East India Company extraordinary rights. It was permitted to build and garrison fortresses, raise, train, and equip troops, to acquire (that is, annex) territory, form alliances, to declare war, and make peace. Additional rights, such as to mint money and to exercise both civil and criminal jurisdiction over any "acquired" areas, made the East India Company a virtually self-governing state, and its bitter Dutch rival was no different.

By 1689, the company had numerous "factories" all over the Indian sub-continent and independently administered vast areas of Bengal and Madras as well as the region of Bombay (Mumbai). The East India Company's continual erosion of the Dutch monopoly over spices coming from their Indonesian holdings led to accusations of piracy and eventually were an irritant—in combination with problems in Africa—that contributed to a series of Anglo-Dutch wars. With trading rivals, other imperial powers, and hostile native princes, the Company needed its own armed forces, which were raised during the 1680s from among the local population. What John Company lacked was a correspondingly powerful navy. In the main,

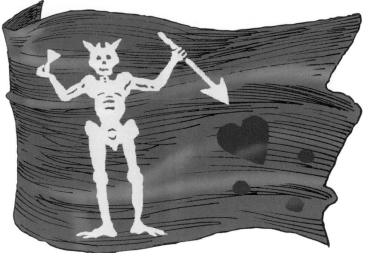

Blackbeard's infamous demonic skeleton stabs a bleeding heart.

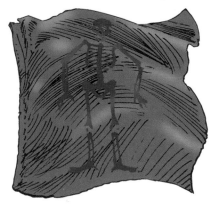

Another use of color, in Edward Low's fittingly blood-red skeleton.

Perhaps the most unusual pirate flag, Thomas Tew's cutlass-wielding arm.

the East Indiamen avoided attack by pirates by being the fastest ships afloat, and by the same token a heavily armed man-of-war could not keep up and so was of little practical use away from the Indian harbors. Eventually, London provided naval contingents along the route, which eventually reduced the threat of piracy.

Early growth of the slave trade

The end of buccaneering in the Caribbean led to an increase in the number of pirates looking elsewhere for rich pickings. One such area was West Africa, where the slave trade was in its heyday. By 1690 a Portuguese monopoly along the slaving coast had been broken open, allowing an influx of English, French, and Dutch slavers. The English even operated the trade under the dubious cover of the R.A.C. (Royal African Company). Originally known as the Company of Royal Adventurers Trading to Africa, it received an English monopoly over the slave

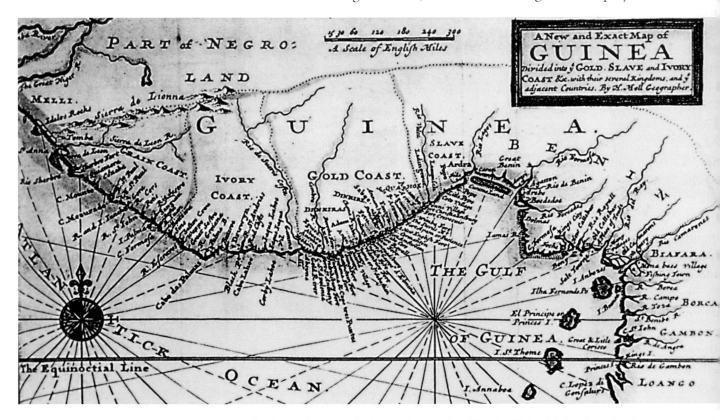

The Guinea Coast of West Africa stretched from the Gambia in the west to Gabon in the east, and included the Grain Coast, Ivory Coast, Gold Coast, Nigeria, and Benin, all rich sources of slaves throughout the late 17th century and all of the 18th.

trade through a royal charter issued by Charles II in 1660 after the Restoration. In fact its most distinguished member was the king's brother, James, Duke of York, so as a royal monopoly it received the protection of the Royal Navy, whose task was to seize rival English slave traders and drive off foreigners—effectively the French, Portuguese, and the Dutch, although by this time the Dutch had largely driven out the Portuguese. Friction was inevitable and came to a head in 1667 in the Second Anglo-Dutch War, the conflict in which Sir Christopher Myngs met his end.

Slaves captured by agents of the R.A.C. to be sold to the Americas were gathered at trading posts on the Guinea Coast, and branded with the letters D.Y. (after the Duke of York) or R.A.C. By the early 1680s, some 5000 slaves per year were being transported, a figure that had doubled by 1689, when the R.A.C. lost its monopoly, to the benefit of other British ports like Bristol. At this point it turned very profitably to also trading in gold, and gained another exclusive right to provide the English Mint, giving the Guinea coast of Ghana its alternative name of the Gold Coast, and the coin the realm nicknamed the "guinea."

Not surprisingly, pirates became an increasingly prevalent threat along the West African coast, despite naval patrols and the fortification by army units of slave-trading stations like the Cape Coast Castle on the Gold Coast. It was only a matter of time before pirates from the Americas and Europe ventured around the Cape of Good Hope and into the warm waters of the Indian Ocean, which they did in the last decades of the 17th century, finding it a perfect hunting ground. Along the ocean's northern shores, in the Arabian Sea, sailed Indian and Arab ships carrying a wealth of potential plunder. But the richest prizes afloat anywhere were the Dutch or English East Indiamen, bringing the wealth of the East to the markets of Europe. For a period of 30 years the Indian Ocean was a hotbed of piratical activity, and from its breadth sprang some of the most enduring pirate legends.

Buried treasure is a central theme in tales of piracy in the Golden Age, but doubloons, pieces of eight, and jewelry were an increasingly rare catch and other goods such as sugar, cocoa, and particularly slaves were just as valuable.

Piracy was hardly a new phenomenon in the region. Long before the first trading contacts between Europe and India, piracy was commonplace in many parts of the Indian Ocean. Pirates operated along the western coast of India and along the coasts of Arabia and Persia. Although heavily armed warships and war galleys of the Indian Moghul empire patrolled the northern Indian Ocean and Arab potentates maintained their own naval patrols, the stretch of water was too vast for such measures to quash the constant piratical activity. The arrival of European and American pirates only made the situation worse.

By 1690 the great Moghul empire—gripped by internal dissension, internecine warfare, and losing ground to the East India Company—had also lost its grip of the region's sea lanes. Although Indian and Arab maritime trade thrived, the ability to protect shipping declined. This was the situation that faced the first Western pirates to round the Cape of Good Hope, and they saw it as a golden opportunity. Men such as Henry Every

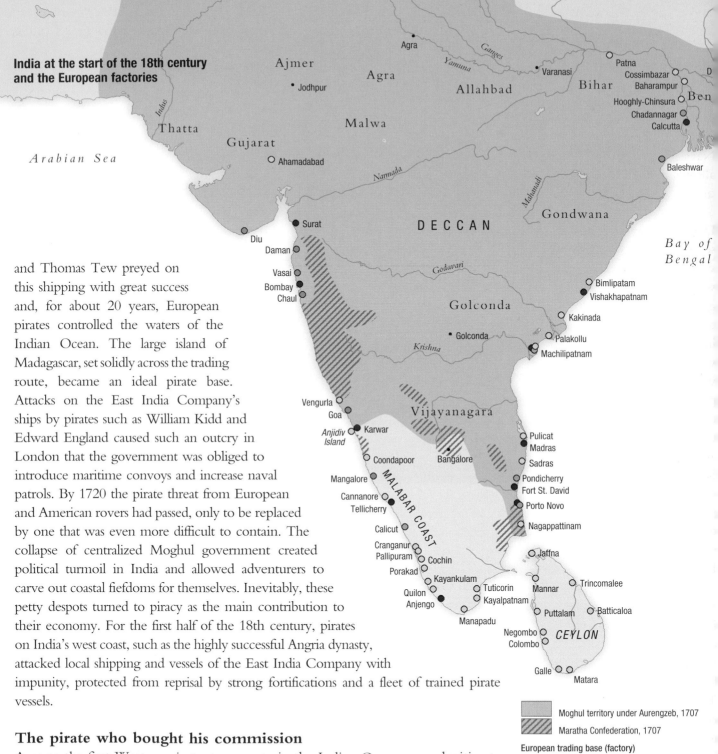

India at the start of the 18th century
and the European factories

Arabian Sea

Thatta

Gujarat

Ahamadabad

Diu

Daman

Vasai

Bombay

Chaul

Surat

Ajmer

Jodhpur

Agra

Agra

Malwa

Allahbad

Varanasi

Patna

Cossimbazar

Baharampur

Hooghly-Chinsura

Chadannagar

Calcutta

Bihar

Ben

D

Baleshwar

Narmada

Godavari

Gondwana

DECCAN

Golconda

Golconda

Krishna

Bimlipatam

Vishakhapatnam

Kakinada

Palakollu

Machilipatnam

Bay of Bengal

Vengurla

Goa

Anjidiv Island

Karwar

Coondapoor

Mangalore

Cannanore

Tellicherry

Calicut

Cranganur

Pallipuram

Porakad

Cochin

Quilon

Anjengo

Kayankulam

Manapadu

MALABAR COAST

Vijayanagara

Bangalore

Pulicat

Madras

Sadras

Pondicherry

Fort St. David

Porto Novo

Nagappattinam

Jaffna

Tuticorin

Kayalpatnam

Mannar

Puttalam

Trincomalee

Batticaloa

Negombo

Colombo

CEYLON

Galle

Matara

Moghul territory under Aurengzeb, 1707

Maratha Confederation, 1707

European trading base (factory)

● British (East India Company)

○ Dutch (Vereenigde Oostindische Compagnie)

● Portuguese

● French

and Thomas Tew preyed on this shipping with great success and, for about 20 years, European pirates controlled the waters of the Indian Ocean. The large island of Madagascar, set solidly across the trading route, became an ideal pirate base. Attacks on the East India Company's ships by pirates such as William Kidd and Edward England caused such an outcry in London that the government was obliged to introduce maritime convoys and increase naval patrols. By 1720 the pirate threat from European and American rovers had passed, only to be replaced by one that was even more difficult to contain. The collapse of centralized Moghul government created political turmoil in India and allowed adventurers to carve out coastal fiefdoms for themselves. Inevitably, these petty despots turned to piracy as the main contribution to their economy. For the first half of the 18th century, pirates on India's west coast, such as the highly successful Angria dynasty, attacked local shipping and vessels of the East India Company with impunity, protected from reprisal by strong fortifications and a fleet of trained pirate vessels.

The pirate who bought his commission

Among the first Western pirates to operate in the Indian Ocean was a legitimate American sea captain named Thomas Tew. Unlike some of his contemporaries, Tew was no hard done by sea-hand, but the scion of a respectable and prosperous Newport, Rhode Island family. With England and France at war, Tew moved south to Bermuda in 1690 to become a privateer and join those already making handsome profits from preying on French shipping bound for Canada. Once ensconced on the island, Tew's adequate funds enabled him to join a consortium to buy a share in the sloop *Amity*, which was being fitted out for a privateering cruise. The consortium appointed Tew captain and Bermuda's governor, a Royal Naval officer named Sir Robert Robinson, granted him letters of marque that allowed him to attack French vessels on the high seas and French slaving stations on the African coast.

In 1691 the *Amity* hauled anchor and sailed from Bermuda with George Drew, another local privateer, bound for West Africa. Their target was the French settlement of Goree (Dakar, Senegal), which was to be attacked in conjunction with the Royal African Company. The two ships became separated in a storm when Drew lost his mast and, now alone, Tew gathered together his crew and proposed they turn to piracy. He foresaw little gain for themselves in attacking the French factory, since the R.A.C. would appropriate what spoils were to be had. It was said he argued that it was better to risk life for plunder than for government. His crew agreed and the *Amity* set course for the Cape of Good Hope, then entered the Indian Ocean. Tew stopped briefly at Madagascar before sailing north and into the Red Sea. In the Straits of Bebelmandeb he fell on an Arab merchant ship, which was captured without any pirate casualties. The haul was impressive; enough to ensure a share of 3000 English pounds per head, with a larger portion reserved for Tew and his Bermudan backers.

Late in 1693 *Amity* again stopped in Madagascar and, according to the *General History*, Tew met the French pirate Misson, who had founded the colony of Libertatia (sometimes given as Libertalia), a form of pirate Utopia. Johnson described it as a fortified harbor, with a marketplace, houses, and docks. The society at Libertatia was an egalitarian one, where all men enjoyed the same rights, even black slaves set free from captured slave ships. However appealing, there is no evidence that either Misson or Libertatia ever existed outside of Johnson's imagination, and the author's literary purpose may have been to underline the leveling nature of pirate society, a theme that runs all the way through his book.

What is known is that by April 1694 Tew had returned to Newport, Rhode Island, where he paid off his crew and fellow consortium shareholders, sold the

An early 18th-century map of the western Indian Ocean shows Madagascar. The island provided pirates with an ideal base from which to attack ships sailing between India and Europe as they passed through the channel between Madagascar and the East African coast.

Visiting New York's governor, Benjamin Fletcher, Thomas Tew—clay pipe in hand—lays out his plans for a privateering commission; from a painting by Howard Pyle. Fletcher said of the affable pirate, "He is what is called a very pleasant man."

Amity, and went to live ashore, the very picture of gentry and a toast among the cream of colonial society. During his sojourn in New England, Tew visited New York and met Benjamin Fletcher, the English governor. Fletcher was later to describe Tew as "agreeable and companionable." After several months and some pressure from members of his old crew, Tew decided to return to sea. Having encountered difficulties in obtaining letters of marque from other colonial governors, Tew went straight to New York in October 1694 and presented his suit to Fletcher, who willingly provided him with a privateering commission to harass and attack French shipping heading for Canada, in return for a share of 300 pounds. Not a particularly scrupulous man, it is unlikely that Fletcher was under any misapprehension about Tew's real agenda. Two contemporary accounts make it clear that all Boston knew Tew was fitting out "three small ships, a sloop, a brigantine, and a barque…" at Rhode Island, ready to sail for the Indian Ocean and the Red Sea. Fletcher's successor, the Earl of Bellamont, said that Tew's real intentions were well advertised in New York.

In November 1694, Tew left in his new sloop that he had also named *Amity*, accompanied by two other privateers turned pirates: Thomas Wake and William Want. Want had served with Tew on the previous voyage and was apparently a trusted associate. The small fleet stopped again in Madagascar, and for the next few seasons Tew cruised independently, in association with his two fellow New Englanders, or as part of a pirate squadron. On this last point, according to Johnson this also included another famous pirate, Henry Every. Certainly by 1696 Tew was regarded as such a serious threat to the crown that in January of that year King William III (1672–1702) gave a certain Captain William Kidd of New York a special commission. In it Thomas Tew (written as "Too") was specifically named as a pirate and, as a pirate-hunter, Kidd was told to seek him out.

Tew's activities are unclear during this period, but it was probably in June 1695 that he entered his old hunting ground of the Red Sea, where he attacked an Arab vessel. Unlike previous prizes, it put up resistance, and Tew was hit by a cannon-ball that ripped open his abdomen, mortally wounding him. As Johnson colorfully describes it, Tew "held his bowels with his hands some small space; when he dropp'd, it struck such a terror in his men, that they suffered themselves to be taken, without making resistance." Their fate has never been uncovered, but the victors surely executed them. Tew was one of the archetypal romantic pirates: dashing, successful (for a time), and able to cheat the gallows through death in action. Like his contemporary Henry Every, Thomas Tew's career served to encourage others to follow in piratical footsteps.

Benjamin Fletcher, however, did not cheat justice for his sponsorship of Tew. Complaints against his corruption made from up and down the American seaboard caused such a stink in the king's ears that he commanded the Council of Trade and Plantations to investigate. The council wrote to Fletcher in February 1697, informing him that: "By information given lately at the trial of several of [Henry] Every's crew, your Government is named as a place of protection to such villains, and your favor to Captain Tew given as an instance of it." Fletcher defended himself, saying: "Captain Tew…came to my table like the other strangers who visit the province. He told me he had a sloop well manned, and gave bond to fight the French at the mouth of the Canada river [St. Lawrence], whereupon I gave him a commission."

The following year Richard Coote, Earl of Bellamont, replaced Fletcher and began to investigate the complaints. In 1698 he reported to the Lords of Trade that the pirates "that have given the greatest disturbance in the East Indies and the Red Sea, have either been fitted out from New York or Rhode Island, and manned from New York." He pointed the finger directly at his predecessor, that Governor Fletcher had issued commissions to Tew and other pirates "when none of them had any ship or vessel in Col. Fletcher's government, yet they had commissions and were permitted to raise men in New York and the design was public of their being bound for the Red Sea. Thomas Tew was a most notorious pirate," went on Bellamont, "complained of by the East India Company…a man of most mean and infamous character, he was received and caressed by Col. Fletcher, dined and supp'd often with him…and they exchanged presents, as gold watches, etc."

Recalled to London in disgrace, Fletcher faced the anger of the Lords of Trade, who agreed that the circumstances and timing of his commission to Tew "makes it highly probable it was not granted for nothing." The right of colonial governors to issue letters of marque in the king's name was not one that assumed the benefit of personal gain. Hanging on to the last shreds of respectability, Benjamin Fletcher said of Tew that he was "not only a man of courage and activity, but of the greatest sense and remembrance of what he had seen of any seaman that I ever met with. He was also what is called a very pleasant man…."

The unluckiest pirate

The man who received the commission from William III to hunt down Thomas Tew eventually won the dubious distinction—whipped up by the popular press of the day—of being one of England's most notorious pirates. But Captain Kidd was excoriated for crimes he never committed, and in fact was a considerable failure

Howard Pyle's portrayal of "Captain Kidd," the man sent to hunt down Thomas Tew, is close to the only known contemporary painting of the privateer (*see over the page*), but the pirate artist has made him meaner of appearance.

as a pirate. He only made one privateering voyage and took only one prize of any substance, but it was enough to warrant his arrest and place him on trial for his life.

William Kidd was born in Scotland in 1645, probably in Greenock, although some argue for Dundee. When he was only a child his father's death condemned the reputable family to poverty and, like many Scottish boys before him, young William took to a life at sea. The details of the first 20 years of his life as a seaman are vague before his first recorded appearance in 1689. Serving on a Caribbean privateer in that year, with England and France at war, Kidd led the boarding party that took a French vessel prize and sailed it to Nevis. Elected as captain, he renamed the ship *Blessed William*, in honor of the Protestant English king. Shortly after this event Kidd was to suffer an indignity that would be visited on him again—under the glib tongue of a sailor called Robert Culliford, his crew insisted they turn to piracy and abandoned Kidd when he refused them.

Portrait of a prosperous privateering captain of the Restoration period. William Kidd ended up with a reputation as a pirate that he did not deserve, and met a pirate's fate at the end of a rope.

By 1691 he had arrived in New York, where he married a twice-widowed girl half his age, who brought a considerable amount of colonial property from her earlier marriages. With two daughters soon following, William Kidd established himself as a sound member of the community, respected as an honest, hard-working captain engaged in lawful privateering when the occasion arose. In 1695 he sailed to England, hoping to win more lucrative privateering contracts, and in London met Richard Coote, Earl of Bellamont. The earl was pitching at the king and the Lords of Trade to have himself appointed as governor for New York and Massachusetts to replace the peculating Benjamin Fletcher. His platform was to strike at piracy wherever he encountered it, while attacking French interests whenever possible. With complaints coming in from every quarter about Thomas Tew's activities among other pirates, William III was happy to give Bellamont's protege a royal commission in this respect. The *Antigua*, Kidd's own ship, was sold to raise funds, but with royal patronage he and Bellamont were able to raise finance from other investors who included several earls and barons; sufficient money to build and crew a new privateer.

The 300-ton, 34-gun *Adventure Galley* was commissioned and fitted out in London with oars as well as sails, hence its name. There is no evidence to prove it, but this choice of vessel points to William Kidd either being well informed on Mediterranean maritime techniques or easily persuaded to experiment boldly on the advice of others. Since pirates were more often encountered in the shallows of estuaries and among the sandbars of islands, the oars would be a key advantage, giving the galley maneuverability in battle under wind-shaded conditions. The king signed letters of marque, allowing Kidd to attack pirates and any French he encountered in the Indian Ocean. The language was suitably vague here and there, the implication being that the shareholders would turn a blind eye to the occasional piratical act if it produced a profit, a small recompense as the fiscal constraints of the contract meant that Kidd and his crew would otherwise see little benefit. In spite of this small chink of leeway, the otherwise restrictive terms strongly influenced Kidd's future

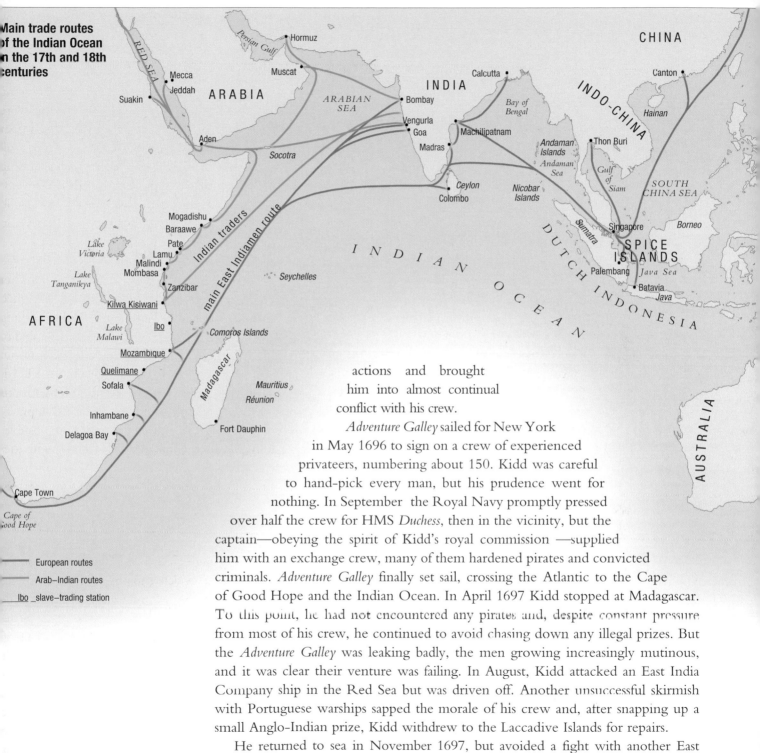

Main trade routes of the Indian Ocean in the 17th and 18th centuries

European routes
Arab–Indian routes
Ibo _slave–trading station

actions and brought him into almost continual conflict with his crew.

Adventure Galley sailed for New York in May 1696 to sign on a crew of experienced privateers, numbering about 150. Kidd was careful to hand-pick every man, but his prudence went for nothing. In September the Royal Navy promptly pressed over half the crew for HMS *Duchess*, then in the vicinity, but the captain—obeying the spirit of Kidd's royal commission —supplied him with an exchange crew, many of them hardened pirates and convicted criminals. *Adventure Galley* finally set sail, crossing the Atlantic to the Cape of Good Hope and the Indian Ocean. In April 1697 Kidd stopped at Madagascar. To this point, he had not encountered any pirates and, despite constant pressure from most of his crew, he continued to avoid chasing down any illegal prizes. But the *Adventure Galley* was leaking badly, the men growing increasingly mutinous, and it was clear their venture was failing. In August, Kidd attacked an East India Company ship in the Red Sea but was driven off. Another unsuccessful skirmish with Portuguese warships sapped the morale of his crew and, after snapping up a small Anglo-Indian prize, Kidd withdrew to the Laccadive Islands for repairs.

He returned to sea in November 1697, but avoided a fight with another East Indiaman. Another evasive encounter resulted in an argument between Kidd and a

Built at the Deptford shipyards in London, 1695, the *Adventure Galley* was an ocean-going, ship-rigged galley armed with 34 guns. Her construction, seen here in cutaway, was evidently hurried because seaworthiness through timber rot was a continual problem.

gunner, William Moore. Kidd hurled an insult at Moore, calling him a "lousy dog." Moore retorted: "You have made me so and you have brought me to ruin and many more." Kidd was so enraged that he picked up a heavy bucket and struck the gunner over the head, killing him. After capturing three small prizes off the Indian coast, in January 1698 Kidd snared the *Queddah Merchant* with its lucrative cargo. In doing so he was following the dictates of his commission because the *Queddah Merchant* was sailing under French colors. However, her captain was an Englishman, and when Kidd offered to give up the prize for that reason, the rebellious crew forced him to keep her. On hearing of the incident, the East India Company forced the government's hand to brand Kidd as a pirate, making any pardon he might beg impossible.

After a further fruitless cruise, Kidd reached Madagascar in April 1698, where he encountered the only pirate of his pirate-hunting expedition, none less than Rober

Culliford sailing the *Mocha Frigate*. But instead of securing a captive and avenging the theft of his first ever prize in Nevis, history repeated itself. Kidd's men mutinied and signed up with Culliford, who sailed off, leaving the pirate-hunter with the worm-eaten *Adventure Galley* and 13 men still loyal to him. Salvaging every last scrap from the badly rotted galley, they abandoned her for the *Queddah Merchant*, which Kidd renamed the *Adventure Prize*. They left Madagascar, giving up the Indian Ocean and the cruise, and sailed to Boston, where Kidd tried to arrange a pardon with Richard Cootes, Earl of Bellamont, now governor of New York and Massachusetts. Instead, Bellamont had him arrested and sent to London to stand trial. Rumors that Kidd buried his plunder on Long Island before sailing to Boston may be accurate, although Bellamont probably recovered the goods after Kidd was arrested.

In early 1700, Kidd was thrown into prison in London amid a flurry of news-sheet speculation. Placed in a vulnerable position, Kidd's noble shareholders wanted no further part of his problems and went to some lengths to ensure his notoriety by planting misinformation. Stories abounded of his merciless cruelty, but if atrocities there were, it had been members of his unruly crew who had committed them. While the Tory opposition tried to make Kidd name his political backers and testify against them, his alarmed backers from the Whig party conveniently "lost" incriminating papers to prevent a political scandal. Most importantly, documents proving the two ships he had taken were lawful French prizes, thus refuting the East India Company's assertion of piracy, went missing. These were eventually discovered among other dusty relics in London in the early 20th century. To avoid further embarrassment to king and nobility, Kidd was speedily tried, convicted of the murder of William Moore, and hanged at Execution Dock in London's Wapping on May 23, 1701. His body was then displayed in a gibbet on the banks of the River Thames, a warning to other pirates. A victim of miscalculation and intrigue, Captain Kidd is one of the unluckiest pirates of his era.

The pirate who knew when to stop

Henry Every (or John Avery, Long Ben, or sometimes Benjamin Bridgeman) is often regarded as the ultimate successful pirate: he captured the richest prize of his day, eluded the authorities, and lived to tell the tale. He became the subject of *The Successful Pyrate* (1712), a play by that doyen of piratology Charles Johnson, and provided inspiration for many looking for an easy life of adventure and plunder. Above all, unlike Thomas Tew and other contemporaries, he knew when to stop. Every's early life remains shrouded in mystery, although he probably learned his sea legs working on Royal Navy ships. One account places him at the bombardment of the Barbary port of Algiers in 1671, another claims a Caribbean buccaneer background for him, and he has been described as an unlicensed slave-trading captain of the early 1690s. Until the end of that decade the Royal African Company held a monopoly on this profitable trade, but interlopers who risked breaking the slave-trading laws could reap immense profits.

An illustration in Johnson's *General History* depicts Henry Every sheltered from the tropical sun under a makeshift parasol held by a black slave. In the background, the pirate's crossed bones flag flies from a captured trading factory.

By 1694 Every had apparently abandoned slave trading and—although the claims of an early privateering career based in the Bahamas have no proven basis—by June he was serving as first mate on a privateer named the *Charles*, anchored at La Coruña in northwestern Spain, licensed by the Spanish to operate against the shipping of the French colony of Martinique, in the West Indies. However, neither Every nor the *Charles* made it to the Spanish Main. One night when the drunkard of a captain lay in a rum-soaked stupor, Every led a mutiny and the crew took over the sloop, renaming her the *Fancy*, with Every as her new captain. The *Fancy* was an ideal pirate ship, designed as a fast privateer and armed with 46 guns. The pirates sailed her south, capturing four vessels off the Cape Verde Islands on the way to the Cape of Good Hope. One ship was a French pirate, the other three were English vessels, and yet Every wrote an astonishing letter, dated February 18, 1695, which he gave to a London-bound ship, and it was published in the news-sheets. In it, he claimed he had no hostile intentions toward English or Dutch ships, but said that "my men are hungry, stout, and resolute, and should they exceed my desire I cannot help myself." It was clearly a bargaining point should he ever be captured, and he concluded with the phrase, "as yet an Englishman's friend, Henry Every." He added a postscript, giving his location as Johanna Island in the Comoros and a warning that "Here is 160 odd French armed men who waits the opportunity of getting any ship, take care of yourselves."

The *Fancy* locked in battle with the Moghul treasure ship *Gang-i-sawai*, acts as a background for Every to pose as a respectable English gentleman on the shore. The Indian treasure ship was carrying more than a king's ransom in valuables and coins.

Having entered the Indian Ocean later in 1695, Every sailed up the East African coast and into the Red Sea, where he met many other pirates, including several from the American colonies. Every forged an alliance and formed them into a squadron powerful enough to intercept the well-armed Moghul treasure fleets that sailed between India and the Middle East. The pirates lay in wait for the annual treasure fleet that was due to return to India from Arabia carrying gold, silver and jewels, which had earlier been exchanged for Indian or Oriental silks and spices. The Indians scattered on sighting the pirates, and nightfall covered their escape, but fortune favored Every and when dawn broke two Indian ships were within range. The smaller, *Fateh Mohammed*, was quickly overcome, but the larger *Gang-i-sawai* only surrendered after a brutal fight. The survivors were tortured to reveal hidden caches of treasure then killed, and women were raped, a brutality fueled by the religious and racial differences between the pirates and the Indians.

The contrast between their fate and that of the women portrayed in Johnson's lay would be hilarious if it were not so horrific. In *The Successful Pyrate*, the *Gang-sawai* is carrying two ladies of European extraction, who banter with the pirates, exchanging suggestive comments intended to amuse the theater audience.

To his astonishment and the crew's delight, Every found they had captured the Grand Moghul Aurengzeb's main treasure ship, containing over 600,000 pounds in gold, silver, jewels, and other luxuries. Each pirate in the fleet received a share of over 1000 pounds, a staggering sum of money for the time, with a larger share going to Every and the *Fancy*'s crew. The allied pirate fleet disbanded and the *Fancy* sailed for the Caribbean, where it was agreed there would be a warmer welcome for a successful "privateer" than back in England. So Every and his crew fetched up in the Bahamas, where England's writ counted for little and the islands' pirate council offered them protection. The crewmen were paid off and dispersed.

Unfortunately for the *nouveaux riches*, Aurengzeb had cut off all trade relations with the East India Company, and to re-establish the position it was necessary to pay reparations and place a bounty on the pirates' heads. Some made the mistake of returning to England, where several were caught and hanged, but Every sailed for Ireland, then vanished. His subsequent life remains a mystery, but it was thought he was able to retire into obscurity with his wealth. Known as the "Arch Pyrate" or by his nickname of "Long Ben," Every is the only pirate who survived to live off his ill-gotten gains. As such, he was one of the most successful pirates of them all and, after Charles Johnson had finished burnishing his reputation, a fine example to many who dreamed of following in his wake.

Edward England—hard head, soft heart

Brutality was a standard condition for almost every pirate, and for crews desperate for quick gain and plenty of it, working for a captain with a sense of mercy was the lot of a loser; Edward England fitted this description. He was a skilled sailor and fierce in battle but a tendency to leniency with captives went against the vicious standards of his profession. In the end his crews turned against him and Edward ended his days starving to death in the slums of Madagascar.

England was probably born in Ireland, as Edward Seegar. As a seaman, he served on a trading sloop based in Jamaica and pursued a legitimate career as a sailor. This ended in 1717, when his vessel was captured by Christopher Winter, a pirate operating out of New Providence in the Bahamas, who otherwise remains a footnote in history. The pirates returned to the Bahamas with their prize and, electing to join them, Seegar changed his name to England in an effort to cover his tracks. He served under Winter until July 1718, when the man who was to do more than anyone else to end the Golden Age of piracy arrived in New Providence. Governor Woodes Rogers, wielding a great big broom, came to sweep the

Edward England as portrayed in a woodcut that featured in Johnson's *General History*. His crew eventually rejected him for being too lenient on their victims.

Bahamas clean of pirates (*see pages 152–54*). Along with several more infamou[s] names, England escaped capture in a stolen sloop and crossed the Atlantic bent o[n] carving out a piratical career with a new crew.

He cruised off the West African coast from the Azores to the Cape Verde Island[s] and collected several prizes. One of these vessels was the snow brigantine *Cadogan*. She was a slave ship from Bristol and Skinner, her captain, was well remembered fo[r] past cruelties by several of England's men. They tortured and killed him and the[n] began a slaughter of the slaver's crew, but England made them stop, and those wh[o] wished to join him were spared. Among them was Howell Davis, who would soo[n] make a name for himself as a pirate to be feared (*see pages 170–72*); he was mad[e] captain of the *Cadogan*. Another of the prizes was a larger ship called the *Pearl*, whic[h] England took as his own flagship, while keeping his sloop as an auxiliary vessel. Th[e] pirates continued on their way, sailing off the Guinea coast, capturing dozens mor[e] prizes. One, the sloop *Victory*, England gave to John Taylor, one of his trusted crewmen[.]

Turning south, the pirates rounded the Cape of Good Hope and entered th[e] Indian Ocean, intending to prey on British and Dutch East Indiamen returning t[o] Europe. A short break in Madagascar allowed the ships to be beached for careening[,] during which period they "liv'd there very wantonly for several weeks, makin[g] free with the Negroe women." England and Taylor went on to cruise in consor[t] off the northwest coast of India. Again, England moved into one of his prizes, [a] 34-gun square-rigged ship which, like Henry Every, he renamed the *Fancy*. The[y] then returned to the Atlantic, arriving off the coas[t] in 1719 between the Gambia river and Cape Coast[.] The hunting was good and ten ships fell into thei[r] hands. England plundered and then let go thre[e] of them with their crews, two others were take[n] as prizes, and the remainder were set afire an[d] burned to the waterline. The two prizes, *Mercur[y]* and *Elizabeth*, were refitted and given new names[,] *Queen Anne's Revenge* and *Flying King*. England the[n] handed these over to his trusted lieutenants Captai[n] Lane and Robert Sample, who both set sail for th[e] Caribbean and their own piratical careers. Shortl[y] after, England and Taylor captured two more ships[,] releasing one and keeping the other, called th[e] *Victory II*, which became Taylor's new flagship.

England and Taylor returned to Madagasca[r] via Johanna Island (now Nzwani in the Comoro[s] Islands; the French called it Anjouan) northwest o[f] Madagascar, which was a popular pirate rendezvous[,] since it sat bang in the middle of the shipping rout[e]

Opposite: There was a fashion in contemporary publications for depicting pirates against a backdrop of their vessel in battle. In this case, Edward England is shown with the *Fancy* in combat with the East Indiaman *Cassandra*.

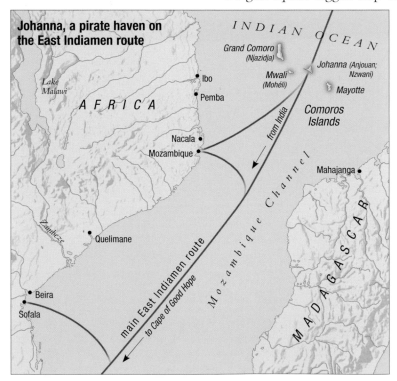

between India and the Cape of Good Hope. Approaching the small island on August 27, 1720, England found three East Indiamen in the harbor, one Dutch and two British, the *Cassandra* and the *Greenwich*. The two smaller ships raised anchor and escaped, but the more heavily armed *Cassandra*, captained by a Scot called James Macrae, bought time for them by opening fire on the *Fancy*. While John Taylor pursued the fleeing vessels in *Victory*, *Fancy* engaged the *Cassandra* in a brutal sea battle. Macrae and England pounded each other with broadsides at close range in a fight that lasted for several hours. Of the two vessels, *Fancy* was the more powerfully armed, so despite the enormous determination and bravery of both captains and their crews, when it became obvious that the pirates were gaining the upper hand, Macrae ran his badly battered ship onto the nearby beach and led his surviving crewmen ashore.

The pirates sent a boat to capture the *Cassandra* and found a cargo reputedly valued at 75,000 pounds. Macrae and his crew hid ashore for ten days, then, short of food and water, they gave themselves up. This was a gamble, since although the *Cassandra* had suffered 37 casualties, over 90 of England's pirates had died so revenge for their lost shipmates was a motive for murder. After a lengthy argument between England and John Taylor (angered at having let prizes escape his clutches) the captain's naturally lenient nature prevailed and he set Macrae and the *Cassandra*'s crew free. As England's pirate fleet gathered way, Taylor fomented rebellion among the men and persuaded most of them to join him and mutiny. Standing little chance against such odds, England was removed from his position. Along with only three steadfast men, he was marooned on an islet off Madagascar in early 1721. The castaways managed to construct a raft and eventually reached Madagascar, where England was reduced to begging for food, and where he died soon afterward.

After abandoning his former captain, John Taylor headed east across the ocean toward the Malabar Coast in *Victory* and with *Fancy* in train, but ran into serious trouble. A squadron of British warships, retreating from a failed mission to dislodge Indian pirates from two small islands off the East India Company's main base of Bombay, offered battle. Outnumbered, Taylor turned tail and fled for safer waters off the East African coast, where he teamed up with Olivier La Bouche. This French pirate had just arrived from the Caribbean and Atlantic, where he had sailed

Marooned, the oil painting by Howard Pyle, is a classic image from the Golden Age of piracy. Up and down the coasts of South America and South Africa, the numerous uninhabited islands made perfect prisons for those who fell foul of their captains—and for hapless captains who provoked mutiny among their crews.

with Sam Bellamy in 1716 and Howell Davis two years later. After capturing a Portuguese ship laden with booty and divvying it between them, the pirates split up, La Bouche for Madagascar, Taylor for the West Indies, and thence to Panama. The governor of Porto Bello granted him a pardon and John Taylor later became a captain in the Panamanian coastguard.

The Afro-Indian pirate kings

Before leaving the warmth of the Indian Ocean for cooler climes along the North American seaboard, it is worth noting that both the Dutch V.O.C. and the East India Company suffered as greatly from more localized piracy as they did from European and colonial American pirates. The Indian Moghul Empire, disintegrating under internal political and external military pressures, left a vacuum at the start of the 18th century, which former vassal states soon began to fill. Of these, the most vigorous was Maratha, which soon established an empire in the center of India. In its earliest phase of expansion outsiders provided the expertise in military and naval matters. In the case of the navy, officers were usually Persian, Arabian (Omani and Yemeni), and African Muslims. One among these was Kanhoji (or Conajee) Angria, an African Muslim, who rose rapidly to become commander of the Maratha Rajah's fleet by 1698. In reality, the "fleet" was no more than an organization of pirates who controlled the 240-mile stretch of India's western seaboard south from Bombay to Vengurla.

When the East India Company objected to his raiding and, in 1704, told the Rajah to order Angria to desist, the virtually independent pirate's reply was typically arrogant: he would seize their ships wherever he came across them. The Angrian maritime fiefdom attracted adventurers from India and from Europe, and by the 1720s the region played host to hundreds of well-armed pirate craft—some of as many as 40 guns—whose captains owed allegiance to the Angria family. From coastal strongholds and small offshore islands, Angria sent large fleets to attack coastal shipping and, where possible, to capture East Indiamen. He viewed Britain with contempt and his treatment of British captives held for ransom aroused particular anger, since he forced them to act as slaves instead of holding them in at least a minimum of comfort until their ransoms were paid.

A Dutch East Indiaman bears down on the Cape through pirate-infested waters. In some cases, those sailing toward India and the Spice Islands were better value as prizes, since they were often laden with silver to pay for future cargoes.

In 1710, he offered the British a direct affront by capturing the tiny islets of Karanja and Colaba off Bombay—headquarters of the East India Company—and then for years terrorized the Indian and British shipping that used the port. His next step was to extort protection money, and even East Indiaman captains were forced to pay a toll to the pirates to gain safe access to Bombay. British humiliation reached its peak in 1712 when Angria's ships captured the private yacht of the East India Company's governor of Bombay. But there was something of a silver lining—the ransom was heavy, almost 4000 pounds, but came with an agreement of truce for all East India Company ships, and so for the next four years Angria restricted his attacks to Indian shipping. Although this was a respite for the company, the activities of Angria and his pirates were considered a major embarrassment to the British in the eyes of other Indian potentates, so when a new company governor was appointed in January 1716, British policy changed. Governor Charles Boone ordered that naval resources should gather for an assault on the pirate nest, and in return Angria began to harass East Indiamen again. Two company attacks on Angria's stronghold of Colaba were repulsed, and in late 1716 Angria even blockaded the port again, forcing Boone to pay another humiliating tribute to unlock the harbor's mouth.

In late 1717 another British attack on Angria's coastal strongholds was repulsed by gunboats, and the situation reached a stalemate that a further assault in 1721

Pyrate barbecue—Kanhoji Angria hated the East India Company with a passion and showed no mercy to any English captives who were not worth the price of a ransom. Back home, news-sheet readers shuddered with a delicious sense of horror at scenes like this, of Angrian pirates roasting the captain of a captured prize on a griddle.

ailed to alter. However, there was a small reward for the British in that as they were returning to Bombay, some of the squadron ran into John Taylor, with the result related earlier. A Royal Naval squadron containing four ships of the line under the command of Commodore Thomas Matthews carrying 6000 soldiers, in conjunction with Portuguese land forces, was also sent to attack Angria in 1721. It too was repulsed and in January 1722, Boone was recalled to London. Commodore Matthews followed a year later to have charges of corruption leveled at him in conjunction with the failure at Karanja and Colaba. He was accused and convicted of negotiating with Indian pirates and effectively betraying the mission.

When Kanhoji Angria died in 1729, his pirate realm—now an independent state—was considered unassailable; the perfect pirate haven. His two sons succeeded him, but Sumbhaji and Mannaji never saw eye to eye. The division of their father's territory gave Sumbhaji the island strongholds to the north near Bombay, and Mannaji chunks of the mainland further to the south; the power struggle began. Bit by bit Mannaji was forced to give ground, so that by 1735 Sumbhaji controlled everything except a small coastal enclave, which he left his brother to rule. By the time Sumbhaji Angria's consolidation was complete, the East India Company had also grown stronger and a new breed of fast-sailing warships frequently escorted their merchant vessels. Nevertheless, Sumbhaji continued his father's policy of harassing shipping around Bombay, and in 1736 he captured the East Indiaman *Derby* by bringing his vessels in from the target's stern so that the British guns could not be brought to bear. The *Derby*, filled with the annual gold shipment for Bombay, was the richest Indiaman prize ever taken.

Toolaji Angria picked up the reins with even more viciousness when his half-brother Sumbhaji died in 1743. He attacked East Indiaman convoys, driving off or capturing the escorting warships. The British government could not tolerate such instability in a region it was coming to recognize as one of the most vital parts of its empire. In the 1750s, following an alliance with the Indian Maratha Confederacy, an overwhelming land and sea assault was launched on the Angrian strongholds. One by one they fell to Anglo-Indian army brigades or Royal Navy gunnery, until by February 1756 only Angria's main fortress at Vijayadurg remained, and it too was stormed after a crippling bombardment. Taken prisoner, the British incarcerated Toolaji Angria in a dungeon, broke up his pirate fleet, and transported his vast treasury to Bombay.

There are many in India today who regard the Angria family with great affection, national heroes who satisfy the sense of anger at the British imperialism that followed. But more than this, the Angrian dynasty represented the most successful pirate or buccaneer group of the 17th and 18th centuries, anywhere. For half a century they maintained a secure pirate haven, repeatedly humiliated the supposedly all-powerful East India Company, and in the process slowed the spread of British control in India.

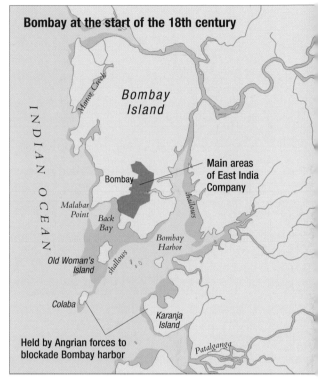

Colaba is now incorporated with the city of Mumbai, linked by a wide causeway via Old Woman's Island, more or less as indicated by the shallows.

CHAPTER EIGHT

And More Notorious Pyrates

The "Golden Age" of piracy in the Atlantic Ocean

As related briefly in the previous chapter, the arrival of Woodes Rogers in the Bahamas acted as a catalyst on the comfortably ensconced pirate community of New Providence. The result was an almost immediate diaspora of criminals from the islands as pirates headed off to safer hunting grounds, some like Edward England to Africa and the Indian Ocean, others like Charles Vane to the Carolinas. It seems extraordinary that one person should have had such an effect on so many hard men, but Rogers was no ordinary seaman or governor.

Woodes Rogers was born in about 1679 in the small Dorset port of Poole, on England's southern coast. Shortly after his birth, his merchant and ship-owning father moved the family to burgeoning mercantile Bristol, where the young boy grew up with the tang of salt in his nose and the mingled smells of hemp sacks and goods from all over the world. When he came of age, Rogers married a naval officer's daughter and in time took his father's place in the family business. Apart from cargo-carrying vessels, the firm also owned privateer vessels that pursued French shipping in the waters of the English Channel and the far off Caribbean. As prizes became harder to capture, Rogers looked elsewhere to find a profit.

Raised on the wharves and amid seafaring folk, his head no doubt filled with yarns of heroes like Hawkins and Drake, Rogers proposed an expedition to South America's Pacific coast. In 1708 the family teamed up with other Bristol merchants to fit out two 36-gun, 300-ton privateers, the *Duke* with Rogers at the helm and the *Duchess*, commanded by Stephen Courtney. Given the expenditure and risk involved in the venture, Rogers was keen to have the best experience available, and he secured it in the form of the former buccaneer and explorer William Dampier, to serve as sailing master (pilot). Dampier, the first man to sail right around the world twice, knew both sides of the Spanish Main and the Pacific as a well as any.

In the 1670s Dampier had crewed with buccaneers of Central America, twice visiting Campeche, then crossed the Isthmus of Panama to attack Spanish shipping along the Pacific coast and raid settlements in Peru. In 1683 he was back in the Pacific, having rounded Cape Horn serving under a privateer named Cook. They raided Spanish settlements in Peru, the Galapagos Islands, and Mexico. Their number swelled by other buccaneers, the expedition set out across the Pacific in 1686 to prey on the East Indies, including stops in the Philippines, China, the Spice Islands (Indonesia and the Celebes), and New Holland (Australia). Eventually, in 1691, Dampier returned to England, via South Africa. The publication of a journal of his adventures six years later was so well received that the Admiralty offered him the command of a mission to explore Australia, which set out in January 1699, heading first for South America to round Cape Horn.

The expedition was successful in fulfilling its instructions, but Dampier's ship, HMS *Roebuck*, foundered in a storm off Ascension Island early in 1701, marooning her crew for several weeks until a passing East Indiaman rescued them. With the outbreak of the War of the Spanish Succession, Dampier applied for a privateer's commission and was given the the 26-gun *St. George* and a crew of 120 men. He was also responsible for the 16-gun *Cinque Ports* and complement of 63 men; they sailed in April 1703, engaging a French man-of-war en route to South America and capturing four Spanish ships in the Pacific. When the two vessels resupplied at one of the uninhabited Juan Fernández Islands, some 400 miles off the coast of Chile, the sailing master of the *Cinque Ports*, Alexander Selkirk, concerned that his ship was no longer seaworthy, argued with Dampier and then opted to remain behind. Dampier returned to England after his second circumnavigation in 1707 with only the *St. George*—marooned Selkirk's fears had proved correct and *Cinque Ports* sank with all hands at some point after leaving the Juan Fernández Islands.

William Dampier was eager to accept the position of sailing master with Woodes Rogers, particularly because the expedition would take him around the globe for his third time. Rogers was probably considered the rich owner rather than a sea captain, but he proved to be an excellent commander and a skilled seaman, and his crew came to respect him. The *Duke* and *Duchess* rounded Cape Horn during January 1709 and, in February, anchored in the waters of the Juan Fernández Islands, in the process rescuing the castaway Alexander Selkirk, who by then had been marooned for longer than he had anticipated: four years and four months. On his return to England, his experiences were the inspiration for Daniel Defoe's *Robinson Crusoe*.

Keeping away from land, the privateers sailed up the South American coast and captured several Spanish prizes as they headed north. In May, Rogers turned his sights on the city of Guayaquil in Equador, which he captured and held to ransom. The privateers then headed north up to the Californian coast with the intention of ambushing the annual Manila galleons sailing between the Philippines and Acapulco in Mexico. In January 1710 they attacked two of the galleons and captured one, the *Nuestra Señora de la Incarnacion*, commanded by Jean Pichberty, "a gallant Frenchman," but were driven off by the second, larger ship. Rogers' flotilla of

William Dampier, the first man to circumnavigate the globe twice, and then for a third time; painting by Thomas Murray.

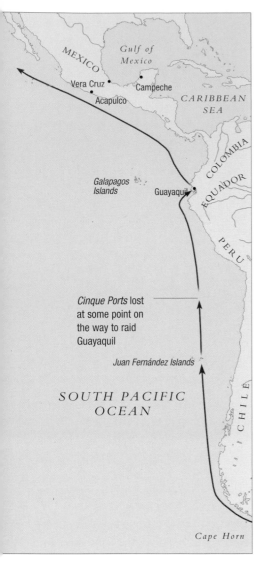

ships and prizes continued sailing west, to return to Bristol in October 1711 amid much public acclaim. However, his success was tempered by a bitter wrangle with the Admiralty. It transpired that the East India Company had lodged a complaint, accusing him of breaching their trade monopoly in the Indian Ocean. Rogers was one voice against the might of John Company, with its aristocratic shareholders. The Admiralty sided with them. In the end, the Bristol merchants received only a third of what they should have earned. In addition, financial mismanagement of the family business during his absence soon forced Rogers to file for bankruptcy. From 1713 he commanded a slave ship sailing between Indonesia and Africa.

Whatever the Admiralty's stance in the Rogers-East India Company affair may have been, the way in which he had handled his expedition placed Woodes Rogers high in the government's estimation. There was trouble brewing in the Bahamas, where settlers and landowners, fed up with the lawless state of the islands, were pressing London for some action. Rogers seemed to be the man for the task and so was appointed to be the first royal governor of the Bahamas late in 1717. At this time, anything approaching a form of authority for the Bahamas was to be found on the island of New Providence, and the only form of governing council—if it could be called that—was manned by pirates; men like Benjamin Hornigold, Charles Vane, Henry Jennings, Sam Bellamy, and Edward "Blackbeard" Teach.

Rogers was under no illusion. He knew the islands were a haven for lawlessness, and the establishment of any kind of authority would be an extremely hazardous undertaking—not only to his person but also to his pocket. It was common practice in the early 18th century for governments to make high-placed appointments but expect the appointee to pay all the costs associated with the position. Thus a colonial governor was expected to pay his way and make a return on his investment through successful, that is honestly profitable, government of his province. Naturally, it was a system open to all kinds of abuse—exemplified by the case of New York's governor, Benjamin Fletcher—from subtle embezzlement to outright theft; taking bribes was the least colonial malfeasance. Fortunately for Woodes Rogers, both his reputation and the fact that many believed the Bahamas offered enormous opportunities for improvement had investors flocking to his consortium. And so, apart from a small Admiralty-paid escort (that left soon after his arrival in New Providence), Rogers and his financial backers paid for the enterprise out of their own pockets.

The new governor arrived in August 1718, escorted by three Royal Navy warships, a frigate, and two sloops, and otherwise armed with papers offering the pirates the king's amnesty if they would give up their lives of crime. The worst pirates had already left or were to sneak away over the next few days. Only Charles Vane resisted the arrival, sending a fireship against the frigate and firing on it as he escaped. The rest—eager to disassociate themselves from Vane's actions—promised to give up piracy in return for a pardon, and even cheered Rogers when he stepped ashore. Over 600 were pardoned, including Hornigold and Jennings, and some

even helped Rogers to defend the island against Spanish or pirate attack by forming a militia and an anti-piracy squadron. Rogers quickly consolidated his power and formed a governing council from among respected settlers, penitent pirates, and from his own small company of militia. When the naval squadron departed, many former pirates also slipped away and reverted to their old ways, but a mass-hanging of turncoat ex-pirates in December 1718 and a bungled Spanish attack in the following year helped to unite the new colony.

Sadly, the enterprise provided no immediate returns—and Rogers' general honesty stopped him from resorting to underhand dealings—and so in 1721, with no further support forthcoming from Britain, Rogers and his family returned to London, where he was thrown into the debtors' prison. He was freed after a lengthy appeal and the salary paid to him permitted a return to New Providence for a second term. His attempts to improve agricultural production on the islands came to nothing, and he died there in 1732. Despite all his earlier achievements, Woodes Rogers is best remembered as a pirate hunter. At his first posting, he had promised that he and his

Woodes Rogers is depicted getting his crewmen to frisk Spanish ladies for their jewelry during his successful privateering raid on Guayaquil in 1710. The ladies gasp, horrified at the affront to their dignity, but the seamen suspect they have hidden valuables in their clothing in places considered inaccessible to decent men.

153

Contemporary engraving of Edward Teach posed against a background of his ships anchored off Ocracoke Island.

fellow colonial governors would hunt down and destroy or bring to trial the ten worst pirates who had fled at his arrival, including Blackbeard, and this oath he saw kept. Almost single-handedly, by example, Rogers cleaned up the Bahamas pirate haven and greatly contributed to the end of the Golden Age of piracy. His war cry *Expulsis piratis restituta commercia* ("pirates expelled, commerce restored") became the islands' motto until the Bahamas achieved independence in 1973.

The most famous pirate of them all

It is ironic that Blackbeard is invariably considered to be the most notorious pirate of all time, for he was far from the cruellest. On capturing a prize, Blackbeard was likely to take any valuables, navigational instruments, weapons, wine, and rum casks, before allowing the crew and any passengers to sail away unharmed. To outright bloody slaughter, he preferred marooning a crew and burning their ship as punishment for resistance. Blackbeard worked hard at establishing his fearsome, demonic image, but no evidence exists to suggest that he ever killed anyone who was not trying to kill him—with one important exception. It was alleged of Teach that he would not tolerate females aboard his ship, and if a woman was taken captive she was strangled and her body pitched over the side. If this accusation were actually true, Blackbeard was not alone in his aversion to the fairer sex at sea—his contemporary, Stede Bonnet, also only saved males for ransom or inclusion in his crew.

Other pirates caused far more mayhem, captured richer cargoes, more ships, and more valuable prisoners, but Edward Teach has come to represent the genre more than any other. His enduring popularity most probably stems from his appearance. In 1717 a victim described him as "a tall, spare man with a very black beard which he wore very long." Blackbeard tied his beard up with black ribbons, and added to his menacing appearance by wearing a crimson coat and bandoleers slung over his shoulders that held three brace of pistols. To this already devilish image, Johnson's *General History* adds the claim that Blackbeard wove burning lengths of slow match into his hair that stuck out from under his hat.

So much for the image. "Blackbeard" was the nickname given to Edward Teach (or Thatch), a seaman born in Bristol, one of England's busiest ports by the early 18th century. He reportedly served aboard a British privateer based in Jamaica, but in the peace of 1714 following the end of the War of the Spanish Succession, like many other privateers, Teach found himself unemployed. He arrived in New Providence in the Bahamas in 1715–16 which, largely ignored by any authority, was already a thriving pirate haven. With a choice of captain to serve under, Teach signed on as a crewman with Benjamin Hornigold, who enjoyed a short but solid reputation as a successful man, fair in his dealings with others. In one anecdote a victim recounted how Hornigold pursued and attacked his ship. When they struck their colors and waited in abject terror, the crew was amazed that all the pirate wanted was their hats, to replace those his own crew had lost in a drunken spree the night before.

Teach left New Providence a deck hand, but returned the captain of a captured sloop, which Hornigold placed under his command. In 1717 they plundered six ships off the American coast and raided deep into the Caribbean, during which voyage Teach proved himself a charismatic leader. In the November of that year, in the eastern Caribbean, Hornigold and Teach took a 26-gun, richly laden French "guineyman" with the name of *Concorde*. From the captain of this, or another prize, they heard that the British Crown had decided to take the Bahamas in hand. Woodes Rogers, a man of fearsome reputation, was coming as governor, but with the king's amnesty for repentant pirates. Benjamin Hornigold, who had probably never been entirely happy with a criminal reputation, decided to return to New Providence and ask for a royal pardon. Teach declined, and after dividing the shares of booty, the two split up. Teach made the *Concorde* his flagship, ramped up her armament to 40 guns, and renamed her *Queen Anne's Revenge* (a popular ship's name of the time).

Hornigold's faith in Woodes Rogers paid off—he received his pardon and received a governmental commission to hunt pirates. Among others, he pursued Stede Bonnet and Charles Vane, but seems to have avoided those like Blackbeard who numbered among his proteges. At some point in 1719, while sailing off the coast of Mexico on a trading voyage, Hornigold's ship vanished, perhaps after striking a reef, and the entire crew was presumed lost.

New Providence may have been a sensible destination for Hornigold, but the imminent arrival of Governor Rogers meant that Teach had to find a new base. In January 1718 he sailed to North Carolina and established a lair on Ocracoke Island, near the settlement of Bath Towne, which provided a ready market for the plunder seized from prizes. This boost to the local economy, plus a bribe to the colony's governor, ensured safety from prosecution. By March, Teach was cruising in the Gulf of Mexico, where he captured several prizes, including the sloop *Revenge*, which belonged to the "gentleman" pirate Stede Bonnet. It is probable that at first Teach invited Bonnet to sail with him, but then stole his command when he discovered that the educated landowner was a poor leader and incompetent sailor. Having placed another in command of the *Revenge*, Teach obliged Bonnet

Ocracoke and Blackbeard's hunting grounds

OCACOCK INLET. Latitude 34°.55'N°

3 Here is 9¼ Feet over the Shoal

Ryals Shoal

SOUND

PAMTICOE

Beacon Island Shoal

Ocacock Island

Core Bank

A Scale of Miles

New York
Pennsylvania
Philadelphia
Maryland
Washington
Virginia
Chesapeake Bay
Richmond
North Carolina
Bath Towne
Pamlico Sound
Ocracoke Island
Wilmington
South Carolina
Georgetown
Charleston
ATLANTIC OCEAN
Savanah
Georgia

Settled areas, 1713

British

Spanish

modern state border

St. Augustine

Florida

Grand Bahama

Abaco

New Providence

Nassau

Florida Keys

Andros

Bahamas

Straits of Florida

Bahamas settled by British, but not under authority of the Crown until 1718

CUBA

to become his guest aboard *Queen Anne's Revenge*, where he remained in comfortable confinement until she was wrecked six months later.

On the northward return toward Ocracoke along the Atlantic coast in May, Teach decided to blockade the port of Charleston, South Carolina. Standing off the entrance to the harbor of Beaufort Inlet, Teach took eight vessels, capturing a number of prominent local citizens in the process, which he held for ransom. Among his demands was a chest of medical supplies, which might give substance to popular rumors that Teach had contracted a form of venereal disease. The pirates returned to Ocracoke but lost *Queen Anne's Revenge* after running her aground on a tidal sandbar. One of the smaller vessels of the flotilla, the ten-gun sloop *Adventure*, was also lost while trying to assist the stranded flagship. There is confusion and no certain evidence as to what happened to Stede Bonnet at this point. Some claims suggest that before leaving Beaufort Inlet Teach stripped Bonnet's sloop *Revenge* of her accumulated booty and provisions and sailed away aboard a smaller vessel.

Salt marshes on Ocracoke Island—the narrow entrances to Pamlico Sound with its sandbanks and uncharted shallows made it difficult for any ship to sneak up on Blackbeard's hideout.

Perhaps it was Teach's intention to let his guest-prisoner go and take his chances, but it is said that the freed pirate managed to rescue some 25 crewmen Blackbeard had marooned on a deserted sandbar as punishment for an unstated reason; with these hands as a crew, Bonnet went aboard *Revenge* again and resumed his lawless ways.

In Bath Towne, Teach sold his stolen ships and cargo, bought a house, and was even granted a pardon by the governor, Charles Eden. Not that this should be thought of as a brush with respectability, but perhaps—with the period of amnesty over—Edward Teach desired security; his Blackbeard persona, however, would not let him rest, and more ships were taken prize off the Carolinas.

In October 1718, another notorious figure came to visit Teach, fellow pirate Charles Vane. Many colonists feared that the week-long bout of festivities that resulted represented the thin end of a wedge that would make a new pirate haven of the Carolinas. Resentment over this brazen display of lawlessness and the apparent weakness of Eden's authority swelled. The governor of neighboring Virginia Alexander Spotswood—a similar breed of Englishman to Woodes Rogers—decided to take firm action and follow Rogers' example. According to a later account in *The*

Boston News-Letter of February 23, 1719, he hired two sloops "…well manned with Fifty pickt Men of His Majesty's Men of War lying there, and small Arms, but no great Guns, under the Command of Lieutenant Robert Maynard of His Majesty's ship Pearl, in pursuit of that Notorious and Arch Pirate Capt. Teach…."

On November 22, 1718, Maynard aboard the *Pearl* and a midshipman commanding the sloop *Ranger* arrived off Ocracoke at dawn. As luck would have it, there were so many pirates in Bath Towne that Teach was able to get a head-start in the confusion. Aboard his sloop *Adventure*, he escaped through an unmarked channel, while Maynard's sloops ran aground trying to follow. According to Maynard, Teach shouted, " 'Drank Damnation to me and my men!' whom he stil'd Cowardly Puppies, saying he would neither give nor take Quarter." With the rising tide, the sloops broke free and continued the pursuit. Teach fired grapeshot into the pursuing *Ranger* that killed several of her crew, including the midshipman in charge. A shot from Maynard's sloop cut Teach's jibsheet and forced the pirates to lose their way and run onto a sandbar. Seeing that he was fast closing on *Adventure*, Maynard ordered most of his men to duck out of sight. The ruse worked. Believing that the navy crew had fallen from shot or shrapnel, Teach jumped the narrowing gap as the *Adventure* came alongside, followed by his men. As the fooled pirates boarded the *Pearl*, Maynard's crew rose up and a brutal hand-to-hand fight began.

Woodcut showing a moment from the week-long pirate party held when Charles Vane and his crews joined Blackbeard's in September 1718 at Ocracoke. The good Protestant citizens of Bath Towne were scandalized that the pirates brought in women from nearby settlements for their entertainment, yet this buccolic illustration suggests nothing more than one might expect from a typical 18th-century puritan community dance.

Teach and Maynard exchanged fire, and a lucky ball from the lieutenant's pistol wounded the pirate. Then out came swords and the fight continued until Maynard's blade snapped. At that moment of peril, a naval rating made a swipe at Teach and delivered a terrible sword wound to his neck and throat, from which he soon died. The 13 surviving pirates, seeing their leader lying in a pool of his own blood, threw down their weapons and begged for quarter. Maynard rounded up all the pirates still in Bath Towne, then returned to Williamsburg in Virginia, with Blackbeard's decapitated head hanging from the bowsprit of his sloop. The pirates were tried, and in March 1719 they were hanged in Williamsburg. In an odd postscript, Maynard's sloop *Pearl*, soon after transferred to the Caribbean under another command, was to fall prey to the pirate Charles Vane.

The gentleman pirate who bought his own ship

Before running across Blackbeard in the Gulf of Mexico, Stede Bonnet had enjoyed a short but successful period as a pirate—but he was a very strange example of the profession. For a start, he abandoned the life of a respected plantation owner near Bridgetown in Barbados, then instead of stealing or capturing a ship, as any decent pirate might be expected to do, Bonnet purchased and fitted out a ten-gun sloop from his own pocket. Odder still, rather than agree a contract with his potential crew, listing the shares each man might expect from prize money, he offered to pay a salary. No wonder they called Bonnet the "gentleman pirate." According to Johnson, he was a major in the island militia and "a gentleman of good reputation…a master of plentiful fortune, and had the advantage of a liberal education." If this is true, it is amazing that a successful and established plantation owner would suddenly turn to piracy. At his trial the judge described him as an "esteemed man of letters," and some of his former neighbors wondered whether a bout of bad tropical humors had disturbed his mind. Others alleged that he ran away from his shrewish wife, who made a misogynist of him—which might explain his cruel treatment of female captives.

During the spring of 1717, Bonnet set sail aboard his sloop *Revenge*, together with a crew of 70 seamen. He sailed for the Atlantic coast of the American colonies, where he captured and plundered several ships off the Virginia Capes, then off Long Island, New York, and by August 1717 he was off South Carolina, where he took two more small vessels before rounding Florida and entering the Gulf of Mexico.

Here, at some stage, he met Edward Teach. Although it has been hinted earlier that Bonnet was captured by Teach, this remains unclear, although a Boston paper of November 1717 reported that he was a virtual prisoner on Blackbeard's ship. It appears that one of Teach's men was put in charge of *Revenge*, while Bonnet accompanied Teach in *Queen Anne's Revenge*. Bonnet must have sailed with Teach during his cruise in the Caribbean and been at the blockade of Charleston in May 1718, but either there in one version or on the return to Ocracoke in another, Bonnet was set free, along with his ship, by a set of circumstances never made clear.

Opposite: Blackbeard's final battle was against the Royal Navy after Lieutenant Maynard tricked the pirate into boarding the naval sloop, thinking it was almost unmanned. Wounded in a pistol volley, Blackbeard was finally dispatched by a sword blow from a Scots sailor.

In Europe, after only four years of peace, a new conflict broke out, grandly called the War of the Quadruple Alliance. New it might have been, but the cause was an old one. The treaty of 1714 that ended the War of the Spanish Succession had obliged the Frenchman King Philip V of Spain (1700–46) to renounce his claim to the French succession, but when his grandfather Louis XIV died, Philip reneged.

Encouraged by his prime minister and his ambitious wife, Philip declared invalid the succession of his nephew, the child Louis XV. Naturally, Britain was opposed to any union between her traditional enemies of France and Spain, as were the Dutch. The Habsburgs, embroiled in a bitter war with Turkey, kept out of the conflict. To add to British woes, Philip backed the Jacobite cause of exiled James Francis Edward Stuart, known as the Old Pretender (1688-1766), to restore the Catholic Stuart dynasty to the British throne.

For many American pirates, this new war was a godsend, a chance to turn at least semi-legal as privateers. Bonnet approached the governor of North Carolina for a pardon, which was granted, and he set off for St Thomas in the Virgin Islands with letters of marque empowering him to attack Spanish shipping. On his way south he paused briefly off Ocracoke during June 1718 and, acting as a pirate turned pirate-hunter, tried tracking down Blackbeard. But this was an itch he could not scratch. Unable to satisfy his bitter grudge against Blackbeard, Bonnet gave up his mission to St. Thomas, instead reverting to piracy off the American colonial coast. In order to disguise himself he changed the name of his sloop to the *Royal James* and adopted the identity of Captain Thomas.

He captured three prizes off Virginia, then another six vessels. Keeping two of them, Bonnet sailed into the Cape Fear river for repairs, where he seized a local ship and tore it apart for the necessary timbers. News of pirate activity nearby soon reached the authorities at Charleston in South Carolina, the city still smarting from Blackbeard's blockade and attack a few months earlier. The reaction was swift

Local merchant ship owner Colonel William Rhett was authorized to attack the pirates with his two armed sloops, *Henry* and *Sea Nymph*. These had barely raised sail when Charles Vane's Jolly Roger was sighted off the city; *Henry* and *Sea Nymph* went in hot pursuit, but Vane managed to slip away.

Colonel Rhett returned to his earlier mission and sailed up Cape Fear during the evening of September 26, 1718. Bonnet retreated upstream but the river became shallower and eventually the *Royal James* shoaled, forcing the pirates to stand and fight. It was no easy task for the Charleston men, but after a mammoth five-hour battle the pirates surrendered, were taken away in chains to Charleston, and thrown into prison. Somehow, Bonnet managed to break out, but was quickly taken and tried. "Esteemed man of letters" or no, his attempted escape prevented any chance of his bargaining for a pardon. Besides, the resentment felt by the citizens of Charleston following their humiliation at Blackbeard's hands helped to seal Bonnet's fate. Sir Nicholas Trot, judge of the Vice-Admiralty Court, refused to show leniency. Only three of the pirate deck hands were acquitted. The condemned men included some who had only joined the pirates weeks before. Stede Bonnet, landowner turned pirate, was found guilty and hanged on White Point near Charleston in November 1718, along with 30 of his crew.

A newspaper account of Stede Bonnet's execution was accompanied with a suitably gruesome illustration of his corpse swinging when he was hanged in Charleston in November 1718. A bunch of flowers clutched in his hands symbolizes repentance.

A pirate unloved and dogged by misfortune

Charles Vane, chased off by Colonel Rhett before he cornered Bonnet, may have escaped a similar conviction at angry Charlestonian hands, but fate had an equally grisly fate in mind for the pirate. Nothing is known about Vane's early life, apart from his having an English background. He is first mentioned as serving in the crew of Henry Jennings during 1716 in the attack on the camps of Spanish salvors, recovering sunken treasure from the wrecks of the previous year's treasure fleet. The *flota* had foundered in a hurricane that struck it close to Florida's southeastern coast, taking a vast cargo of silver to the bottom. The Spanish governor of Havana dispatched a salvage crew to recover the lost fortune. Spanish pressure brought to bear on the Port Royal authorities had forced Jennings from his base in Jamaica to find refuge in the Bahamian pirate haven of New Providence. During the War of the Spanish Succession, Jennings hunted Spanish and French merchantmen and earned a reputation among the pirate community of New Providence. With the war's end, like most of his compatriots, he returned to piracy. When he heard of the disaster off Florida, Jennings—who had every reason to hate the Spanish—determined to prevent Havana from recovering its drowned wealth.

And so, with Charles Vane in tow, Jennings struck with some 300 men in three small ships. The sneak assault was timed to land on the unsuspecting salvagers once they had retrieved the silver from the shallow seabed. Jennings men drove off the 60-strong Spanish guard and won a haul that added up to about 350,000 pieces of eight. To this they added a passing Spanish galleon carrying a further 60,000 silver coins. After participating in this success, Charles Vane made his first independent cruises early in 1718 and earned quick notoriety. In May, a report made to the governor of Bermuda by two captains whose vessels had been attacked by pirates within hours of one another named Vane as the culprit. Their claim that Vane needlessly tortured several men on the two Bermuda sloops and then had them killed fits with what seems to have been an impetuous and ill-tempered behavior that made him unpopular even among his own crews.

In July of the same year Vane captured a French square-rigged ship. As luck would have it, he was bringing his prize back to New Providence in August, just as Governor Woodes Rogers was sailing into the harbor for the first time. Vane was faced with a choice: hand over his plunder or flee. But after such a successful start, was he to give up the life of a pirate captain? His answer came quickly. The French ship was emptied of any final items of worth and then set on fire and sailed straight for Rogers' flagship. As it tried to avoid the fireship, Vane and his pirate crew turned to head for the open sea, firing at the British flagship and jeering at its navy crew. Vane escaped amid the smoke and confusion. Meanwhile, as related earlier, his former leader Jennings accepted the king's pardon, and turned his back on piracy.

Evading pursuit, Vane and his unrepentant pirates escaped to the Carolinas where, like Blackbeard, they fed their appetites on ships leaving and entering Charleston. Vane captured four vessels in quick succession, one of which he handed over to a subordinate named Yeats. Not long after, they captured a large brigantine bringing almost a hundred slaves from West Africa for sale in Charleston. Soon after this event, Yeats—now considering himself the very finest of pirates too—fell out with Vane, who insisted on Yeats' subordinate position. Determined on his

A competent seaman but an unpopular captain, Charles Vane fell out with his crew and eventually they voted him out; woodcut from Johnson's *General History*.

independence, Yeats sailed away at night a few days later while the other pirate ships lay at anchor, taking with him a good number of Vane's crew and a lot of the gathered loot, including the slaves. This falling out was the first indication that rancor existed between Vane and his crewmen. He gave chase, but abandoned the pursuit when Yeats evaded him, possibly by sailing into Charleston harbor and giving himself up in return for a pardon, with the "rescued" slaves acting as a sweetener.

A number of armed vessels sent after Vane by colonial governors during late August and early September 1718, including those commanded by Colonel William Rhett, failed to catch the pirate. And, as if mocking the authorities, Vane sailed into Pamlico Sound to meet Blackbeard on Ocracoke Island for the week-long bacchanalian party that indirectly caused Blackbeard's downfall.

By that October, Vane was cruising in the vicinity of New York, where he captured two small ships off Long Island, but no other potential prizes were spotted until November 23. At first sight, Vane ordered the Jolly Roger aloft, expecting the lone ship to heave to and surrender, but instead its master brought his vessel alongside, dropped the gun ports and opened fire. The pirates had caught a heavily armed French man-of-war in their net. No doubt Vane was wise to turn and flee the scene as fast as possible, but there were many in the crew who questioned his decision as the act of a craven. On the following day a furious argument broke out and the quartermaster, "Calico" Jack Rackham, accused his captain of cowardice. The crew demonstrated the extent of Vane's lack of popularity by voting for Rackham as captain. Mutinies of this kind often resulted in the execution of the deposed captain and any suspected supporters, but Rackham gave Vane a small prize sloop and let him go with the handful of men who remained loyal to him, including the former mate, Robert Deal.

Starting from scratch again, Vane and about 15 hands sailed south and through the Florida Straits. After rounding Cuba's western tip they cruised between Jamaica and the Yucatán peninsula. In November the pirates captured a sloop, which Vane handed to Deal, and two small local craft,

With the "judge" perched in the crook of a tree, a pirate crew holds a mock court to try one of their number for a crime.

which were abandoned. In the Gulf of Honduras the pirates captured two small vessels out of Jamaica, one being the sloop *Pearl*, which had presided at Blackbeard's end. Both were released with their crews after being plundered.

They wintered on the small Honduran island of Baracho and sailed in February 1719, intending to make for the Windward Passage between Cuba and Hispaniola. But after a few days at sea a hurricane struck and the sloops lost contact with each other. Vane was wrecked on a reef and only he and a single seaman survived. Stranded on a small uninhabited island in the Gulf of Honduras for several months, the two men survived by eating turtles and fish before rescue hove in sight.

This turned out to be the sloop of a former privateer named Holford, who was well known to Vane. Holford intuited that if he picked up the two men it could not be long before Vane would be "caballing with my men, knock me on the head and run away with my ship a pirating." So Holford sailed away, abandoning both men to their fate, and it was another ship a few days later that happened on Vane's signal and rescued them. But Vane's misfortune was not over: his rescuer caught up with Holford and offered an invitation to sup with him. As the two captains sat down to dinner, Holford spotted Vane scrubbing the deck. Holford's host, horrified at having taken a notorious pirate aboard, begged his guest to relieve him of the burden. Holford agreed and transferred Vane to his own ship—in chains. Holford turned the pirate over to the authorities in Jamaica to stand trial. Vane's former mate, Robert Deal, had also survived the hurricane, only to be captured by a warship, taken to Jamaica, and executed. Both Vane and his one surviving crewman were found guilty and hanged at Gallows Point, Port Royal on March 22, 1720. Their corpses were then suspended in chains at the small islet of Gun Cay as a warning to other pirates.

The cutthroat women and "Calico" Jack Rackham

"Calico" Jack Rackham outlived his former captain by about eight months. His first act as a pirate captain was to attack and take the French vessel from which Charles Vane had fled in November 1718, but "Calico" Jack—so called because of the striped cloth he favored for his breeches—was in this period of larger-than-life figures, something of a lesser pirate whose fame rests more on his choice of crew than on his own abilities. His eventual capture made his name when it was discovered that two of his crew were women. Almost as famous as Blackbeard, the two female pirates Anne Bonny and Mary Read caused a sensation at their trial, the excitement stemming from the revelation that they had lived as men for years. The stir they created quite eclipsed their mediocre captain. Rackham was typical of the pirates whose small sloops preyed on coastal shipping. Although his roots are obscure, by 1718 he had arrived on New Providence, serving under Vane and becoming elected as quartermaster.

"Calico" Jack Rackham, a pirate more renowned for the two women in his crew than for exploits of his own.

After letting Vane and his few loyal supporters go, Captain Rackham continued the cruise until he carelessly lost his sloop to two Royal Navy ships. These surprised the pirates while all hands were ashore, including Rackham.

By May 1719 Rackham had returned to New Providence to plead for a pardon, which was granted as part of the widespread pirate amnesty offered by Woodes Rogers. While there, he met Anne Bonny, the illegitimate and headstrong daughter of an Irish lawyer from South Carolina. Anne had married a seaman, James Bonny, and run off with him when he turned to piracy, and ended up in New Providence, where she met Jack Rackham. The arrangement is unclear, but there is evidence that when Rackham returned to sea, Anne accompanied him as his mistress. This was in August—after three months ashore Rackham was fed up with his circumstances. He felt that a criminal life at sea was infinitely preferable to one of unemployment in New Providence, so he stole the sloop *William* and returned to piracy. For the next 15 months, "Calico" Jack and his crew cruised off the coast of Cuba, managing to snare several small vessels. Astonishingly, Anne Bonny was not the only female on board the *William*.

Almost everything known about Mary Read's early life comes from Charles Johnson's *General History*, and is almost certainly fictional. Apparently born in England, Read's impoverished mother "bred her daughter dressed as a boy" in order to benefit from a stipend from a relative. As a teenager, Read first worked as a boy in domestic service, then signed up as a naval rating before running away to join the army. The infantry unit soon left for a tour of duty in the Netherlands, where the young cadet fell in love with a messmate, to whom he-she had revealed her secret. They married but he died shortly after, and newly widowed Read, disguised again in male garb, took passage as a seaman on a Dutch ship bound for the West Indies. As they neared the Americas, English pirates attacked and took the ship prize. Hearing

With pistol, ax, sword, and breasts, the female pirate Anne Bonny fascinated the early 18th-century public.

English spoken among the Dutch, the pirates adopted the young "man" and after serving with them for a while, Read accompanied them to New Providence, arriving as "Calico" Jack Rackham was preparing to sail in August 1719.

Read accompanied Rackham and her fellow female pirate on the *William*, but in late 1720 Rackham's luck ran out—and again it was to the Royal Navy. While at anchor off the western tip of Jamaica, the naval sloop came up to the pirates while most of the nine crew-members were sleeping off a drunken celebration after taking some petty prize. According to testimonies, as the naval vessel dropped anchor and sent a pinnace to investigate, the women roused the drunks and used the *William* to cut the naval sloop's anchor cable as they escaped.

After a chase they were overtaken by the pursuers, led by Captain Barnet. Rackham's sloop was boarded and, reputedly, Anne Bonny and Mary Read were the only members of her crew to offer resistance, the rest being worse the wear for drink or too hung over to defend themselves. The navy tars overcame the two women, and "Calico" Jack Rackham's pirates were taken to Port Royal to stand trial.

Anne Bonny and Mary Read dressed as men when they were acting as pirates, but were otherwise said to behave as women (both had lovers on Rackham's crew). This contemporary engraving, designed to maximize the sensational aspect of their story, makes them very unfeminine.

Their capture caused a sensation and turned the female pirates into celebrities. What had everyone so excited was the astonishing revelation that Anne Bonny and Mary Read had escaped the traditional restrictions imposed on the lives of contemporary women. In other words, not only were they female criminals, swaggering pirates to boot, but they had broken the rules of society. In court it was reported that "they were both very profligate, cursing and swearing much, and very ready and willing to do anything." Victims testified that they wore men's clothing in action, but otherwise dressed as women.

Jack Rackham tried repenting again, but his plea was ignored and he was hanged on November 27, 1720, together with the rest of his male crew. Anne and Mary were also condemned, but then reprieved when it was discovered that both were pregnant. Subsequently, Mary died in a Jamaican prison in 1721, probably of a fever and still pregnant, but Anne's fate is unknown.

Samuel Bellamy and the Whydah

Due to a tragedy, Samuel Bellamy remains one of the Golden Age's more interesting pirates. Although his career was pretty run-of-the-mill, the discovery in the 1980s of his galley-ship *Whydah*, which was wrecked with huge loss of life including his own off Cape Cod, has given historians fascinating insights into a pirate's shipboard life of the early 18th century. Bellamy was born in Devon, an English county with a strong seafaring tradition but, as with most pirates of this period, the events of his youth are unclear. Indeed, the early days of his pirate career are also misty, but it has been suggested that working on the salvage

Below right: The bronze bell from the *Whydah Galley*. Its recovery from the seabed off Cape Cod identified the wreck beyond any doubt as Sam Bellamy's famous ship.

Archeologists recovered a variety of artifacts from the *Whydah* wreck site. **Above**, a sword hilt is still in fine condition; **below**, a large round shot and the wadding used to pack it into a cannon.

of a Spanish shipwreck acted as the catalyst. He argued with the project leaders, so Bellamy and a small group with him decided to turn pirate. Given the date—if this described event actually happened (again, from evidence offered in Johnson's *General History*)—Bellamy was probably involved in the 1716 assault made by Henry Jennings on the camps of salvors working on the wrecked 1715 Spanish treasure fleet off Florida's southeast coast.

Certainly, by 1716 Bellamy had reached New Providence, where he sailed with the pirate Benjamin Hornigold, whose crew included Edward "Blackbeard" Teach. Hornigold had a degree of conscience, and his small pirate squadron fell apart in 1718 when he refused to attack British vessels and sought a pardon from Woodes Rogers. Bellamy and Blackbeard decided to go their own way, and Bellamy was elected captain of Hornigold's former sloop, the *Mary Anne*. For the rest of the year Bellamy cruised off the Virgin Islands, accompanied by another vessel under the command of the French pirate Olivier La Bouche, who had also been companion on occasion to Hornigold. The partnership proved moderately successful, and Bellamy and his consort captured several ships throughout the autumn and winter of 1716–17. Like many pirates, Bellamy felt his station in life demanded a larger flagship than a sloop, so when he moved into the captured square-rigged ship *Sultana* he handed control of his former vessel to his quartermaster, Paul Williams.

The three pirate vessels continued their voyage until early 1717, when a storm separated the two British pirates from their French colleague. La Bouche, as has been related on pages 146–7, later joined forces with John Taylor in the Indian Ocean. In February or March 1717, Bellamy and Williams captured the *Whydah*, a large British slave vessel returning home on the last leg of her triangular slave rading voyage. She carried money, sugar, and indigo, and the rich prize became Bellamy's new flagship. *Whydah* was a 300-ton ship-rigged galley, and she was quickly adapted to carry the 28 guns moved aboard from other ships, turning her from a slaver into a formidable pirate ship, with the oars offering an enormous advantage in the wind-shaded shallows of the American river estuaries. Bellamy and *Whydah*'s former captain became friends, and it is said that the pirate let the slave captain go free, and even gave him the *Sultana* in which to sail home. Charles Johnson puts a pretty speech into Bellamy's mouth, as he expounds to a merchant captain on the nature of piracy and rants against the great and good of Britain: "Damn them for a pack of crafty rascals, and you, who serve them, for a parcel of hen-hearted numbskulls. They vilify us, the scoundrels do, when there is only this difference, they rob the poor under the cover of law, forsooth, and we plunder the rich under the protection of our own courage. Had you not better make then one of us, than sneak after these villains for employment?"

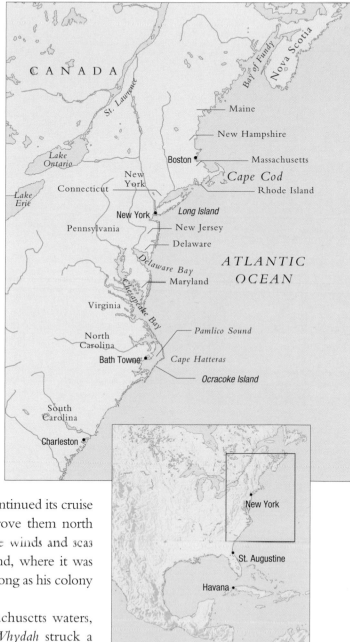

No matter the speciousness of this Robin Hood-style defense, Johnson's words give the reader a clear indication of the common feeling among the dispossessed who made up the majority of pirate crews, that somehow they were the cheated, not the thieves; that, at least, they were no worse than the aristocrats who ran their world. Perhaps the greatest attraction to the all-too brief and brutal career as a pirate was the social leveling a life at sea brought about. A moment later Johnson has Bellamy say, "I am a free prince, and I have as much authority to make war on the whole world, as he who has a hundred sail of ships at sea, and an army of 100,000 men in the field."

In two ships Bellamy and Williams sailed north along the Atlantic coast of the American colonies, capturing four more vessels off Virginia. One of these was added to the pirate squadron, which continued its cruise northward. In April 1717 they were hit by a sudden storm that drove them north past New York and toward the New England (Maine) coast. As the winds and seas subsided, the two captains decided to sail back south to Rhode Island, where it was rumored the local governor took a lenient view of pirate activities, so long as his colony profited from them.

The pirates never made it. After taking several prizes in Massachusetts waters, tragedy struck. On the night of May 17, in a heavy fog, the *Whydah* struck a sandbar 3 miles south of the village of Wellfleet, on Cape Cod, and one of the prize vessels sailing with the flotilla ran aground further to the south. The Atlantic surf capsized *Whydah* and her crew of 146 pirates all drowned, apart from two who were imprisoned as soon as they reached the shore. Samuel Bellamy was lost in the shipwreck. The two survivors were tried in a Massachusetts court, together with seven pirate survivors from the wrecked prize ship. Two were acquitted and the remaining seven hanged in Boston.

In 1984, the well-known wreck hunter Barry Clifford recovered the remains of the *Whydah*. Finds included coins, weapons, and even the ship's bell, which marked the last resting place of Samuel Bellamy. These objects may be seen in a museum in Provincetown, on Cape Cod.

Dashing and deceitful, Howell Davis successfully misled Portuguese and English fort commanders in West Africa that he was a legitimate privateer.

Howell Davis—Terror of the West African coast

As Edward England, abandoning the New Providence of Woodes Rogers, cruised off the West African coast in 1718, it may be remembered that he captured several prizes (*see page 144*), among them the slave ship *Cadogan*. England prevented the pirates from torturing the slaver's crewmen, one of whom was the *Cadogan*'s mate, Howell Davis. He was said to have been born in about 1690 in Milford Haven, a seaport in southwest Wales, and so in time found himself signing on ships operating out of Britain's great slaver port, Bristol. Spared by Edward England, Davis and some others elected to join the pirate band. According to Johnson's *General History*, England gave Davis the *Cadogan* as a prize, and the two then parted company, England for the Indian Ocean, Davis for Brazil. However, he never made South America because the crew either rebelled or persuaded him to change his mind and head for Barbados instead. On reaching the island, Davis was imprisoned on suspicion of piracy. On his release three months later, he made his way to that former pirates' haven, New Providence. But Woodes Rogers had done his work well, and there was little in the colony to attract an aspiring pirate.

In late 1718 Howell Davis took passage on the *Buck*, a sloop bound for the West Indies crewed largely by ex-pirates. As it lay off Martinique, he successfully encouraged the 35 seamen to return to their old trade and take over the vessel. The men then held a council of war to elect a new captain and their decision, aided by "a large bowl of punch," went in favor of Davis. His first task was to select a good base from which to operate, and this he found in a cove in eastern Cuba. From there, they cruised eastward to the Virgin Islands and Hispaniola, where two French ships were seized. The second prize was a 24-gun ship, vastly superior to the *Buck*, but Davis reputedly used deception to capture her by pretending that an earlier prize

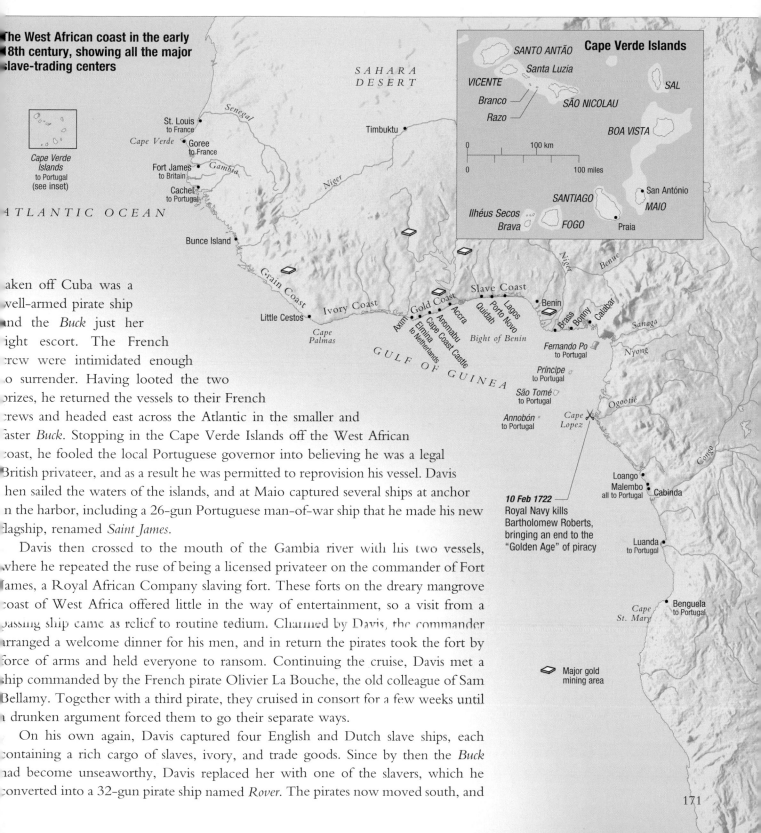

The West African coast in the early 18th century, showing all the major slave-trading centers

Cape Verde Islands
to Portugal
(see inset)

SAHARA DESERT

Senegal

St. Louis
to France

Cape Verde Goree
to France

Fort James
to Britain

Gambia

Cachel
to Portugal

ATLANTIC OCEAN

Bunce Island

Timbuktu

Niger

Cape Verde Islands

SANTO ANTÃO

Santa Luzia

VICENTE

Branco

Razo

SÃO NICOLAU

SAL

BOA VISTA

100 km

100 miles

San António

MAIO

Ilhéus Secos

Brava

SANTIAGO

FOGO

Praia

Niger   *Benine*

Grain Coast

Little Cestos

Ivory Coast

Gold Coast

Axim
Elmina
to Netherlands
Cape Coast Castle
Anomabu
Accra
Quidah
Porto Novo
Lagos

Slave Coast

Benin

Brass   Bonny   Calabar

Sanaga

Cape
Palmas

GULF OF GUINEA

Bight of Benin

Fernando Po
to Portugal

Nyong

Príncipe
to Portugal

São Tomé
to Portugal

Annobón
to Portugal

Cape
Lopez

Ogootié

Congo

10 Feb 1722
Royal Navy kills
Bartholomew Roberts,
bringing an end to the
"Golden Age" of piracy

Loango
Malembo
all to Portugal   Cabinda

Luanda
to Portugal

Cape
St. Mary

Benguela
to Portugal

Major gold
mining area

aken off Cuba was a well-armed pirate ship and the *Buck* just her light escort. The French crew were intimidated enough to surrender. Having looted the two prizes, he returned the vessels to their French crews and headed east across the Atlantic in the smaller and faster *Buck*. Stopping in the Cape Verde Islands off the West African coast, he fooled the local Portuguese governor into believing he was a legal British privateer, and as a result he was permitted to reprovision his vessel. Davis then sailed the waters of the islands, and at Maio captured several ships at anchor in the harbor, including a 26-gun Portuguese man-of-war ship that he made his new flagship, renamed *Saint James*.

Davis then crossed to the mouth of the Gambia river with his two vessels, where he repeated the ruse of being a licensed privateer on the commander of Fort James, a Royal African Company slaving fort. These forts on the dreary mangrove coast of West Africa offered little in the way of entertainment, so a visit from a passing ship came as relief to routine tedium. Charmed by Davis, the commander arranged a welcome dinner for his men, and in return the pirates took the fort by force of arms and held everyone to ransom. Continuing the cruise, Davis met a ship commanded by the French pirate Olivier La Bouche, the old colleague of Sam Bellamy. Together with a third pirate, they cruised in consort for a few weeks until a drunken argument forced them to go their separate ways.

On his own again, Davis captured four English and Dutch slave ships, each containing a rich cargo of slaves, ivory, and trade goods. Since by then the *Buck* had become unseaworthy, Davis replaced her with one of the slavers, which he converted into a 32-gun pirate ship named *Rover*. The pirates now moved south, and

171

off the Gold Coast (Ghana) at a place called Anomabu captured the London-bound slave ship *Princess*, whose crew included another Welshman, Bartholomew Roberts. The tropical waters off the Guinea Coast were unkind to a ship's timbers and the now rotten *Saint James* was replaced by another rich Dutch slaver they captured.

The fleet continued on into the Gulf of Guinea, finally arriving at the Portuguese island of Príncipe. Here, Davis used his tried and tested deception on the local governor, claiming the *Rover* was a privateer engaged in an anti-piracy patrol. Davis even finessed his ploy by seizing a French ship that entered the harbor on the grounds that it had traded with pirates. Whether this Portuguese official was a natural cynic or whether news of the fake British privateer had circulated, this time the lie failed. The day before the pirates planned to depart, Davis and a band of his crewmen were ambushed and killed by Portuguese militia, who were following up a report that the pirates planned to kidnap the governor. The remaining crewmen elected Bartholomew Roberts as their captain, who took a brutal revenge on Príncipe before escaping.

One captain whose ship Davis captured in 1719 said of this colorful and intelligent pirate that he was a man "who, allowing for the Course of Life he had been unhappily engaged in, was a most generous humane Person." There were, no doubt, many who would disagree, especially considering that Howell Davis had been the mentor of Bartholomew Roberts, who carved out a reputation never surpassed for its achievements or its bloodthirstiness.

The last great pirate of the Golden Age

In an extraordinary period of some 30 months, Bartholomew Roberts captured more than 400 vessels, making him one of the most successful pirates of all time. While he was loose on the high seas, in the waters of the American colonies, the Caribbean, and the

In Johnson's *General History*, Howell Davis is depicted leading his treacherous attack on Fort James, the Royal African Company's slave-trading center at the mouth of the Gambia river.

coast of West Africa, ships' masters sailed in terror of sighting his fearsome Jolly Roger, snapping at the masthead.

Born John Robert in 1682 in a small village on the coast of Pembrokeshire, Wales, he apparently went to sea in 1695. When or why he changed his name to Bartholomew and added an "s" to his second name is unknown. His life from the age of 13 is a blank until 1718, when he was recorded as a mate aboard a sloop sailing out of Barbados. In 1719 Roberts was third mate aboard the *Princess*, taking on slaves at Anomabu when she was captured by Howell Davis. After escaping the ambush on Príncipe in which Davis was slain, as elected captain Roberts's first act earned him the nickname Black Bart. He led the crew back to Príncipe and in the pitch darkness of a tropical night slaughtered a great many of the male population and looted anything of value. A few days later he captured a Dutch Guineaman, then two days later an English vessel that strayed across his path. The pirates then anchored back at Anomabu to take on water and provisions, and took a vote on whether the next voyage should be to the Indian Ocean and the East Indies or to Brazil. Brazil won.

The expedition on the other side of the Atlantic turned out to be both a massive success and something of a setback for Roberts. After some two months prowling off the Brazilian coast, Roberts and his second in command, Walter Kennedy on the *Rover*, were about to give up searching and depart for the West Indies when they crossed the large bay of Los todos Santos (Salvador) and encountered a fleet of 42 Portuguese ships about to set sail for Lisbon, escorted by two 70-gun men-of-war. Roberts quickly took the nearest of the vessels and, at the point of a sword, her master pointed out the richest ship in the flotilla. It was not an easy target, armed with 40 guns and more than 150 hands, but the pirates' surprise held. Roberts and his men boarded and captured their prize to find its hold stacked with 40,000 gold coins and a great deal of exquisite jewelry, some pieces designed specially for the king of Portugal. The men now wanted to spend some time enjoying their share of the booty, so Roberts sailed for Île du Diable (Devil's Isle). Around the bulge of Brazil from Los todos Santos, this was one of the very worst of pirate havens, packed

More successful that his mentor, Howell Davis, dapper Bartholomew Roberts as depicted in Johnson's *General History*.

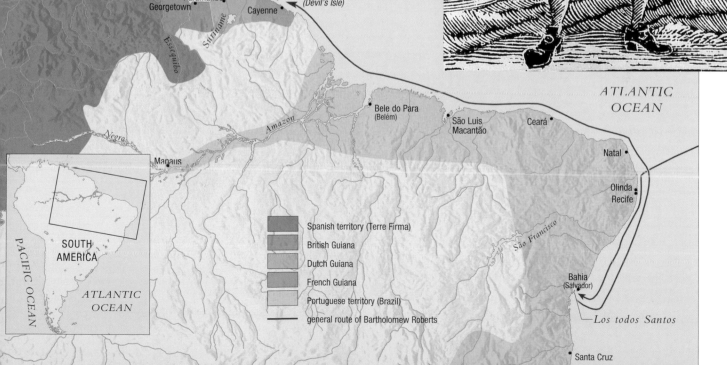

Île du Diable (Devil's Isle)
Paramaribo
Georgetown
Cayenne

Essequibo
Suriname

ATLANTIC OCEAN

Negro
Manaus

Amazon
Bele do Para (Belém)
São Luis Macantão
Ceará

Natal

Olinda
Recife

São Francisco

SOUTH AMERICA

PACIFIC OCEAN

ATLANTIC OCEAN

Spanish territory (Terre Firma)
British Guiana
Dutch Guiana
French Guiana
Portuguese territory (Brazil)
general route of Bartholomew Roberts

Bahia (Salvador)
Los todos Santos

Santa Cruz

Iron leg shackles, called bilboes, were used to keep African slaves closely hemmed in for transportation across the Atlantic. The bilboes came in a variety of sizes and strengths to accommodate men (top), women, and children (bottom). By making them lie flat on the deck of the hold for the entire voyage, a slaver could cram as many as 250 slaves into the hold. As a result, slave ships made fine pirate prizes when the cargo was finally sold in the West Indies and the American colonies. For the slaves, the change of master made no difference, although some were allowed to join up.

with all the dregs of society, ready to offer comforts of every kind in return for the sailors' gold.

After a few weeks' rest and recreation, and much relieved in weight of booty, the two ships headed for the mouth of the Suriname river, where they sighted a brigantine. Roberts in the fast sloop went in pursuit, leaving Walter Kennedy in the *Rover* to hold position. The target got away and Roberts found himself in contrary winds, so it was over a week later that they were able to return, only to find that Kennedy and the *Rover*'s crew had disappeared, along with what remained of the plunder. Black Bart shrugged off the disaster—after all, they had spent most of their money. As though to emphasize the point, he renamed his sloop *Fortune* and then sat his remaining crew down to hammer out a new, binding set of pirate articles that would avoid a similar situation—the most comprehensive of its kind to have survived intact (*see page 234*).

Roberts sailed the *Fortune* in a northerly direction around the edges of the Lesser Antilles, capturing ships on the way. The French pirate Montigny la Palisse in his sloop *Sea King* joined the piratical spree late in February 1720. And then they were met by two British naval vessels out of Barbados. *Sea King* sustained considerable damage to its rigging and la Palisse abandoned the fight. *Fortune* also suffered damage and killed and wounded sailors. Roberts broke off the engagement and managed to escape, even though he had to dodge two French naval sloops from Martinique out looking for him. Ever after, he swore vengeance on the people of Barbados and Martinique and had his infamous flag made up to advertise his enmity (*see page 130*).

After making repairs quietly in Santo Domingo, Roberts continued northward, selling the prize ships and cargo in New England in early 1720. He then proceeded to haunt the fishing grounds of Newfoundland, boarding more than 170 vessels. Exchanging a prize for a French ship, which he armed with 28 guns and renamed *Royal Fortune*, he sailed back down the American coast and took even more ships. Next, it was the Caribbean's turn as he entered the sea in the summer, capturing 15 French, British, and Dutch vessels in rapid succession. In that September he started a six-month rampage through the Leeward Islands, attacking St. Kitts and Martinique, and capturing at least a hundred ships. One of these was a 52-gun man-of-war carrying the French governor of Martinique. Roberts hanged him from the yardarm of his command ship, then tortured and killed most of the crew. Taking the prize as his new flagship, Roberts named her *Royal Fortune*—the second of several craft he gave that name.

In April 1721 Bartholomew Roberts crossed the Atlantic to West Africa, arriving near the mouth of the Senegal river in early June. He was chased by two French ships but, poorly armed, they were quickly taken and renamed *Ranger* and *Little Ranger*. Roberts now sailed toward Sierra Leone, overtaking a large slaver and then the frigate *Onslow*, which was carrying soldiers bound for Cape Coast Castle on the Gold Coast. Some of these opted to become pirates, but to prove that the social leveling enjoyed by seamen was confined to sailors, the landlubbers were offered only quarter-shares. Roberts renamed *Onslow* to be the fourth *Royal Fortune*; perhaps he should have left it at "third time lucky…."

The deadly spree came to an end on February 10, 1722, when the British warship HMS *Swallow* caught up with the pirates off Cape Lopez, in modern Gabon. *Royal Fortune IV* and *Little Ranger* were beached for careening, but Challoner Ogle of the *Swallow* came across *Ranger*, commanded by James Skyrme, well out of sight of the other pirates on the shore, and immediately engaged him. One of Skyrme's legs was taken off by a cannonball and ten pirate hands were killed. In his last act, Skyrme struck *Ranger*'s colors and the surviving crewmen were captured. In the few days between this preliminary action and the main battle, Roberts had refloated the other vessels, taken another prize, and was back at anchor. Most of the pirates were drunk from a night's celebratory carousing when at dawn the *Swallow* hove into sight off the beach. At first, any who saw her approaching assumed it was Skyrme returning in the *Ranger*, so Ogle was able to get the drop on Roberts.

As soon as he realized the danger, Roberts prepared himself, dressing in his trademark finery. Johnson said of him: "Roberts made a gallant figure, a sword in his hand, and two pairs of pistols slung over his shoulders." The dandy pirate captain ordered his ship to head towards Ogle's, hoping to sail past him and out into the open sea and escape. As the ships passed, the *Swallow* fired a broadside of grapeshot at close range, some of which hit Roberts, killing him instantly. The crew were familiar with his express wishes to be buried at sea and, also to avoid his corpse being taken, those nearest to him pitched his body overboard. The surviving pirates surrendered after exchanging broadsides in a running battle that lasted for almost three hours. The three captured ships produced a large haul of gold dust valued at over 14,000 pounds. In what was the largest pirate trial and execution of the era, held in West Africa at British slave-trading center of Cape Coast Castle, 54 hanged, 37 earned sentences of penal servitude, the rest were acquitted; 70 African pirates were sold into slavery.

Roberts was one of the most successful and colorful pirates of all time. He was an unusual character for this age, described as tall, good-looking, tee-total, and always well dressed (*see page 233*). He possessed a ruthless skill in the piratical arts of intimidation and seamanship, and was highly regarded by the crews of all his fleet. Although he was not the last pirate of the period, his demise marked the beginning of the end of the Golden Age of piracy. Bartholomew Roberts had a piratical career that was brief, violent, and unmatched in scale of prizes by any other; his motto was "A merry life and a short one."

Artists had little to go on when it came to portraying heroes or villains for the illustrated news-sheets of the time, which explains the similarity of stance between this and the woodcut on the previous spread. Here, Bartholomew Roberts stands before a vista of *Ranger* and *Royal Fortune* (foreground), herding a flotilla of captured slave ships off the coast of West Africa. Such prizes were worth a fortune when the slaves were sold to plantation owners in the Americas.

CHAPTER NINE

Violence and Savage Justice

Bringing an end to the Golden Age

The ferocity of hand-to-hand fighting at sea was never better captured than in this account of Blackbeard's last fight:

Maynard and Teach themselves begun the fight with their swords, Maynard making a thrust, the point of his sword went against Teach's cartridge box, and bended it to the hilt. Teach broke the guard of it, and wounded Maynard's fingers but did not disable him, whereupon he jumped back and threw away his sword and cut Teach's face pretty much; in the interim both companies engaged in Maynard's sloop, one of Maynard's men being a Highlander, engaged Teach with his broad sword, who gave Teach a cut on the neck, Teach saying, "Well done lad;" the Highlander replied, "If it be not well done, I'll do better." With that he gave him a second stroke, which cut off his head, laying it flat on his shoulder.

The weapons available to both pirate and pirate hunter were identical—indeed, often enough the pirate had stolen them from a naval source. Navy vessels, therefore, were as desirable a prize as a merchantman, although a stiffer fight could be anticipated. Pirates preferred to capture victims without a fight, and poorly armed merchant ships surrendered rather than risk the slaughter that usually followed an unsuccessful defense. After raising the Jolly Roger, a shot across the bows usually proved enough to bring the victim's surrender. With its colors struck, the captured vessel was ordered to lower her boats to ferry a pirate prize-crew across.

Pirate ships went heavily armed, and in some cases they felt that it was worth their while attacking less compliant and more powerfully armed opponents. Gauging the risks was part of the pirate captain's job. Charles Vane paid the price of shying away from a fight, while Edward England relished the prospect, but paid the price for leniency toward the men he captured. If there were to be a battle, the preferred method of attack was to come alongside the target and board it as quickly as possible to avoid damaging the prize through gunfire. Ropes with grappling hooks thrown by the pirates pulled the two ships together. Once the pirates swung aboard, a fierce hand-to-hand fight would ensue, and since they were often better armed and more numerous than their opponents, the pirates usually prevailed.

Firearms were popular boarding weapons, and included muskets, blunderbusses, and pistols. Blackbeard is reported to have carried three pairs of pistols, as well as a sword and a knife. The most popular edged weapon was the cutlass. A cheap, clumsy, but effective cutting weapon, it was the maritime blade of choice. Naval officers and pirate captains often favored the more gentlemanly smallsword, designed to be thrust with the point. Half-pikes, axes, knives, and even marine belaying pins were used in a desperate hand-to-hand fight. The deck of a small ship could be devastated with the hand-thrown explosive device called a "grenadoe."

Though a pirate captain only employed gunnery as a last resort, it was the principal form of attack for a naval vessel or a powerfully armed merchantman intending to resist. Even small trading vessels carried artillery pieces (guns or cannons; a cannon referred only to a specific size and type of ordnance). The frequent warfare of the 17th and 18th centuries meant that arming a vessel was essential, and also meant that most sailors were skilled in firing the weapons. A four-wheeled truck carriage used a simple elevating system and wooden spikes to aim the gun at sea, although elevation of the piece was often little more than waiting for the ship to crest the top of a wave before firing. Rammers and sponges were kept beside the guns, ready for action when required.

A four-pounder, the typical gun size on a pirate sloop, could fire a roundshot about 1000 yards. In addition to roundshot, which damaged the hull, chainshot or barshot tore apart the sails and made escape impossible, while at close range anti-personnel grapeshot cut down the enemy crew.

The shortsword, or stabbing dagger, was a handy weapon in close combat. Artillery ranged from roundshot (1), used to smash hulls and masts, to the spinning double cannonball (2) and chainshot (3), both of which brought down rigging. Grapeshot (4) wrought havoc among crews, inflicting dreadful wounds

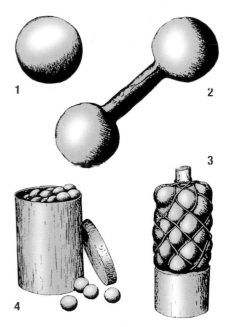

Curbing piracy and providing a deterrent

Despite having the best of it in terms of armament, numbers, and sheer ferocity for several years, most pirates of the Golden Age knew that they could not evade justice forever. Although a few notorious pirates such as Henry Every were never caught, most eventually felt the full force of Admiralty law. The excesses of the Golden Age, while undoubtedly exciting public attention for the sensational aspect, were met with universal anger among the merchants who suffered the most. The mercantile backlash was predictable, backed by an increasingly firm anti-pirate stance by regional governments, major national powers, and their navies.

It has been demonstrated that in the early part of the age several colonial governors along the American Atlantic seaboard and in the Caribbean islands regarded pirates as a useful source of income, bringing captured produce to their markets. What changed the minds of colonial authorities was the economic boom that developed following the end of almost constant warfare in 1714. It opened up European and American markets and increased maritime trade almost threefold within 15 years, but a large number of former privateers turned to piracy. When piracy began to hinder the economic development of the American colonies and cut into the profit margins of European merchants and investors, the climate changed.

On both sides of the Atlantic, a growing clamor for anti-piracy legislation and maritime security led to a major clampdown on piratical activity. Out went the blind-eye merchants like Benjamin Fletcher and in came a fresh breed of governors, such as Woodes Rogers in the Bahamas and Alexander Spotswood in Virginia, who led the way by establishing anti-pirate naval patrols and maintaining a tough judicial line when pirates fell into their hands.

At the outset, it was the colonists who had to foot the bills for many of these naval patrols, but in a short space of time Europe's maritime powers began to contribute finance to help stamp out piracy. Britain's Royal Navy was the

A fine example of an 18th-century handgun that any pirate would have killed for; the short-barreled Belgian flintlock pistol.

leading maritime force in the early 18th century and, together with the navies of France, Spain, and the Netherlands, its patrols helped to extinguish piracy in the West Indies, then later from the American Atlantic coastline, the coast of West Africa, and the Indian Ocean. It was this concerted effort that finally brought to book those major pirate figures Blackbeard, Bartholomew Roberts, and Stede Bonnet.

In addition to increased naval patrols on the high seas and in threatened coastal regions, other strategies were also devised to cut the level of piracy. Borrowed from the Spanish *flota* system, the British adopted convoys for a number of years in the Indian Ocean, soon followed by the Dutch and then by most nations in the Caribbean. By making piracy too difficult and too dangerous, occurrences of pirate attacks lessened dramatically. It was also realized that if a pirate's existence was made to appear extremely unattractive, it would adversely affect recruitment and cut back the numbers of seamen willing to take the risk of a pirate's life. This was accomplished by making the trials and executions of captured pirate crews very public, and very grisly.

Pirate crews apprehended in the late 17th century were commonly spared execution, with only their ringleaders facing the death sentence. But pirate excesses and the consequent outcry at the start of the 18th century put any sense of leniency aside. Throughout the Golden Age mass executions of entire crews became increasingly frequent. It has to be said that the public approval at such events did not spring entirely from relief that criminals were receiving due justice, there was also the far less noble frisson that any public execution aroused. Crowds regularly attended any execution of a convicted criminal, so how exciting was the despatch of 54 men at a go, as happened when the crewmen of Bartholomew Roberts met their end in 1722?

With the occasional exception of men who knew when to retire, such as Henry Every, or accept a pardon and start a new life, such as Benjamin Hornigold, almost every pirate met death in battle or on the gallows. The pirate's life was nasty, brutish, and short, and by emphasizing the near certainty of a painful and gruesome end Europe's admiralties gained an effective psychological deterrent aimed at seamen who might otherwise have considered piracy as a life option. The whole process of the trial and execution of pirates, as well as the frequent public abuse of their corpses, is well documented, and executions attracted a widespread and morbid interest among contemporary observers. The procedure also followed a set pattern, which was designed to obtain the maximum propaganda value from the judicial process and so add to the deterrent's effectiveness.

A model of a powerfully armed Royal Navy frigate of the kind in service against pirates in the North Atlantic at the end of the 17th century and start of the 18th century.

The process of maritime capital punishment

Pirates who were caught in the early 18th century faced the prospect of a highly publicized trial and, if found guilty, almost certainly faced execution by one of several different procedures, according to the laws of the country in which they had been convicted. In England the process of hanging took place in a particular manner that was later exported throughout the British colonies in the Americas, the West Indies, India, and West Africa. France and Spain had similar systems, although certain aspects, such as the type of execution and the increased use of lifetime sentences in slavery, differed from the English judicial model. For example, the Spanish used the garrote to execute, while the French made extensive use of penal service in their colonies for those who were left with their heads intact.

From 1701 Admiralty Courts were established in the English American and Caribbean colonies to oversee all trials involving crimes committed "below the high water mark," extending Admiralty authority. After the start of 1716 colonial courts supervised a string of mass pirate executions. In addition to those already mentioned, some of the more prominent executions in the New World included eight pirates captured by Woodes Rogers in New Providence, Bahamas (December 1718), Charles Harris and 25 pirates in Newport, Rhode Island (July 1723), 11 pirates from the crew of George Lowther on St. Kitts (November 1723), and William Fly and two pirates in Boston, Massachusetts (July 1726).

However horrible these mass executions may have been, they were far removed from lynchings. In most countries, piracy trials were conducted according to Maritime or Admiralty law. In England, condemned men were taken from their prison in London—usually the Marshalsea gaol—to Execution Dock in Wapping, on the banks of the Thames, where a wooden gallows stood on the foreshore above the low-water mark (i.e., within the boundaries of Admiralty law's authority). After a brief prayer from a chaplain or priest, the pirate was allowed a last speech, and then hanged. His body was left for a day-and-a-half to be "washed by the tides as Admiralty law proscribes," and then buried in an unmarked grave. The cadavers of more prominent pirates played their part in the propaganda campaign. Following the tide washing, the corpse was cut down, tarred, bound in chains, and placed inside an iron cage. This was suspended from a gibbet, often located at the entrance

Execution Dock in London's Wapping wharf district, where pirates were hanged "above the low water mark" until dead. On the way from the Marshalsea prison to the noose, they were accompanied by a jeering throng throwing mud, excrement, and rotten vegetables at them.

Pirates taken in the Far East faced a kinder fate than many of their contemporaries in the West. Professional executioners could usually decapitate the condemned in a flash, with a single sword blow to the neck.

Hanged and drying: Captain William Kidd's corpse took a long time to rot away, all the while advertising to would-be pirates the almost certain fate that awaited them.

to a port, like the shore of the Thames near London or at Gallows Point or Gun Cay outside Port Royal, Jamaica. The body was left to rot inside its cage, a process that took up to two years, depending on the climate.

This was the fate that befell William Kidd's corpse, "whose body was visible for years after his execution." The sun, rain, and frost rotted the body, and seagulls pecked out its eyes, but the tar and cage kept the bones in place, "as a great terror to all persons from committing ye like crimes." Pirates later said they would sooner die in battle than "be hanged up drying, like Kidd."

By 1730 all of the most notorious pirates and their crews had been hunted down and either killed in action or executed following their conviction in public trials. The Golden Age of piracy was effectively ended through a combination of naval patrols and harsh judicial punishment.

CHAPTER TEN

Everyone Hates Britain

French and American privateers pound the Royal Navy

The concerted effort of the major maritime powers brought the most notorious of Johnson's "pyrates" to book by the late 1720s, and the period later romanticized as a Golden Age ended. Security on the high seas, however, was by no means guaranteed, since this more or less coincided with the end of the War of the Quadruple Alliance, which ended Spanish domination of the western Mediterranean, as well as bringing the once-powerful Spanish navy to its knees. From this point on, Spain's control of the Spanish Main was also to slip from her imperial grasp as one province after another won independence in a series of century-long wars. The Spanish Main was again a prime target for Caribbean pirates. But the main drive to a renewed surge in piracy was once again war.

The causes of what became known as the War of the Austrian Succession (1740–48) are not the subject of this book, save to say that the familiar—though often unwilling—partners of Great Britain and the Dutch United Provinces were, among other nations, pitched against Spain and France. This was great news for any number of seamen, since letters of marque were issued to hundreds of colonial privateers. The Caribbean was the hunting ground, where weakening Spanish control offered the best opportunities, although they also ventured into the Atlantic.

Shipping in the 18th century carried a range of cargoes in American waters. Cane sugar, raw cotton and finished linens, American spices, and massive amounts of tobacco went east to Europe. In the opposite direction, the slave trade still carried its miserable cargo from Africa to the Americas throughout the century. Indentured workers still figured, but a new cargo of women intended for the colonial wedding market bulked up passenger manifests. And, as more women arrived and settled into their pre-arranged marriages, demand increased for luxury goods such as the latest Parisian fashions and delicate teas. Rum was shipped in both directions, while the colonists imported gin and wine from Europe. Other European imports included manufactured goods, tools, and weapons. The large variety and volume of maritime trade ensured rich pickings for pirates and privateers.

For much of the 18th century, the British Royal Navy was consistently victorious in a series of large fleet actions against the French and Spanish navies. With ships of the line leaving the yards at a high rate, the Royal Navy was able to maintain a close blockade of enemy coasts and virtually eliminate rival maritime trade. It was the winning strategy that led to Britain's complete dominance of the world's oceans by 1800. Faced with this overwhelming naval achievement, Britain's enemies were forced to rely on raiding British commerce, rather than through fleet battles. France immediately sought a solution through privateers in its struggles with Britain. This not only suited the circumstances, it also maintained a veneer of international legitimacy, especially in the West Indies and Caribbean. Because the 1686 Treaty of Whitehall had decreed that conflict in the New World would not lead to war between the two nations, its provisions in effect sanctioned the actions of privateers, whether the two countries were at war or not. In any case, the combination of substantial French settlements in the Caribbean and the vulnerability of British maritime trade in the area made it a particularly attractive option for privateers.

French privateers operating in the Caribbean to the south and out of Canadian bases to the north hunted British shipping, and through their respective colonial governors both the French and Spanish crowns issued letters of marque by the hundred. In the Lesser Antilles the French islands provided perfect privateer bases during the War of the Austrian Succession, while the fortress of Louisburg protected

HMS *Hibernia* fighting a privateer, 1814; by an unknown British artist. American privateers were more than a danger to merchantmen, they also tied up valuable naval resources to act as convoy escorts.

Opposite: During the early 18th century, colonial cities such as Boston, seen here in a map after the one prepared by Captain John Bonner in 1722, were growing rapidly in prosperity. A corresponding sense of civic pride and independence was soon to lead to an overwhelming wish to be free of irksome taxes paid to the British crown.

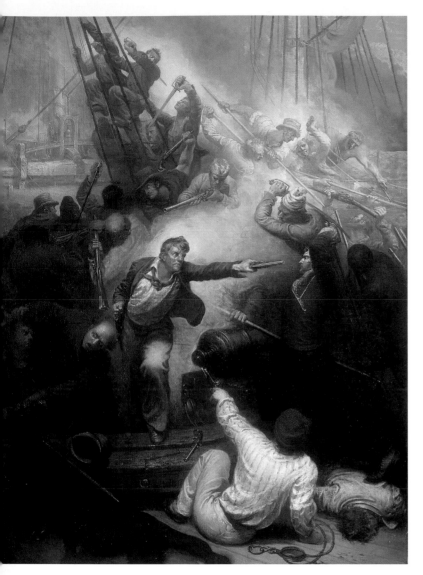

Samuel Drummond's oil painting of Captain William Rogers capturing the *Jeune Richard*, painted in 1807, captures all the drama and violence of a boarding action.

the French Canadian privateers and provided a safe base from which to attack shipping of the American colonies. During the Seven Years War (1756–63), French privateer raids were so dangerous that they influenced British strategy, which included the decision to capture the privateer havens of Louisburg, Martinique, Guadeloupe and Dominica. France then supported the American colonists in their revolution against Britain after 1778, and French privateers benefited from a Royal Navy weakened by cutbacks and inefficiency. British losses from Spanish and French privateers during what the colonists called the American War of Independence and which King George III dubbed the Revolutionary War amounted to an estimated five percent of her mercantile fleet.

A French privateer in the Indian Ocean

Privateer action in the face of Royal Navy domination was not restricted to the New World. For centuries, the port of Dunkirk in France had been a privateer base, and it served more than 60 French privateers during the Revolutionary War, sailing under French or American letters of marque. Privateers operating out of Dunkirk captured hundreds of British prizes right under the Admiralty's nose, in the waters of the English Channel and the Irish Sea. After America's revolution came France's overdue explosion of civic unrest. The French Revolutionary and Napoleonic Wars began in 1796, and the French found their harbors blockaded and their navy in neglected condition at a time when Britain's had been rebuilt and reinvigorated. The British kept a powerful naval presence in the Caribbean, so French privateers looked elsewhere for opportunities to harass British shipping and found it in the old battleground of the Indian Ocean.

The most successful French privateer was Robert Surcouf (1773–1827), a seaman of the Breton port of St. Malo. He enlisted on a merchantman to India when he was 15, and then until 1791 worked in the Mozambique–Madagascar slave trade. At the outbreak of war he was based on the Île de France (Mauritius) and found himself as second officer of a frigate engaged against two British naval vessels. Surcouf distinguished himself sufficiently to be promoted to captain and was given the tiny four-gun ship *La Créole*. Although denied letters of marque, Surcouf sailed into the lucrative trade routes of the Indian Ocean, where he encountered three East Indiamen escorted by the 24-gun *Triton*. Through the ruse of not showing his colors until the British ship fired a warning shot, Surcouf came alongside and gave the Indiaman a broadside. In spite of the extreme differential in firepower, the Frenchman won the day and the British ships lowered their flags. The prizes were taken to Mauritius, where they were confiscated, since Surcouf lacked a privateer's license. He sailed to France and was promptly issued with one.

Surcouf returned to sea in August 1798, in command of the 18-gun *Clarisse* and a complement of 105 men. On his way to the Indian Ocean they captured four ships in the South Atlantic, and then two more off the Indonesian island of Sumatra in February 1799. In November he took an Indiaman with a cargo estimated to be worth more than a million francs before dodging away from the 56-gun frigate HMS *Sybille*. As the *Clarisse* returned to Mauritius, a British brig and an American merchantman fell into the privateer's hands. His success brought further promotion in 1800 and the command of the *Confiance*, a fast 18-gun frigate, in which he captured nine British ships. These included the large 38-gun East Indiaman HMS *Kent* with 400 men and a company of naval riflemen onboard. Outnumbered more than three to one, on October 7 the French boarded and seized control of the British ship, in the Bay of Bengal. For this exploit, Robert Surcouf became a French military legend, while the British Admiralty declared him a pirate with a hefty bounty on his head. Returning to France during the brief peace of 1802–3, the now-wealthy privateer turned his home town of St. Malo and other small ports into French privateer havens, and continued to harass British shipping for the remainder of the Napoleonic Wars. The emperor even made him a baron.

Robert Surcouf was not alone among his compatriots. British shipping suffered badly from French privateers—mercantile losses exceeded 2000 ships during the first six years of the Napoleonic Wars. French privateers also captured hundreds of neutral American vessels, which prompted America to fight the undeclared, so-called Quasi War in 1798 to drive off their French attackers. The British also used privateers during the wars with France and the American Revolution. By 1809, when Britain and Spain made peace, the owners of privateer vessels were complaining that they had been so successful in devastating French shipping that there were no more prizes to be taken. This famine was eased during the war between Britain and the United States started in 1812, but this time it was the Americans who were the principal beneficiaries.

The battle between the *Confiance*, commanded by Surcouf, and HMS *Kent*, by Ambroise-Louis Gameray. Celebrating the hero of St. Malo, a statue of Robert Surcouf stands in his home town. To the French, he was an inspiration; to the merchantmen and British ships-of-the-line he captured or destroyed, he was a pirate with a price on his head.

John Paul Jones—the Continental Navy's first-appointed 1st Lieutenant—was also the first officer to raise the American ensign, the Grand Union flag, seen below. This painting of c.1890 was done long after Jones' death, at a time when his memory was being reinstated following a long period of neglect.

A new-found liberty defended at sea

Following the rebellion of the American colonies in 1775, the Continental Congress and individual colonies began to build a naval force, which would be required to confront the power of the Royal Navy. Although the fledgling Continental Navy accomplished relatively little during the seven years of war, one navy man emerged as America's first true hero—John Paul Jones.

Born as John Paul on the southwest coast of Scotland in 1747, like so many Scots before him, he went to sea as a young boy aged barely 12. For the next 20 years he made numerous voyages on merchant ships and slavers, calling in at many ports including Fredericksburg in Virginia, where his older brother ran a plantation. In 1768 the young sailor's fortune was the result of an ill wind, when both captain and first mate of the Scottish brig he was sailing on succumbed to yellow fever. When John Paul brought the vessel safely to port, the grateful owners made him the ship's master. In 1770, during a second voyage to the West Indies, an incident led to Paul flogging a seaman, who later died of his injuries. This unfortunate event led to accusations of cruelty that were to dog him for a long while afterward and probably drove him out of a profitable business in Tobago. He fled back to America and Fredericksburg, where he changed his identity, adding "Jones" to his nomenclature.

In 1775 John Paul Jones went to Philadelphia, where the newly founded Continental Navy had its headquarters, to volunteer his services to fight the British. He became a 1st Lieutenant aboard the 30-gun frigate USS *Alfred* and sailed from the Delaware river in February 1776 to attack British merchant vessels in the Bahamas. As the ship prepared to sail, Jones became the first man to hoist the American ensign on a naval vessel, the Grand Union flag. Over the course of the following months, Jones commanded a number of ships, taking many prizes and freeing American prisoners held in British prisons on Nova Scotia, before he was given the 18-gun USS *Ranger* on June 14, 1777 (the day America adopted the Stars and Stripes flag). With his reputation, Jones had hoped for a more prestigious vessel than *Ranger*, and so it was with some disappointment that in early 1778 he sailed for Brest in France with orders to harass the Royal Navy in its own waters.

He left Brest that April and headed north into the Irish Sea. Off Carrickfergus the Americans sighted the 20-gun brig HMS *Drake* at anchor in the harbor, but contrary winds dashed any attempt to engage the British warship. Jones landed at the northern English port of Whitehaven, where he burned shipping in the harbor and destroyed a small fort. Next, he made landfall on the Scottish coast near his birthplace of Kirkcudbright. The plan to kidnap the Earl of Selkirk, who lived nearby, and ransom him for American sailors impressed by the Royal Navy was foiled by the nobleman's absence. According to Jones, his crew were determined to plunder the estate and in the end he allowed them to take the family silver in return for not burning anything. He later arranged to return the valuables to Lady Selkirk, but the British still named the act plain and simple piracy, and Jones responsible for

t. Leaving Scotland, *Ranger* returned to Carrickfergus and, with the help of better weather, attacked the *Drake*. After a short gun battle, the Americans captured the British ship, imprisoned her crew, and returned to Brest with the prize.

Jones was given the command of a new ship, a converted French Indiaman renamed *Bonhomme Richard*. In August he put to sea again, in company with four French privateers, and captured three British merchant ships off the coast of Ireland and northern Scotland. By early September he was in the North Sea, but had become separated from all but one of his French consorts, the *Pallas*. He tried to repeat his earlier raids by landing on the Scottish coast in the Firth of Forth at Leith, near Edinburgh. On this occasion bad weather forced him to abandon the attack and the two ships continued to cruise southward down the Scottish and English coasts.

On September 23, 1779, off Flamborough Head, the two ships met a British convoy escorted by two men-of-war. Jones steered for the 50-gun *Serapis* while his French consort *Pallas* engaged a 20-gun sloop. Suspecting the accuracy of his French artillery, Jones resolved to fight at close quarters. An attempt to board failed, and the ships began a gunnery duel at point-blank range. A broadside from *Serapis* cut *Bonhomme Richard*'s mainmast and holed the privateer below the waterline. Apparently sinking and with her ensign shot to a rag, Captain Pearson of the *Serapis* signalled Jones "Has your ship struck [colors]?" Jones replied, "I have not yet begun to fight," and the slaughter continued. He then rammed the *Serapis*, and withering musket fire from the

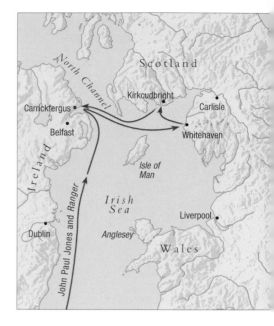

John Paul Jones in his French-rigged warship *Bonhomme Richard* exchanges broadsides with HMS *Serapis* off Flamborough Head in 1779.

rigging devastated its decks. A hand grenade exploded part of the *Serapis*'s magazine and Pearson eventually conceded defeat. Both ships were shattered; the *Bonhomme Richard* eventually sank and the *Serapis* limped toward a friendly port. Jones entered the history books as the most successful American naval commander of the Revolutionary War.

On his return to France early in 1780, Jones was fêted and his deeds were even honored by a ballad that popularized him as an American "pirate." Louis XVI, an ardent supporter, awarded Jones the Order of Military Merit and knighted him with the title "Chevalier." In 1787 the Continental Congress had a commemorative medal struck for the "valor and brilliant services" of Chevalier John Paul Jones. He went on to serve in the Russian navy and fought with distinction against Ottoman Turks in the Black Sea. Discredited by false charges of assaulting an underage girl, he left Russia for Paris, where the great American revolutionary died a broken and almost forgotten man on July 18, 1792. (Six months later, on January 21, 1793, his admirer the king met his own death at the hands of French revolutionaries.) France and Russia hailed him a hero, Britain called him a pirate, even the American Congress appeared to deny Jones the respect he deserved. It was a century before his remains were brought home to his adopted land and John Paul Jones was awarded American recognition.

The Privateer Fly, oil painting by Francis Holman (1729–84). From the shipyards of Baltimore came the finest cutters and sloops. Fast and maneuverable, they were the ideal privateer ships.

American privateers create havoc

At the same time in 1775 that the Continental Congress was constructing the Continental Navy, they were also busy commissioning privateers, who proved to be far better value than the navy and a lucrative source of revenue. Over 3000 British ships and their cargoes were captured and brought into American ports by privateers during the war for independence, successes that were to be repeated during the War of 1812 (1812–15), when purpose-built long-range privateers proved particularly effective as snipers of British shipping.

As early as April 1775, rebel whaleboats captured a British schooner off Martha's Vineyard, near Boston, and by early 1776 larger and better-armed privateers were cruising in the Atlantic and the Caribbean, while smaller ships concentrated on harassing British and British-Canadian fishing fleets off Newfoundland. As well as valuable merchant cargoes, captured British supply ships provided much-needed muskets and powder for George Washington's Continental Army.

Unlike Continental Navy crews, the deckhands on a privateer received no pay—their only source of income was prize money. It was a form of commission hat ensured compliancy, discipline, and motivated the sailors to supreme effort hen it came to a fight. Immense profits could be made; the Salem privateer *Rattlesnake* alone took prizes worth over $1 million in a single cruise. Ports such as alem, Boston, and Baltimore grew rich as a result of their privateer fleets, although rench ports and colonies also provided safe privateer havens and shared in the enefits. In response to these attacks, the Royal Navy slowly introduced a convoy ystem for protection, but thousands of British ships continued to sail unescorted. he larger merchantmen went armed, but privateers had heavier artillery and igger crews, which gave them the edge in action. Shipping losses were part of the eason for the erosion of Britain's will to continue the struggle against the American evolutionaries following the defeat of her army at Yorktown in 1781.

The War of 1812 was largely a naval conflict, and a boon to privateers. Ship wners were eager to repeat the privateering successes of the American Revolution nd within two months over 150 commissioned vessels had put to sea. At first, many ere poorly armed, so they relied on boarding and hand-to-hand combat rather han gunnery to subdue and capture the enemy. However, victories were often loodless because, after the recent state of peace, many British merchant ships sailed

narmed, making them readily surrendered rgets—and the vast size of the mercantile eet meant that prizes were plentiful.

American ship owners soon began to ommission specialized craft, designed from 1e keel upward as privateers. Some of these, ke the heavy schooners *Paul Jones*, *Saratoga*, *orktown*, and *Revenge*, were able to carry ver 150 men and an armament capable of ngaging British frigates when the need arose. altimore was the main privateer port on 1e Atlantic seaboard and, taking advantage f lessons learned during the American evolution, leading shipwrights developed 1ese new privateers in the city's shipyards. he profits of chandlers and shipwrights 1ultiplied exponentially. Baltimore-built

Any shortcomings of the fledgling American navy during the War of Independence were more than made up for in the War of 1812. This painting by Thomas Birch (1779–1851) depicts an incident that shook confidence in British naval supremacy, which occurred on August 19, 1812. Having closed with "His Britannic Majesty's frigate" *Guerrière* off the coast of Brazil, the USS *Constitution* ravaged and captured the 38-gun British warship in under a half hour. After evacuating her captain and surviving crew, the *Guerrière* was fired and sank. The exploit earned the *Constitution* the nickname "Old Ironsides."

hooners were renowned for their speed and easy handling, such as the 350-ton rivateer *America*, armed with 20 guns and carrying a crew of 120. She took 40 prizes om the British during the war that returned her owners a profit of over $600,000.

The most successful privateer of the War of 1812 was the Boston brig *Yankee*, hose 40 prizes totalled over $3,000,000. Other purpose-built heavy privateers such the schooners *Prince of Neufchatel*, *Chasseur*, and *Lyon* contributed to the growing ll on British merchant shipping. The best of the specialized privateer schooners of the War of 1812 were as well designed for speed as later clipper ships or trans–Atlantic racing yachts, a tribute to their designers.

At the time Napoleon Bonaparte abdicated in April 1814, there were more than 500 privateers operating out of the American ports. With the French collapse, the British Admiralty was free to concentrate attention on troublesome America. (Famously, Napoleon made a comeback, but his short-lived resurrection resulted in land battles; the Royal Navy was barely involved.) The blockade had proved effective against France, and so it did on the other side of the Atlantic. By the end of the year American maritime commerce was at a standstill. Over 1300 British ships

The New York-built *Prince of Neufchatel*, a privately owned privateer, seen here engaging the 40-gun British frigate HMS *Endymion*. In spite of her far superior armament and renowned speed, the *Endymion* was unable to subdue the American privateer, which escaped after inflicting serious damage to the enemy. The *Endymion*'s captain later said that he lost as many men in his efforts to seize the *Prince of Neufchatel* as he would have done had his ship engaged a regular man-of-war of equal power.

...ad been captured by privateers during the war—although British privateers had also ...arried American shipping, and the losses led ship owners on both sides of the Atlantic ...o demand an end to the war. Peace was finally achieved at the end of 1814 (although ...he last action took place early in 1815, the news not having arrived in time).

The War of 1812 was the last great surge of American privateering, and apart ...rom attacks by Confederate raiders during the American Civil War, state-sponsored ...iracy became a thing of the past. Almost all American and European privateers ...beyed instructions and curtailed their activities, but it was a different matter in ...Central and South America when peace was declared. Latin American privateers ...ourished, even expanding their attacks to include non-Spanish shipping, and a ...ew wave of sea-going terror washed over the Caribbean and the Gulf of Mexico.

CHAPTER ELEVEN

The Last American Pirates

Filling the voids created by peace after war

The Americas in the first half of the 19th century

- former Spanish province
- former Portuguese territory
- **1821** date of independence from Spain/Portugal
- USA territory gained from Spain
- British territory
- French territory
- Dutch territory

PACIFIC OCEAN

Denver

Salt Lake City

Sacramento
San Francisco

Santa Barbara • Los Angeles

San Diego

1848 to USA

El Paso
Ciudad Juárez

Mazatlán

Acapulco

Monterrey

MEXICO
1821

Tampico

Vera Cruz

Mexico City

Gulf of Mexico

Matagorda Bay

Galveston

San Antonio
Texas
1836
1845 to USA

New Orleans
(see inset, right)

Memphis

Birmingham
Alabama
Mississippi

Pensacola

UNITED
STATES

Territory of
Orleans
1804
Louisiana
1812

Florida
1810–19
(to USA)

Jacksonville
St. Augustine

Nassau

Key West

Havana

*Bahamas
Britain*

Miami

CUBA
1898

Kings
(Port Ro

British
Honduras

Mérida

GUATEMALA
1821

Guatemala
City

EL SALVADOR
1821

HONDURAS
1821

Managua

NICARAGUA
1821

Piracy in American or Caribbean waters was never stamped out completely afte the Golden Age, but for almost a century there were only occasional, isolate incidents. However, as the previous chapter outlined, the Napoleonic Wars an the War of 1812 created employment for thousands of privateers, and when the las conflict ended in 1815 most found themselves facing unemployment. Many turne to piracy, operating from remote harbors in places like Cuba and Puerto Rico Although a number of them, such as Jean Laffite, were American (or nominally so) the majority came from the Spanish-speaking regions of the Caribbean and Sout America. Jean Laffite is an interesting character. He lived much of his life beyon the law and yet—in the way of a licensed privateer—sold his skills to a prope authority in the defense of New Orleans in the last action of the Anglo-America War of 1812, becoming something of a national hero in the process.

Like so many pirates, Laffite's early years are vague. He was born in about 178 in France, traditionally in the southern city of Bayonne, close to the norther Spanish border, which gives some support to the tradition that while his fath was French his mother was Spanish, and probably Jewish. However, Haiti has als

ATLANTIC
OCEAN

DOMINICAN
REPUBLIC
1822

PUERTO RICO
1898 (to USA)

Guadeloupe (France)
Dominica (Britain)
Barbados
(Britain)

Martinique
(France)

San
Juan

nto
mingo

CARIBBEAN
SEA

Trinidad
(Britain)

Prince

*Dutch
Antilles*

Cumaná

Caracas

Maracaibo

VENEZUELA
1821

Cartagena

COLOMBIA
1819

Bogotá

ANAMA
821

OSTA
ICA
821

ECUADOR
1822

Esmeraldas
Quito

Guayaquil

PERU
1821

PACIFIC
OCEAN

Cuzco

Lima

Callao

Cayenne

Paramaribo

French
Guiana

Georgetown

British
Guiana

Dutch
Guiana

Manaus

BRAZIL
1822
(from Portugal)

BOLIVIA
1825

La Paz

Arica

Chuquisaca
Potosí

CHILE
1818

Antofagasta

La Serena

Santiago
Valparaiso

Valdivia

PATAGONIA

Buenos Aires
1536

PARAGUAY
1811

Asunción

Rio Grande

URUGUAY
1828

Montevideo

ARGENTINA
1816

Córdoba

Buenos Aires

Mar del Plata

Punta Alta

ATLANTIC
OCEAN

Malvinas
1820 to Argentina
Falklands
1833 to Britain

Baton Rouge

Picayune

Biloxi

Mississippi

Amite Creek

Pearl

Mississippi Sound

Lake
Maurepas

Lake
Pontchartrain

Donaldsonville

Convent

Metairie

New Orleans

Lake
Borgne

Chandleur
Sound

Chandeleur Islands

JEAN LAFFITE
N.H.P. & PRESERVE

Lake
Salvador

Barataria

Pointe a la Hache

Breton
Sound

Grand Bay

Barataria
Bay

Mississippi
Delta

Caillou
Bay

Terrebonne Bay

Timbalier Bay

West
Bay

G U L F   O F   M E X I C O

---

een identified as his birthplace. By 1809 he and
rother Pierre were living in New Orleans where they
an a smithy, a business that also acted as a cover for a massive
peration involving the smuggling of slaves and the fencing of
tolen goods. Working the swamps to the south of New Orleans
round Barataria Bay, the Laffites attracted a great number of the less
esirable denizens of the Louisiana bayous. By 1810 Jean had made himself
he chief spokesman of a group of pirates, privateers, and smugglers said to number
nore than 3000 men, operating from what they called the kingdom of Barataria.

Over the next few years the Baratarian pirates raided shipping in the Gulf of
Mexico, concentrating on Spanish ships and slave traders, while Laffite supervised
he sale of the plunder as it came in. The sale of slaves generated valuable income,

The wounded, dying, and dead litter the deck as Jean Laffite leads his men aboard a captured prize, in a contemporary woodcut. Astonishingly, Laffite is regarded as an American hero for his part in defeating British invaders at the battle for New Orleans in 1815; so much so that a park is named after him, the Jean Laffite National Historical Park and Preserve near New Orleans.

but since the United States Congress had banned the importation of slaves in 1808, plantation owners attended auctions held in secret near Barataria, where they could purchase new slaves and pirate booty was traded to the nearby city's merchants. This operation grew too extensive to remain hidden for long, and when the Territory of Orleans, as the region was known, became Louisiana, the 18th state to join the Union in 1812, its first elected governor, William Charles Cole Claiborne, ordered the Laffite brothers' arrest in November on charges of piracy and illegal trading. Released on bail due to the efforts of New Orleans' best lawyers, the brothers escaped and the trading continued, but this time they hid the auctions even deeper in the bayous. Laffite clearly had a sense of humor; when the governor put a price of $500 on his head in 1813, the pirate's response was to post bills on every corner offering ten times as much for Claiborne's head.

This stalemate lasted until 1814, by which time the Anglo-American war had dragged on for two years, mostly well to the north of the Gulf states. In this time an American invasion of Canada had been repulsed, and then after a series of successful frigate actions, the fledgling US Navy found itself blockaded in its home ports by the superior British fleet. The British raided the American coast in Maryland, captured the capital of Washington, and burned the White House. The

British were determined to repeat this success at New Orleans in order to disrupt the booming trade of the Mississippi river. In September of that year, British officers offered Laffite a pardon and financial reward if he would help them to storm New Orleans. Instead, Laffite informed the Louisiana authorities—his actions probably less influenced by patriotism than by the threat to his lucrative New Orleans market.

Governor Claiborne—a man with less humor than Laffite—had not forgotten the bounty snub and his response to the offer of help was to send the schooners *Carolina* and *Louisiana* into Barataria Bay to capture the pirate fleet as it lay at anchor. Laffite and his colleagues hid in the bayous until the departure of the two ships—which represented Louisiana and Mississippi's entire naval force—then reclaimed their settlement. But it was not to be business as usual. News that the British were gathering a large invasion force in Jamaica galvanized resistance in New Orleans. In December the federal government sent Major-General Andrew Jackson to mastermind the city's defenses, and he mustered militias from Kentucky, Tennessee, and Mississippi to bolster that of Louisiana. Looking to conscript every last man, Jackson offered Laffite's Baratarians a truce in return for their fighting help. Early in January the British force landed east of the city and were bloodily repulsed in the resulting Battle of New Orleans (January 8, 1815).

For their efforts, Laffite's pirates were rewarded with official pardons issued by President Madison a month later. While many seized the opportunity to give up piracy, the Laffite brothers chose to continue, but within a year or so found themselves hoisted by their own petard. The army units they had helped stayed

Pirate schooners in Galveston harbor come under fire from the USS *Enterprise*.

A painting by Augustus Baird depicts one of several instances when American merchantmen were lured into range by a few pirates dressed as women, while the rest of the villains lay on deck out of sight.

in place and the military presence to enforce the law made the Mississippi delta unhealthy for pirates and smugglers. Resigned to a move, the brothers stole a vessel and sailed to Texas. This region, technically still a Spanish possession but in fact a lawless frontier sprawling between America and Mexico, was home to some of the most desperate men in the Americas—an ideal pirate refuge.

Jean Laffite's pirate attacks resumed and by 1817 he held Galveston as his new secure port. He moved into the large Maison Rouge, which he seized from Spain's governor of Texas, the French pirate Louis-Michel Aury (*see the sidebar opposite*). With considerable strengthening, the Red House's upper floor became a fortress with cannon commanding Galveston harbor. In about 1820, Laffite is said to have married Madeline Regaud, who may have been the widow or daughter of a French colonist. And in the same year, a force spearheaded by Captain Biddle in the brig USS *Enterprise* bombarded and destroyed Galveston after one of the pirate's captains attacked an American merchantman. Laffite escaped capture on his flagship the *Pride*, but his subsequent life is unknown. Although it is considered likely he died in Mexico, rumors persisted that he survived and returned to the United States under an assumed name.

Cut-price robbers and murderers of the Caribbean

The Napoleonic Wars exercised a profound effect on the former Spanish Main. The Peninsular War (1807–14) ravaged Spain, fatally weakening her control over the once enormous New World empire. So quickly was the impact felt that the crucible-mix of peoples who made up the Spanish Americas were able to pick up the cudgels of independence almost immediately and free themselves from the Spanish yoke. By the end of 1808, with Spain fully occupied against Napoleon's armies and fighting for her life, the first of a long string of Latin American Wars of Liberation erupted.

By 1822 Mexico, Peru, and Chile were independent states, Honduras, Guatemala, San Salvador, Nicaragua, and Costa Rica (after a brief liaison with Mexico) had founded their own state, the United Provinces of Central America, and Simón Bolívar's rebel army had liberated Ecuador, Colombia, and Venezuela by 1825. Cuba and Puerto Rico remained under Spanish control, but guerrilla fighting plagued the islands. The emerging Latin American states hired privateers like Louis-Michel Aury to fight on their behalf against their Spanish oppressors, a pool largely expanded with the ending of the War of 1812. This meant that after 1815 there were hundreds of privateers operating in the Caribbean, and many saw little point in restricting their attacks to Spanish shipping. Beyond the confines of the Caribbean, the oceans were considered to be safe for commerce after the end of the Napoleonic Wars. The growing demand for materials driven by the Industrial Revolution in Europe and the emergent industry of America created an extraordinary demand for ships' cargoes. Consequently, the Caribbean and American shipping lanes were filled with a greater amount of vessels than had ever been seen before.

Many of the new Latin-American pirates were small-time robbers, content to attack ships that carried little in the way of plunder. Captain Lander of the American brig *Washington* reported that in an attack of 1822 Hispanic pirates stole $16, some food, cooking equipment, clothing, and a compass. This was not larceny on a grand scale, but these pirates frequently murdered their victims to prevent anyone identifying them later. While men like Bartholomew Roberts plundered wealthy cargoes and spared the crew during the Golden Age, in the 1820s merchant sailors were often slaughtered simply for the shirts on their backs.

With a fragile economy heavily dependent on commerce with Europe, the United States' emergent maritime trade was particularly vulnerable to pirate attack. Between 1815 and 1820 hundreds of American vessels were attacked and plundered, and marine insurance rates soared. Stories of excessive brutality and murder became commonplace. From 1820 onward, major efforts were made by the U.S. Navy to stamp out piracy in the Caribbean. Aggressive navy patrols and raids on known pirate havens gradually brought the situation under control. Pirates like Jean Laffite were driven from the seas, and although a few notorious scoundrels remained at large, by the late 1820s the threat of widespread piracy had receded.

Louis-Michel Aury

Born in Paris in about 1788, at the dawn of the French Revolution, Louis-Michel Aury served as a "powder monkey" in the Revolutionary Navy, and after his 14th birthday as a cabin boy on privateer ships. By 1810, having saved enough prize money to purchase the command of his own vessel, he sailed for the Americas to support the Spanish colonies in their fight for independence. In 1813, operating out of North Carolina, Aury attacked Spanish ships under Venezuelan letters of marque. In the following year he took a commission as Commodore of the Navy of New Granada (Colombia), but fell out with Latin America's great revolutionary leader Simón Bolívar over payment for his services.

In 1816 the newly founded Republic of Mexico appointed Aury as governor of Texas and he set up his headquarters and a privateering base on Galveston Island. And it was while he was absent from there on a mission that Jean Laffite seized control of Galveston. Aury attempted to establish a new base southwest of Galveston at Matagorda Bay, but this failed and he left Texas in 1817 to join other adventurer-privateers attacking Spanish Florida on behalf of Venezuela. Louis-Michel Aury died after being thrown from a horse in August 1821 on Old Providence Island in the western Caribbean, where three years earlier he had founded a pirate settlement, thriving on the stolen cargoes of Spanish shipping.

Much of the success in this outcome was due to one man, the U.S. Navy's pirate hunter, David Porter.

Pirate hunter accused of piracy

As the losses of American ships increased, ship owners and the American public demanded action. In 1821, President Monroe authorized the establishment of an anti-pirate squadron, and its command went to Commodore David Porter. The pitfalls facing a U.S. Navy pirate hunter in the uncertain political situation of the early 19th century are highlighted by Porter's career. At one moment he was a national hero and a respected naval officer of flag rank, the next he was labeled a pirate. What is certain is that he was the right man for the task of ridding the new country's waters of piracy.

Born on February 1, 1780 in Boston, Massachusetts, David Porter first went to sea as a midshipman in 1798 on the U.S. Navy's *Constellation* during the Quasi-War with France. A year later, participating in the action on February 9 against the 40-gun French frigate *L'Insurgente*, Porter distinguished himself during its capture. He then served as 1st lieutenant onboard the Baltimore schooners *Experiment* and *Amphitheater*. During the Barbary Wars (1801–07) Porter was again 1st lieutenant of the U.S. Navy ships *Enterprise*, *New York*, and *Philadelphia*. He was captured by corsairs in the attack on Tripoli harbor of October 31, 1803, when the *Philadelphia* ran aground. After spending more than a year in a Barbary prison he was repatriated and promoted to command the *Enterprise*.

During the War of 1812, Porter commanded the *Essex* and came to the American public's attention by capturing the first British warship of the conflict, HMS *Alert*, in August 1812. In the following year he took *Essex* around Cape Horn to attack British whalers but met his match off Valparaiso when he ran into the frigates *Phoebe* and *Cherub*. Porter surrendered to the British, but he was soon paroled and given free passage back to the United States, on the condition that he would not again take up arms against the British. Now a naval hero, Porter served in Washington as a member of the Board of Naval Commissioners from 1815 until he was called on to fight pirates once again—this time in home waters. Following President Monroe's authorization, on December 20, 1822, Secretary of the Navy Smith Thompson appointed Captain David Porter "to command the vessels-of-war of the United States on the West India station...for the suppression of piracy." Porter was promoted to the rank of commodore and handed $500,000 to outfit an anti-piracy squadron on Key West off the southern tip of Florida.

Porter, at the age of 42, now commanded a fleet of 16 craft, the largest peacetime collection of American ships that the young country had yet assembled. This U.S. Naval force was known as the Mosquito Fleet, due to its use of small craft of shallow draft: naval brigs, rapidly converted Baltimore schooners, an early paddle steamer, and even a decoy merchant ship armed with hidden guns. The Mosquito Fleet chose Key West as its base because of its central location in pirate waters of the West Indies. The island was then known as Thompson's Island, and soon the fledgling township boasted the busiest naval base in the United States. The phrase "Mosquito Fleet"

Opposite: Commodore David Porter cleared the West Indies of pirates in a two-year campaign that compares in success with that of Pompey the Great in the Mediterranean over 1700 years before. Unfortunately, in exceeding his orders on Puerto Rico, the Spanish branded him a pirate and his own naval commission courtmartialed him.

Opposite: The destruction of the pirate ship *Catalina* by Porter's Mosquito Fleet in 1823 marked a high point in America's anti-piracy program. The *Catalina's* captain, the infamous Cuban pirate Diabolito, and crew escaped to land, where they turned to banditry. The plagued Spanish authorities later complained bitterly that it was the fault of America that so many pirates had been driven on shore.

had extra meaning for the sailors, since in summer months the insects carried yellow fever and malaria, and the island's naval hospital overflowed with fever patients. As if this were not enough, Porter's orders covered a daunting range of tasks: suppress piracy and the slave trade; protect the commerce and citizens of the United States; transport American specie when required. By early 1823 he was ready and his ships scoured the Caribbean, the Bahamas, and the Gulf of Mexico, hitting pirate bases in Mexico, Cuba, Puerto Rico, and further along the Florida Keys.

Cuba was a particularly difficult target, since the Spanish resented the American presence and at times seemed to condone the piratical activities of their seamen. Distinguishing between honest seamen and pirates, who often disguised themselves as fishermen and local traders, proved to be a major headache. Porter walked a political tightrope, but as his successes grew Spanish merchants encouraged the Cuban authorities to support his activities.

One of the Mosquito Fleet's greatest successes was the defeat of the notorious Cuban pirate Diabolito (Little Devil) and his band aboard the *Catalina* in April 1823. The U.S. naval force surprised the pirates off the northern coast of Cuba and forced them to abandon their ship and take to the land to hide. The Spanish authorities then complained to Porter that many former pirates found it safer to become Cuban brigands on land. Porter's fleet ended the careers of other pirates, such as Charles Gibbs, originally of Rhode Island and a once-creditable naval seaman who kept squandering his money, turning to murderous piratical acts to recoup his losses. With hundreds of pirates captured, safe maritime trade was restored and, by 1825, piracy had virtually ceased to exist in American and Caribbean waters.

Unfortunately, Porter fell foul of Spanish politics again when he invaded the town of Fajardo, at the extreme western end of Spanish Puerto Rico, to rescue a fleet officer who had been jailed there. This act was above and beyond his commission from the United States and he was accused by Spain of piratical acts. Porter was recalled and courtmartialed on his return to Washington. He resigned and in 1826 entered the Mexican navy as its commander-in-chief, a position he held for three years. After this stint, he continued to serve his country in several diplomatic posts and died on March 3, 1843 while U.S. minister to Turkey.

David Porter's heroic efforts brought a great measure of peace and prosperity to America's mercantile community, but after his resignation a level of complacency allowed chinks to appear in maritime security. A number of particularly brutal pirates took advantage of the void his departure from the Mosquito Fleet left, and their attacks were the final examples of piracy in Atlantic waters. Of these pirates, the two most notorious were Benito de Soto and "Don" Pedro Gilbert.

Master of the Black Joke

Benito de Soto was a Portuguese seaman who, despite his background, appears to have been raised in a coastal village near La Coruña in Galician Spain. In either case, as a young man he would have been at home in Portuguese-speaking Brazil or Spanish Argentina, and it was from Buenos Aires that he sailed on the brigantine *Defense de Pedro* in 1827, bound for Africa. De Soto was clearly not a man of scruple, for as the laden slaver set our from the coast of Angola, he and the mate took over the ship.

Contemporary woodcut showing Benito de Soto's brigantine *Black Joke* sailing away from the *Morning Star*. The illustration implies that *Morning Star* was scuttled, but in reality she did not sink.

The crew's loyalties were divided, and 18 sailors refused to mutiny. De Soto had them put into an open boat and cast adrift. The boat was said to have capsized while trying to land and its crew drowned. De Soto's villainy was not yet over. As the mutineers celebrated, he staged an argument with the ship's mate and shot him dead, thus eliminating a rival for control of the ship. Both the mate's removal and the means by which it was achieved proved to be a salutary lesson and de Soto was duly elected captain. His first act as the master was to rename the ship—appropriately—*Black Joke*.

The *Black Joke* made a quick passage to the Caribbean to sell the stolen cargo of slaves in Spanish markets. The pirates went south to attack ships in the Caribbean, before passing through the line of the Lesser Antilles. Every vessel they encountered was captured, plundered, its crew slain, and the vessel sunk without ceremony. A string of missing ships marked the pirates' progress. Proceeding southward from the Antilles down the Atlantic coast of South America, they found few prizes. The real hunting ground

200

was in the mid-Atlantic. Sailing ships took a course well out into the South Atlantic, almost reaching the Brazilian coast to take advantage of trade winds, before turning southeast for the coast of South Africa and the Cape of Good Hope. De Soto positioned the *Black Joke* along this busy maritime trade route, where he encountered lucrative prizes returning from India and the Far East carrying spices, opium, or tea. As more ships disappeared it was correctly assumed that pirates were operating in the South Atlantic. Homeward bound East Indiamen were ordered to wait at the small island of St. Helena for a naval escort to convoy them into safer waters—but not every captain heeded the warning.

On February 21, 1832, de Soto came across the bark *Morning Star*, returning home from Ceylon to England. The smaller and faster pirate ship ranged alongside the *Morning Star* and fired at point-blank range. A number of passengers and crew were wounded or killed. De Soto ordered the bark to heave to, then demanded her captain's presence on *Black Joke*'s deck. The captain took some time in getting himself rowed over and de Soto took great offense at this tardiness. When the English captain finally clambered aboard the *Black Joke*, the pirate cut him down with a cutlass. "Thus," he is said to have cried, "does Benito de Soto reward those who disobey him."

The pirate crew then crossed over to the *Morning Star* and boarded her. In an orgy of destruction, they killed some of the men and raped the female passengers. The surviving passengers and crew were locked inside the *Morning Star*'s hold, then she was looted and holed to scuttle her. With that, the pirates returned to the *Black Joke* and sailed off, leaving the trapped captives to their watery mass grave. But not every plan works out. The *Morning Star*'s crew managed to free themselves, heroically manned the pumps, and saved their vessel from sinking. A passing ship rescued them on the following day and for the first time there were survivors to testify to de Soto's crimes, many of them wounded soldiers and officers returning home from India with their wives. Their treatment, combined with the brutal rape of the women, made de Soto the most notorious criminal on the high seas.

The pirates sailed to northwestern Spain to sell their plunder, then headed for the Mediterranean, only to be wrecked off the coast near Cadiz. De Soto and some of his men went on foot to Gibraltar in search of a new vessel; others hid themselves in Spain, but were hunted down and eventually captured. De Soto fared no better—the wounded soldiers from the *Morning Star* had been taken to Gibraltar and one of them recognized him. Found guilty by Gibraltar's governor, Sir George Don, de Soto was then shipped to Cadiz to be hanged along with the rest of his

Since he was addressing an audience of Spaniards, his cry of "Adios Todos!" was likely to be in Spanish, but Portuguese historians like to argue that Benito de Soto actually cried out "Adeus Todos," the same phrase in Portuguese, thus compounding the confusion as to the pirate's real nationality. Whatever, no one in the audience at his execution could be mistaken over his appearance—his head was cut off and stuck on a spike as a grisly warning to other mariners considering piracy as a career.

201

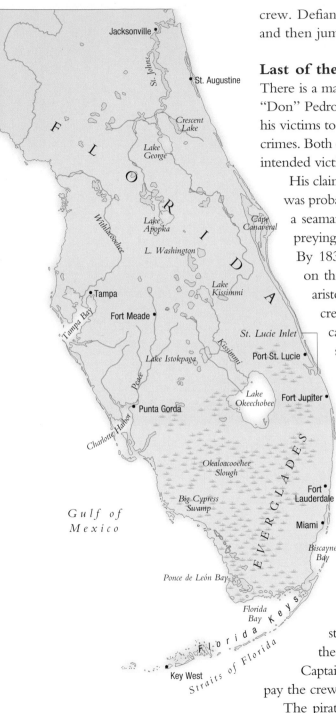

crew. Defiant to the end, the brutal pirate placed the noose around his own neck and then jumped with the final words "Adios Todos!"—"So long everyone!"

Last of the American pirates

There is a marked similarity in the failure of the well-laid plans of Benito de Soto and "Don" Pedro Gibert that led to their downfalls. In de Soto's case, it was the refusal of his victims to drown; in Gibert's case, fire failed to consume the living evidence of his crimes. Both of these vicious pirates eventually met their well-deserved ends when their intended victims survived the crimes to point fingers and bear witness.

His claim to be the son of a Spanish nobleman appears unfounded—Pedro Gibert was probably born a peon somewhere in Latin America in about 1800. He became a seaman and served as a privateer in the service of New Granada (Colombia), preying on Spanish shipping during the province's struggle for independence. By 1830 he was in command of his own schooner called the *Panda*, relying on the less glamorous trades of smuggling and slave trading. He adopted the aristocratic title of "Don" which, according to the testimony of his 11 fellow crewmen, implied his noble lineage, but at his eventual trial the *Panda* captain's name was recorded as plain and simple Gibert, Pedro. For his smuggling operations Gibert established a secure base in a stretch of one of the inshore lagoons on Florida's east coast, probably near St. Lucie Inlet.

Soon enough, passing American shipping became too much to resist and, in addition to smuggling, the *Panda*'s crew worked a variation on the old wrecking theme: lighting fires on the shore to attract attention and then assaulting the vessel when it came to "rescue" them. From there, it was a mere step to striking at ships on the high seas.

Cruising in the waters of the Florida Straits on September 20, 1832, Gibert spotted the American brigantine *Mexican*, en route from Salem in Massachusetts to Rio de Janeiro. As the *Panda* approached, Gibert hoisted the (neutral) Colombian flag, but the *Mexican*'s Captain Isaac Butman decided not to take any chances and turned away. The *Mexican* was armed with two small guns mounted amidships, but when the ammunition was brought up it was found that the roundshot was too large for the guns—perhaps a not uncommon error in the days before strict standardization. Her only chance was to flee, but in the chase that followed the *Panda* proved to be the faster craft. Just before the *Mexican* was overhauled, Captain Butman hid the $20,000 in coins he was carrying, money intended to pay the crew and purchase cargo in Brazil. He then struck his colors and surrendered.

The pirates boarded the *Mexican* and ransacked the ship, but found little to steal. Gibert beat and tortured Butman and some of his crew, and forced them to reveal the location of the ship's hidden paychest. The pirates then made ready to return to their own ship with the plunder, asking what should be done with the prisoners. As reported at the trial, Gibert told them, "Dead cats don't mew. You know what to do." Instead of killing the *Mexican*'s sailors outright, the pirates locked them in the fo'c'sle, then lowered the sails, slashed the rigging and set fire to the ship. Gibert and his men returned to the *Panda* and sailed off, leaving the *Mexican*'s crew to burn to death. Somehow, one of the men squeezed through a hatch and freed his fellows. Captain Butman led the firefighting and got the blaze under control but, no fool, he cannily left part of the fire smoldering so that as the *Panda* disappeared over the horizon, the pirates continued to see smoke rising over their victim. Once they were gone, the *Mexican*'s crew doused the decoy fire and saved what they could of their sails, charts, and navigational equipment. Butman sailed back north, eventually reaching New York. Gibert was now a wanted man.

Gibert remained near Florida for a few months and then in March 1833 he was off the West African coast. By this time slaving was illegal in British territories, but an illicit trade continued to supply the West Indian plantations and Gibert hoped to secure a human cargo. Instead, he ran into HMS *Curlew*. The Royal Navy warship, patrolling Guinea waters, crossed the *Panda*'s wake and turned to engage. Gibert's small crew was no match for the British sailors as they boarded. Gibert and his crew were arrested as unlawful slave traders and shipped to England. It took a few months to establish their true identity, but as soon as it became known, Gibert and his 11 fellow pirates were extradited to the United States to stand trial for piracy. In a Boston courtroom they faced the men they had left to die on the *Mexican*. The outcome was inevitable. Two pirates—described as a "negro cook" and an "Indian" —were acquitted, but six received custodial sentences for murder and piracy, and Pedro Gibert and his three senior officers were sentenced to death. They hanged in 1835, the last pirates to be executed in the United States of America.

A scene depicting the pirates rowing across from the *Panda* to board the *Mexican*.

CHAPTER TWELVE

Piracy in the Far East

From vast powerbases to fragmented tribalism

Opposite: An early 19th-century map of the "East India Isles" shows the complex mass of the Indonesian archipelago and the Indo-China coast up to the island of Hainan—ideal havens for bands of organized pirates.

In the West, the issuing of letters of marque as a means of condoning piracy against another sovereign state was a common convenience—adopted when needed, dropped when not. However, in the Far East the combination of piracy and politics was taken to far greater heights, especially in the South China Sea, where the mix frequently produced pirate states powerful enough to influence the rise and fall of imperial dynasties. Piracy in the waters of the East Indies had a more tribal nature, with different cultures pitched against each other, while also preying on the passing shipping of occidental or oriental merchants. Piracy in the Far East was eventually suppressed by the European powers, first curbed by the arrival of heavily armed Portuguese merchantmen, then English and Dutch warships, and finally the steamships and modern armament that decimated the older fleets of pirate junks.

Edward Cree, a Royal Naval surgeon, painted this watercolor of *A Boatload of Piratical Rascals*, prisoners taken by the fleet after the attack on the pirate force of Shap-'ng-Tsai in 1849 (*page 213*).

Pirates are recorded in Chinese annals as being active in the waters of the South China Sea since before the establishment of the Sui dynasty in AD 589. The end of the Han dynasty in AD 220 created a political void and China fragmented into a number of warring petty states. For almost 400 years local rulers and minor warlords dominated stretches of the Chinese coast, trading where they could and

A Boatload of Piratical Rascals

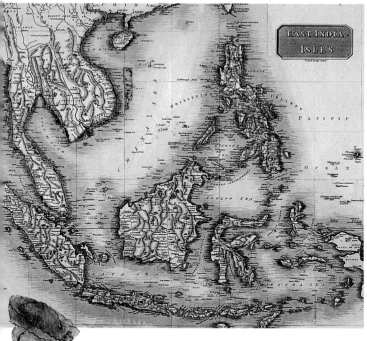

raiding their neighbors' shipping. The great rivers— the Yangtze, Yellow, and Pearl—as wide in some places as small seas, offered enormous opportunities for raiding. While central control was re-established and then lost again during the centuries between the rise of the Sui dynasty and the foundation of the stabilizing Ming dynasty in 1368, imperial power was frequently unable to control the coastal waters of the vast Chinese empire.

In the 13th century there arose a fearsome breed of pirates known as *wako*, from the Chinese for "Japanese bandit," who—in various waves—were to be a continual threat to Chinese and Korean trade for three centuries. Political unrest in Japan from the 13th to the 16th centuries meant that little central authority was exercised to rein in the *wako*, and in many cases local Japanese potentates benefited from the piracy and were therefore disinclined to curb it.

Reacting to Chinese pressure, the Japanese Kamakura Bakufu (government) made some efforts to control the pirates after 1227, even executing some seafarers in front of envoys. But with the collapse of Kamakura power after 1333, pirate raids resumed on an even larger scale. The *wako* pirates attacked Chinese and Korean coastal towns in force, sailing in ships large enough to carry 300 men. Villages were terrorized far from the sea, since pirate junks could sail deep inland, especially on the Yangtze. Although Chinese maritime trade flourished during the 13th and 14th centuries, and Chinese merchants established contact as far afield as the basin of the Indian Ocean, it was only in the 15th century that the Ming rulers regained control of Chinese waters from the pirates who infested it. This control was often based on the poor expedient of paying local rulers to suppress piracy; setting a thief to catch a thief, a policy to be repeated until the 20th century.

By the time of the second phase of activity in the 16th century, the composition of *wako* pirate groups had changed, becoming predominantly Chinese in character, while still operating from Japanese coastal islands. In this period the pirates were greatly aided by the prevailing Ming policy which, after an extraordinary level of maritime activity (*see page 25*), had suddenly closed the ports in 1433, to both foreigners and Chinese ships. The Ming emperor moved the imperial court from Nanjing to Beijing, far away from the great mercantile region. This coincided with a resurgent Confucian preference for isolationism in order to keep dangerous foreign ideas at bay. One consequence of this loss of interest in sea commerce, was an increased emphasis on using the greatly expanded Grand Canal for internal shipping, thus avoiding the dangerous South China and Yellow seas. Further, the

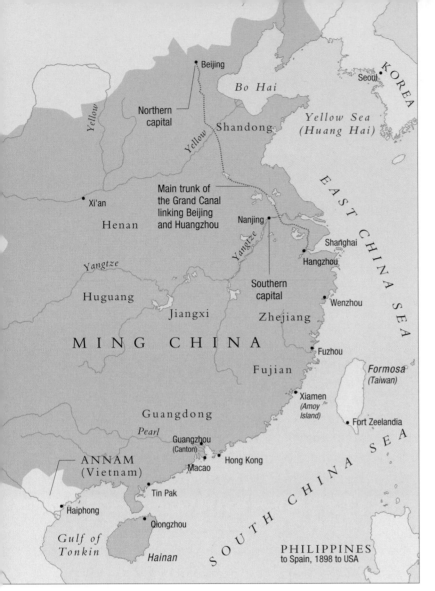

Ming dynasty downgraded the navy, leaving the sea and coasts in the hands of *wako* pirates. Raids as far afield as the Gulf of Siam brought whole coastal regions from Vietnam to Manchuria under *wako* domination.

In the 16th century European sea travelers reached the Far East and opened up trade routes between China, Japan, the Philippines, and Europe. They reported pirate activity in Chinese waters and also further south, in the confined waters of the Indonesian archipelago. There is evidence that that the Portuguese were granted the permission to found a settlement at Macao in the 1550s in exchange for co-operating with Ming forces against the *wako*. While the threat from "Japanese" pirates diminished in the 16th century, rival Chinese pirate empires sprang up along the coast bordering the South China Sea to take their place. Indeed, given the predominantly Chinese composition of *wako* groups it could be argued that only the name by which the pirates were known changed. A Japanese influence is to be seen in the first of the great Chinese pirate-empire builders, Kuo Hsing Yeh.

The pirate who fought to save an empire

Kuo Hsing Yeh, sometimes recorded as Koxinga, was born in 1624, probably in Nagasaki, Japan. His mother was Japanese and his father, Cheng Chih Lung, a successful merchant from Fujian province in southeast China. By the late 1620s Cheng Chih Lung owned a substantial fleet of war and trading junks, based in the busy port of Xiamen (Amoy Island), Fujian. He also traded with Europeans, who were becoming increasingly common in Chinese waters. All this, in spite of the Ming ban on maritime trade, was possible because the government, weakened by its own weight of imperial intrigue and unable to properly face the threat of the invading Manchus from the north, was tottering. The weakness of central authority left Cheng Chih Lung free to expand his powerbase and, by the early 1630s, his ships controlled most of the coast of Fujian and the large island of Formosa (Taiwan) opposite. He was the virtual overlord of the area, maintaining a tightly guarded monopoly of mercantile trade.

His war junks guarded local shipping but also operated as pirates, raiding from the mouth of the Yangtze in the northeast to the island of Hainan in the south. Across this swathe of bustling seas, merchants had to pay protection money to his captains or face the loss of their ships and cargoes. As Manchu gains in the north in 1641 threatened the very existence of the Ming court—which had returned to the safety" of Nanjing—the emperor appointed Cheng Chih Lung to a salaried naval officer's position, with the ironic title "Admiral in Charge of Pirate Suppression." Emperor Zhu Youlang, in desperate straits, needed allies wherever he could find them. When invading Manchu forces captured Nanjing in 1644, Cheng Chih Lung invited Zhu Youlang to set up court in Fuzhou, in Fujian. But the last Ming emperor was a political pawn in a power game. Two years later the pirate-admiral concluded a deal with the new Manchu rulers, who had already declared the Qing imperial dynasty in Beijing. The province of Fujian submitted to Qing authority, but with local power resting in Cheng Chih Lung's hands. In return he almost certainly had Zhu Youlang assassinated. However, it was a poor deal, as the warlord discovered when he later attended the court to receive his reward from the hands of the new emperor; Shunzhi had Cheng Chih Lung thrown into prison and executed for piracy shortly afterward.

The message was not lost on his son. As Manchu forces occupied Fujian, 22-year-old Kuo Hsing Yeh took over the reins of his father's homemade empire and escaped with most of the family's fleet to Formosa. The island—which originally received its European name from a Portuguese seaman who first sighted it from his galleon and cried out "IIha Formosa!" (beautiful island)—had been colonized by the Dutch since 1624. Spanish traders, who had forced their way onto the island's northernmost tip two years later, were finally evicted by the Dutch in 1642. Just a few years after this, the arrival of Kuo Hsing Yeh and his large pirate force was not welcomed. Having no doubt traded in one form or another with Cheng Chih Lung, the Dutch had no illusions about his son and what the outcome of his arrival might mean. For the time being, a state of uneasy truce existed, but friction between the two groups promised a rocky future.

While the Qing dynasty established its control over the mainland, the pirates retained naval supremacy in the Formosa Strait, relatively safe from attack on their island fortress. Kuo Hsing Yeh, determined to avenge his father's treacherous murder, declared war and raised again the Ming banner. Those who still hankered after the Ming imperium heard his war cry, which acted as a rallying point for the rebels. Formosan junks attacked Manchu shipping and effectively blockaded the mouth of the Yangtze river, cutting Nanjing off from all European and Chinese maritime commerce. In 1649 or 1650 the pirates switched from static strategy and launched an amphibious invasion of Xiamen. Kuo Hsing Yeh's rebel forces captured the port and, using this as a base, proceeded to clear Fujian of Qing troops within a year. For the time being, his powerbase was secure. He resumed his father's activities; his pirate fleets dominated the region, and his trading junks sailed as far afield as Japan. The less powerful Manchu navy

Model of a common trading junk to be found almost anywhere along the Chinese coast and the many inlets and river estuaries. Such junks were Chinese pirates' main targets, European shipping being too well armed to be attractive prizes.

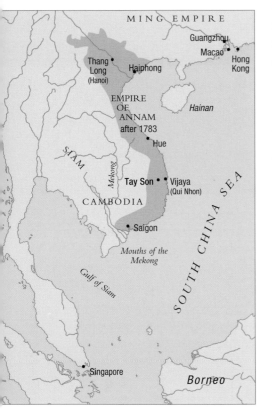

A typical junk pennant.

abandoned the South China Sea and for a decade Kuo Hsing Yeh maintained complete control of its coastal waters, from the mouth of the Yangtze to the Mekong delta.

This state of affairs was not destined to last. Small eruptions of Ming support were a constant irritant to the Qing emperor, and an offensive against Fujian was imperative, although without a naval advantage it remained a tough proposition. In the end, it was Kuo Hsing Yeh who provided the opportunity when he agreed to support a foolhardy attempt to drive the Qing court out of Nanjing. In 1659 he sent a fleet up the Yangtze as part of a combined Ming land and sea assault on the city. His ships were trapped and destroyed. With Ming power finally wiped out in China, the triumphant Qing army swept south, forcing Kuo Hsing Yeh to abandon Fujian for Formosa a second time. No longer possessed of any affability after the Nanjing failure, Kuo Hsing Yeh fell on the Dutch colonists and finally drove them out of Formosa in 1661. He maintained his business monopoly of the region's seas, and his trading and pirate fleets continued to dominate until his death in 1683. Today, Kuo Hsing Yeh is revered as a national hero of Taiwan for his success in driving out foreign imperialism, for his valiant defense of Ming culture and civilization, and also for being a ruthless pirate warlord.

The largest pirate confederation

Kuo Hsing Yeh's achievement of conducting piracy on such a massively strategic level was never repeated elsewhere. By the start of the 18th century the Qing dynasty, having successfully and ruthlessly established its power over the whole empire, was able to temporarily end widespread piracy in Chinese waters. This, however, only drove pirates to other quarters, such as Annam (Vietnam), where political upheaval in the country created an environment attractive to sea robbers. Numerous pirate fleets joined forces with petty rulers to attack their allies' rivals and harass their shipping, a situation also found in the political and tribal rivalry of the Indonesian archipelago. The state of relative peace in the South China Sea endured until about the end of the century, when there was a rapid resurgence of piracy, partly as a result of the Tay Son Rebellion (1771–1802) in Annam. This popular uprising led by three brothers from the village of Tay Son, west of modern-day Qui Nhon, overthrew several China-lackey despots and went a long way toward uniting the country. Under the secure Tay Son banner, Siamese and Chinese armies were repulsed and the brothers welcomed any, especially pirates, who attacked the Chinese.

By now comfortably settled into imperial isolation, the Qing administration proved unequal to the task of suppressing the new pirate groups once again infesting the South China Sea from their pirate havens in Annam. From their midst emerged the piratical dynasty of Ching Yih, who was to lead the largest pirate confederation ever known. While Tay Son provided a safe haven for pirates who operated as their allies, Ching Yih organized pirates into a force powerful enough to resist attack from all-comers, including the forces of the emperor of China.

Ching Yih (also written as Cheng I or Zheng Yi) was probably born in Annam in 1756, the son of a Chinese Tay Son pirate. His father and fellow pirates were engaged in the Vietnamese civil war, but Ching Yih had other plans. In 1801 he married a prostitute, who is known to history as Ching Yih Sao (literally, wife of Ching Yih)—a woman of extraordinary determination and energy, literally her husband's right hand. At the time of their marriage Ching Yih had the command of a modest fleet of pirate junks. He left Annam for the island-dotted coasts of Guangdong province and soon gained control of the pirate fleets who dominated the Chinese coastline, especially among the islands in the mouth of the Pearl River, near Macao and Guangzhou (Canton). Within four years, and with a genius for management, he had combined the fleets into a large naval confederation organized along rigid lines. This was divided into six fleets, each identified by its own color: black, white, red, blue, yellow, and green. Ching Yih allocated each color its own area of operations in order to avoid argument and the possibility that they might fight each other, and each fleet was given its own base. Ching Yih controlled the red fleet, based near Guangzhou, and gave the commanders of the other five the latitude to operate their fleets as they saw fit, while maintaining a loose control over the whole pirate confederation.

The exotic antics of orientals thrilled European newspaper readers, and in this broadsheet illustration of 1836 a wicked Chinese pirate chases a peasant to chop off his head. However, the lurid imagery hinted at the terror tactics employed by coastal pirates to keep the local populations under their subjugation.

The confederation comprised 200 pirate junks at the start, but this force steadily grew. In 1804 Ching Yih blockaded Macao, ostensibly because the Portuguese governor refused to pay protection money. A Portuguese relief force drove the pirates off after several weeks, but nonetheless, Ching Yih had demonstrated his power as a maritime warlord. Portugal was not the only European power with interests in the region—Dutch, British, French, and American trade missions had wharves upriver at Guangzhou, and government-limited concessions with Chinese merchants. Of all the European powers, the only substantial permanent naval presence was that of Britain, which assumed responsibility for patrolling the coast off Macao, but Royal Navy strength was insufficient to reduce the pirate threat

British sailor John Turner survived his encounter with pirates from Ching Yih's band in 1806. The story of his experiences as a captive made sensational reading when he was later rescued and returned to British protection in Guangzhou.

Among many items captured by the Royal Navy in raids on pirate bases was this sword, decorated with a tail of human hair.

appreciably. By 1807 Ching Yih directly commanded over 600 pirate junks and around 30,000 seamen, while the organization as a whole mustered over 150,000 fighting men, making it the largest pirate confederation in history.

Protection money was extorted from ship owners all around the South China Sea, and the confederation effectively dominated the region, politically and militarily. The exceptions were usually European trade ships, since Ching Yih realized that while he was able to repel any Chinese punitive expedition sent against him, the Royal Navy was not so easily deterred. Nevertheless, the European trade mission complained and, during the first decade of the 19th century, the Chinese emperor tried to eradicate the pirate threat. A Chinese naval campaign was unsuccessful, however, and a subsequent imperial amnesty produced only disappointing results. A primary reason for the Chinese initiative's failure was Ching Yih's strategic fleet organization; whenever navy ships attacked a base of one color, fleets of the other colors were summoned and the threat repelled.

The pirate warlord died at the height of his power in late 1807, washed, it was said, overboard in a storm. When his wife Cheng Yih Sao (also rendered as Ching Shih or Zheng Yi Sao) took over control of the red fleet, Ching Yih's bisexual male lover Chang Pao became the new bedmate of the late pirate's wife. Cheng Yih Sao developed into a fearsome pirate leader, and her red fleet dominated the approaches to Macao and the European enclaves in Guangzhou. Unlike her husband, she was not afraid of the consequences of attacking European ships. Within three years, the confederation elected Cheng Yih Sao to lead. Her rules were harsh and strictly enforced, one of which—not surprisingly, given her gender—made the rape of female captives a capital offense, punishable by immediate beheading. Several Chinese expeditions were sent to crush the confederation, but she defeated them all. While the emperor failed by military means, he did succeed through political maneuvers by arranging an amnesty and offering pardons to the pirates. The policy of "divide and rule" worked—offered lucrative imperial markets, many of the senior pirate captains saw the benefits of being legal. Discipline faltered, loyalties split, and colored pirate fleets began fighting one another, which further diminished the organization's influence.

By 1810, the confederation was in disarray. Cheng Yih Sao bowed to the inevitable and accepted a pardon, although she maintained her position at the head of a major smuggling operation well into the 1840s. She died in her 60s, the madam of a well-run brothel in Guangzhou. Chang Pao surrendered the red fleet en masse, received a commission into the imperial navy, and turned pirate-hunter. For the next decade the ex-pirate scoured the waters of the South China Sea, until he destroyed all traces of the massive pirate empire that had been created by his former lovers.

Last of the great Chinese pirates

One of the commodities smuggled by Cheng Yih Sao would almost certainly have been opium, banned in China in the previous century for its deleterious effects on the populace. Despite this, the Chinese market for opium was expanding, and Guangzhou was at the center of the illegal trade. Portugal first introduced porcelain, tea, silk, and other Asian luxury goods to Europe, and by the mid-18th century these items were in high demand, particularly tea and particularly among the British. However, the Qing authorities demanded payment in coin and their refusal to trade in goods was creating a serious imbalance of payments. The British possessed an abundance of Indian-grown opium, which they needed to sell, and so the East India Company positively encouraged addiction in China. This meant it could bully the Chinese merchants, desperate for opium's quick profits, to risk breaking the law and purchase in coin, thus redressing its net outflow of payments to China for tea.

The friction the illegal opium trade created led to the eruption of warfare between China and Britain. The First Opium War (1839–42) resulted in the decisive defeat of the Chinese, and the emperor was forced to sign a humiliating treaty with the Europeans. During the war Hong Kong, situated on an island across the Pearl estuary from Macao, was first occupied by the British in 1841, and then formally ceded in 1842 under the Treaty of Nanjing. It became a crown colony in the following year. China also ceded five more ports in Guangdong to European trade, including Guangzhou, which had previously been restricted to small national

Cheng Yih Sao enforced her pirate rule with great vigor, as this contemporary newspaper illustration attempts to show.

211

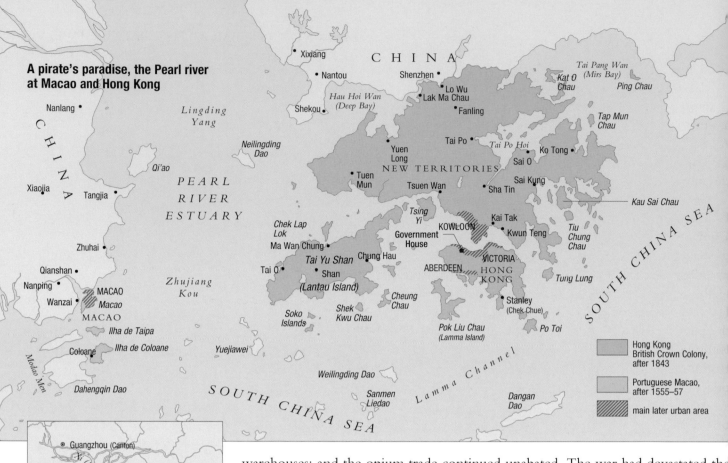

A pirate's paradise, the Pearl river
at Macao and Hong Kong

Hong Kong
British Crown Colony,
after 1843

Portuguese Macao,
after 1555–57

main later urban area

warehouses; and the opium trade continued unabated. The war had devastated the Chinese imperial navy along the South China Sea coast, and the Royal Navy was only concerned with protecting European interests. Consequently, many Chinese turned to piracy, and a new pirate infestation threatened the region.

Like Ching Yih before him, Shap-'ng-Tsai was a pirate who operated along the coasts of Guangdong and Fujian provinces. Based at Tin Pak, 175 miles west of the British treaty port of Hong Kong, he rose to prominence as the leader of a pirate band soon after the war's end. By the end of the 1840s Shap-'ng-Tsai's pirate fleet had grown to include more than 70 vessels, and his group extorted protection money from Chinese traders from Hong Kong to Haiphong in Annam. His men also attacked British and American vessels off the treaty ports, capturing one American and three British opium-carrying clipper ships.

In the vicinity of Hong Kong, traders not only suffered blackmail at the hands of Chinese pirates in the approaches to the Pearl river, but were also subjected to lawless plundering by the crews of the colony's gunboats claiming to be collecting taxes on behalf of the Guangzhou harbor authorities. As a result, the peaceful trading junk of the period had to sail heavily armed, so much so that there was frequently nothing but the cargo to distinguish a trading junk from a pirate.

Shap-'ng-Tsai was uncommonly well informed of everything that was going on in the treaty ports, for several reasons. The pirate ranks were frequently swelled by the enlistment of outlaw European seamen, who came armed with the latest intelligence. The leaders of his piratical fleets made Hong Kong their headquarters, where native chandlers not only supplied them with arms and ammunition and fenced their booty, but furnished them with vital information. A lot of this was gathered through well-paid spies in the mercantile offices and government departments, information such as the shipments of valuable cargo and the movements of tax bullion payments or Royal Navy gunboats to protect them.

Governor Sir George Bonham and the Royal Navy commander of the Far East squadron based at Hong Kong agreed with East India Company officials that steps should be taken to bring the pirate attacks to a close. In September 1849 a punitive expedition comprising a naval squadron of steam warships led by Commander (later Admiral) John Charles Dalrymple Hay entered the pirate base at Tin Pak, only to find that the pirates had flown, forewarned by their spies in Hong Kong. The raid was not a complete failure because the British captured over one hundred junks in the harbor, prizes that the pirates had intended to hold for ransom. In a bizarre twist, the British sold the junks to their former owners under the laws of international salvage. To the ship owners, the result was the same as if the pirates had held onto the vessels. A second pirate base at Bias Bay, east of Hong Kong, was also destroyed, although many of the pirates escaped inland.

T'ien Hou, the provider of fair weather and calmer of storms, appears on this silk flag taken from the flagship of Shap-'ng-Tsai in October 1849.

The Royal Navy pursued Shap-'ng-Tsai and his pirate fleet into the Gulf of Tong King (Tonkin). By October they had discovered the new pirate lair in the delta of the Tong King (Hongha) river, among the channels and delta islands north of the port of Haiphong in Annam. Commander Dalrymple Hay blockaded the mouth of the river to prevent escape, then steamed into action. His force consisted of two steam warships and the East India Company paddle-steamer *Phlegethon*, accompanied by a squadron of imperial Chinese junks. The pirates were caught napping, lying at anchor when the British and Chinese warships arrived. After crossing the sandbar at the river's entrance, the warships bombarded the pirate junks, which were unable to swing around and effectively return fire because of the river's fast current. Over 1800 pirates were killed and 58 pirate vessels were sunk or captured. Shap-'ng-Tsai escaped upriver, accompanied by a handful of pirates and six small junks. He soon took advantage of an offer of the emperor's pardon and a commission into the Chinese navy, a typical Chinese method of combating piracy.

After 1849, Britain maintained a permanent naval presence in the South China Sea, the "China Station" based at Hong Kong. Although incidents of piracy

Vietnamese villagers massacre the survivors of Shap-'ng-Tsai's pirate fleet after its destruction by the Royal Navy.

As headhunters with little interest in ransom payments, the Sea Dyaks were the East Indies' most feared pirates.

continued throughout the remainder of the 19th century, the superior technology of Royal Navy warships ensured that pirates were no longer a serious threat.

Pirate islands of the East Indies

At its southern end, the South China Sea washes against the shores of Malaya, Borneo, and the Indonesian Archipelago, fragmented countries with endless complex coasts, home to numerous small-time, tribal pirates. Shipping from the Spice Islands was particularly vulnerable in the Java Sea, and any vessels sailing between China and Europe had to run the gauntlet of the narrow Strait of Malacca. As British colonial Hong Kong had eventually tamed the northern part of the South China Sea, so Singapore was to do for the East Indies. The islands of Southeast Asia created an ideal pirate haven. Bands of local tribal pirates preyed on the shipping of colonial European powers and the craft of other local peoples. During the 18th and 19th centuries, apart from enclaves controlled by Europeans, most of the region was split into a patchwork of small tribal districts. The arrival of the Dutch irretrievably damaged the two largest power blocks, those of the Javanese and Malayan rulers, and the archipelago's political fragmentation continued until the late 19th century.

Frequently changing alliances between these groups and almost incessant warfare meant that no single power dominated the archipelago and its sea-lanes. Many of these minor kingdoms and tribal groupings used piracy as a means of support, and it frequently formed part of their official tribal policy. The increased presence of Europeans, mainly through the establishment of Dutch trading posts, altered the unstable nature of this regional patchwork. With their lack of respect for local alliances, the colonial Europeans continually interfered through first their support of, and then abandonment of local potentates. The consequence was that, by the 19th century, Europeans were distrusted and their ships singled out for pirate attack.

The Ilanun of the Philippines were the most feared of all the pirates in the East Indies, closely followed by the Balanini pirates of the Sulu Sea, northeast of Borneo. And yet there is evidence to suggest that these people had not always been piratical. Early observers, including the buccaneer William Dampier, who later sailed with Woodes Rogers, described the Ilanun people as being peaceable, so their reliance on piracy must have developed during the 18th century. They not only plagued the waters of the Philippines but also raided far out into the South China Sea. Ilanun raids were often designed to gather slaves, which were then traded in the markets of Sumatra and Java. The Ilanun augmented these large-scale raids with attacks on Spanish shipping around Manila, and the occasional foray against passing Dutch and British Indiamen. Like many East Indian pirates, they used *prahus*, shallow-drafted canoes rowed by slaves. Based on the small island of Jolo, the Balanini pirates were also well placed to engage in slave raiding and attacks on Spanish vessels sailing to and from the Philippines. Their preferred craft was the *corocoro*, a fast-sailing vessel fitted with outriggers that could be powered by sail or oar. A *corocoro* could displace as much as 100 tons and carry as many as 60 pirates, although most were smaller.

Other pirate groups included the Bugis of Sulawesi (the Celebes), who combined trading with piracy, depending on economic conditions. They were described as "the most mercenary, bloodthirsty, inhuman race." To the west, the Atjeh (Achin) and Riau pirates of Sumatra—called sea dacoits—specialized in harassing ships in the Malacca and Sunda straits. The Dyak pirates of Borneo used a variant of the *prahu* called the *bangkong*. By the 1830s, the Dyaks were the most feared pirates of the region.

Predictably, as European trading expanded enormously in the East Indies, pressure from ship owners, merchants, and insurers led to the establishment of a permanent naval base to protect shipping and drive off the pirates. In 1819 Stamford Raffles founded the British colony of Singapore, which was ideally placed to dominate the waters of the Strait of Malacca. In 1836 a combined Royal Navy and East India Company squadron was based in the port, charged with sweeping the strait of pirates. Following the success of this operation, the British launched punitive expeditions against the Dyaks and the Malay pirates and destroyed their power bases. By the 1860s Spanish and British naval expeditions had wiped out the Ilanun and Balanini pirates, and although piracy was never completely suppressed, the Indonesian archipelago was considered safe for shipping. Descendants of the Philippine and Indonesian pirates would revert to piracy during the late 20th century, but they would be armed with assault rifles, not spears.

TO A GENEROUS PUBLIC.

I am a poor young man who have had the misfortune of having my Tongue cut out of my mouth on my passage home from the Coast of China, to Liverpool, in 1845, by the Malay Pirates, on the Coast of Malacca. There were Fourteen of our Crew taken prisoners and kept on shore four months; some of whom had their eyes put out, some their legs cut off, for myself I had my Tongue cut out.

We were taken about 120 miles to sea; we were then given a raft and let go, and were three days and three nights on the raft, and ten out of fourteen were lost. We were picked up by the ship James, bound to Boston, in America, and after our arrival we were sent home to Liverpool, in the ship Sarah James.

Two of my companions had trades before they went to sea, but unfortunately for me having no Father or Mother living, I went to sea quite young. I am now obliged to appeal to a Generous Public for support, and any small donation you please to give will be thankfully received by

Your obedient servant,

WILLIAM EDWARDS.

P.S.—I sailed from Liverpool on the 28th day of May, 1844, on board the Jane Ann, belonging to Mr. Spade, William Jones, Captain. Signed by Mr. Rushton, Magistrate, Liverpool, Mr. Smith, and Mr. Williams, after I landed in Liverpool on the 10th December, 1845.

J. Southward, printer, of Upper Pitt Street, Liverpool published this sad tale of a young British sailor who fell victim to Malay pirates in the Strait of Malacca.

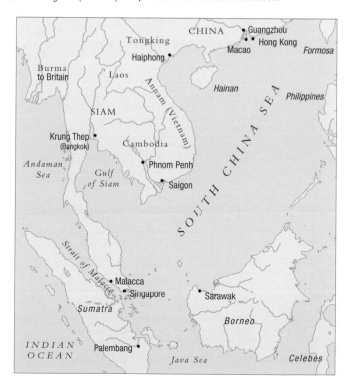

215

CHAPTER THIRTEEN

Home, Sweet Home

Pirate havens from the 15th century to the modern era

Suitable entrepôts for the storage and disposal of plunder have been a by-product of piracy throughout the ages. The names of the islands and ports in and around the Spanish Main that hosted pirates in the 15th to 19th centuries became synonymous with high adventure and carefree lawlessness. Yet in most cases these settlement started as officially sanctioned operations before they turned into something far less savory. The following represents only a short list of the most infamous.

Named by the French after its resemblance at a distance to the shell of a turtle Île de la Tortue (Turtle Island), or Tortuga to the English-speaking buccaneer who later frequented it, lies off the northwestern coast of Hispaniola (modern Haiti). At first a refuge to (mostly Huguenot) French cattle hunters (*boucaniers* evading Spanish troops, the island housed a small settlement by 1620, when its inhabitants took to attacking passing Spanish ships. Spanish punitive raids on the island throughout the 1630s failed to drive out the early buccaneers and in 1642 the French West Indies authority, based at St. Kitts and Martinique, appointed

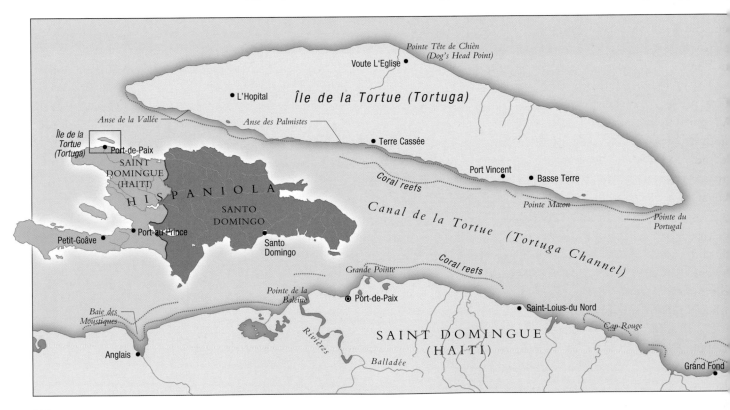

ean le Vasseur to be governor. He constructed a fortress to guard the harbor nd successfully repulsed a Spanish attack, which fact encouraged more French uccaneers to seek refuge on Tortuga. Leaning toward he view that buccaneers could protect the island far etter than a generally absent French navy, le Vasseur roke ties with Martinique, and made the island an ndependent haven for new buccaneers. Many of his uccessors continued to follow this autonomous policy.

Tortuga acquired an international reputation after Englishman Elias Watts secured a commission as governor in 1656. He recruited English and French ailors as both buccaneers and settlers, and sponsored he start of the main buccaneering period, a phase that asted for two decades. Watts only lasted three years efore another Frenchman expelled him, but from that oint on seamen of all the main European maritime owers flocked to Tortuga. During the 1660s, French ettlements spread along the northern and western oasts of Hispaniola. For some 12 years, these colonists ooked to Tortuga for protection and paid for the rivilege, but by the early 1670s Petit-Goâve had eplaced it as the principal buccaneer entrepôt because t provided better markets for the sale of contraband. Tortuga remained in use on a maller scale by privateers and pirates until the early 18th century.

In 1494, during the second voyage of exploration made by Christopher Columbus, the Spanish crew first saw Tortuga and named it "Turtle" because of its humped shape rising from the sea. The name was doubly appropriate because the island's beaches were populated by giant turtles during the egg-laying season. The large beasts made fine pirate food.

The New World's Sodom

When Oliver Cromwell's English soldiers under the command of General Venables aptured Jamaica from the Spanish in 1655 (*see page 99*), they found an easily efended natural harbor on the southern shore at its eastern end. A narrow, rojecting spur enclosed a deep bay, and the quickly built facilities became Port Royal. Since Spanish reprisals were anticipated, the English extended courtesies o those English buccaneers operating out of Tortuga and lured many away by ffering a safe haven. Port Royal was in many respects better situated than Tortuga or raiding on the Spanish Main and soon dozens of buccaneer ships were based in he harbor. Even after peace was declared with Spain in 1660, Jamaican governors ontinued to encourage attacks on the Spanish as a means of aggressive defense, a olicy bound to attract even more sailors of fortune, few of them with any scruples.

By the mid-1660s the buccaneers made Port Royal a thriving, lawless boomtown f 6000 people and brought huge profits to plantation owners and investors alike. While the island's elite hid behind their perfumed handkerchiefs amid pleasant lantation mansions, the rest of the seething mass enjoyed every depravity known.

Above: Port Royal, rebuilt but on a much reduced scale after the 1692 earthquake that destroyed the buccaneers' haven. Kingston is visible on the far shore; painting by Paton Richard (1717–91). **Below:** This plan of Port Royal shows the pre-earthquake town and—shaded—the area of the old town that remained drowned in the 18th century.

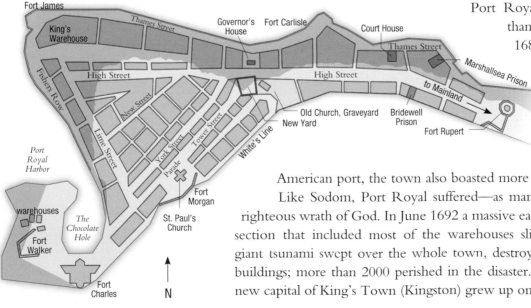

A visiting preacher claimed, "This town is the Sodom of the New World…it population consists of pirates, cut-throats, whores, and some of the vilest persons in the whole of the world." Morgan's sack of Panama led to Governor Modyford's arres and as the new resident governor, Morgan's brief to end buccaneer activities pushed many into full-blown piracy. Suddenly, English vessels were no longer inviolate and attacks on English shipping increased to such an alarming extent that the Jamaican landowners were forced to take measures to protect their business interests. The anti piracy law passed in 1681 began the concerted arrests, convictions, and executions that effectively drove the pirates off to seek other havens in the Bahamas or the Carolinas

Port Royal became a commercial rather than a buccaneering port by the mid 1680s, by which time its population equaled that of Boston. But the visiting preacher would still have found grounds for his disapproval. Along with more marketplaces and warehouses than any other American port, the town also boasted more bars and brothels… and wealth.

Like Sodom, Port Royal suffered—as many at the time saw it—from the righteous wrath of God. In June 1692 a massive earthquake struck and the northern section that included most of the warehouses slid into the sea. Shortly after, giant tsunami swept over the whole town, destroying any but the most substantial buildings; more than 2000 perished in the disaster. Port Royal was rebuilt, but the new capital of King's Town (Kingston) grew up on the shore to the east to dwarf it

Libertatia—no pirate utopia on Madagascar

Whether there was any substance to the pirate utopia of Libertatia or whether it was just a social experiment expressed in the writing of Captain Charles Johnson, there is no denying the contribution of Madagascar to pirate history. Lying astride the rich trade routes between India, the Middle East, and Europe, the large island made a natural and ideal base for pirates. The major trade routes to and from the Far East were squeezed into the relatively narrow—and therefore crowded—channel of some 250 miles in width, between Madagascar and the East African coast. The island is over 300 miles wide at its broadest, and over a thousand miles long, with numerous inlets and safe anchorages. At the time of the Golden Age (1690–1730), the native population was scattered throughout the vast interior and sparse enough for the pirates to disregard as a threat, and the wildlife and fruit plentiful enough to feed everyone.

As the buccaneering era ended in the Caribbean basin in the 1680s, former buccaneers ventured into the Indian Ocean and used bases in northern Madagascar to prey on Indian shipping. These were also within easy range of the Red Sea, where Arab–Indian traffic yielded a substantial haul of plunder. By the 1690s pirates were arriving in Madagascar in increasing numbers and anchorages were established at Ranter Bay (now the Baie d'Antongil), St. Augustine's Bay, and St. Mary's Island, all on the island's east coast. St. Mary's, in particular, was easily defended, and it was reported that by 1700 the islet was home to 17 pirate vessels and 1500 pirates. The nearby but more remote anchorages at Réunion and Mauritius to the east, and Johanna Island in the Comoros to the northwest, were equally important.

With the turn of the century, the navies of England, France, and the Netherlands made repeated campaigns to eradicate the pirate threat in the Indian Ocean and by 1711 it was reported that only 60 or 70 pirates remained on Madagascar. Many of them moved elsewhere, particularly to India, where they entered into service with the Angrian pirates; others settled on the island and took up farming. Perhaps this last gave rise to the notion of a pirate utopia. In his *A General History of the Robberies and Murders of the Most Notorious Pyrates* (1724), Charles Johnson relates the tale of French pirate Captain Misson, who established a pirate republic on Madagascar that he called Libertatia. The settlement described by Johnson was an early leveling and egalitarian community, in which pirates and other inhabitants supported the rights of the people, made and enforced their own laws, and enshrined the concept of liberty. In effect, Libertatia was a utopia built on socialist principles, before the phrase had

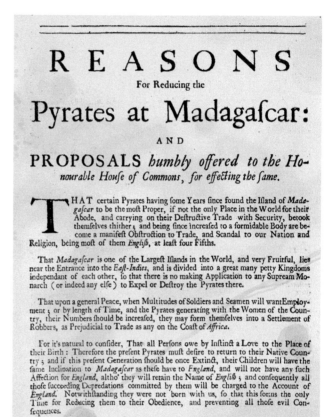

A document dating to the first years of the 18th century proposing that the British parliament should offer an amnesty to all "pyrates" residing in Madagascar—one way of ridding the Indian Ocean of the problem.

A life of peace and leisure is the promise held out in this woodcut of *A Pyrate and a Madagascar Woman*. Captain Johnson's utopian vision of Libertatia was a fiction but a number of pirates accepted governmental amnesties, took local wives, and settled down on Madagascar to earn an honest living. Their life, however, was almost certainly a deal tougher than this idyllic illustration suggests.

been coined. Captured slaves were manumitted, everyone enjoyed the freedom to worship as they saw fit, and wounded and elderly pirates were cared for, so that the could die in peace and security.

Unfortunately, neither Captain Misson nor Libertatia existed. The historia Christopher Hill argues that Johnson's chapter is really a political essay disguised a a pirate history, with echoes of the English Revolution of the mid-17th centur nd an expression of the oppressively harsh conditions faced by early 18th-century eamen. We see no hospice care for poor abandoned Edward England (*see page 46*), and in 1711 the pirates on St. Mary's Island were reported as living in squalor, most of them very poor and despicable, even to the natives."

Where have all the pirates gone?

When the English authorities tightened their grip on Jamaica and closed Port Royal o buccaneers, a handful moved to the north of Cuba to find a new home in the Bahamas and settled on New Providence during the 1680s. The first settlement vas short-lived, destroyed by a Spanish expedition in 1684, but more English uccaneers moved there from Tortuga in 1698. The small settlement of Nassau cted as a spasmodic market for some pirates, but its critical mass was insufficient or survival, and by 1704 it was all but abandoned. What a difference only a few ears can make! When Henry Jennings sailed into Nassau in 1716 he found a perfect haven for pirates, vith a harbor deep enough for small ships but too hallow for warships, a good supply of food and water, nd high hills to provide lookout points. He was not lone; those pirates who had already discovered the nchorage were soon joined by many others, and for few hectic years in the second decade of the 18th entury it was the hotbed center of pirate activity in he Americas.

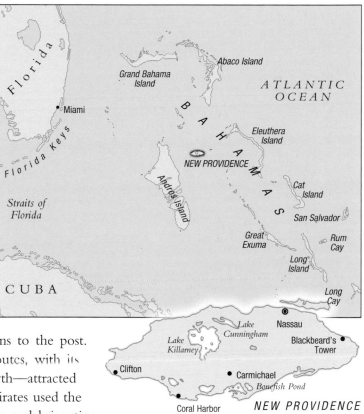

Aside from its natural advantages as a pirate tronghold, there were almost no settlers to upset. Any indigines had died out long before and its tiny andmass of about 60 square miles was not enough o support any plantations, so most landowners lived n larger Eleuthera, further to the east. Until 1718 Bahamian civic leaders were appointed from among hese landowners and, since they went in fear of he pirates, they invariably appointed one of their captains to the post. Consequently, New Providence—close to major trade routes, with its ne harbor and no central authority to curb piratical growth—attracted ust about every pirate in the region. By 1717 over 500 pirates used the sland as a base, serving in a score of ships, mainly sloops and brigantines. The patrons of the makeshift shanty taverns of Nassau would have read like a eritable pirate *Who's Who*. Traders and merchants accompanied the freebooters, nd the settlement of Nassau blossomed into a freewheeling market in contraband oods, slaves, and liquor. Proper accommodation was sparse; the few timber shacks f Nassau town were surrounded by a village of tents made from ships' sails and

With the harbor of Port Nassau in the background, the son of Woodes Rogers holds out a drawing of the town's planned expansion he has prepared for his father's approval. William Hogarth's painting captures the formal elegance of an early Hanoverian-period English family, setting a fine example to all colonists.

spars. Nevertheless, everyone was on an earning spree, from the chandlers to th few whores. Shipwrights earned a wage repairing ships or cutting holes in thei hulls for artillery, making them into pirate ships, while armorers repaired guns an swords. Even those not directly engaged in piracy flourished through trading wit the pirates. And then Woodes Rogers arrived, the first crown-appointed governor and the days of New Providence as a pirate haven were over. With the pirates gone the island returned to being a Bahamian backwater. Today, Nassau thrives on it piratical history, and museums, bars, and restaurants all over New Providence bea testimony to the strong links the island has with its past.

Pirate lairs in the Gulf of Mexico

Barataria and Galveston on the United States shores of the gulf, and the norther shore of Cuba made ideal bases for pirate activity during the last wave of pirac that swept the Caribbean basin in the 19th century. Pirates of the period needed reliable market for the sale of their plunder, ideally a substantial city, preferably in region that relied on a slave economy, because slaves continued to be a regular form of plunder. However, the export of slaves to many countries of the Americas was considered illegal, much as slaves were still in demand, so pirate havens also had to be remote from areas of authority, a factor often incompatible with the requirement of a ready market.

A handful of areas provided the special needs of the last American pirates. The most notorious of these was Barataria, the salt-march bay south of New Orleans that provided a base for Jean Laffite. As an inlet to the west of the Mississippi delta, linked to the river by a network of small creeks, canals, and hidden backwaters, the bay's secret communications were perfect. The pirates used the island of Grand Terre as a base, aided by the local Cajun population, who acted as guides to the bayous and alligator-infested lagoons that provided security from attack. The same waterways gave easy access to New Orleans and its market for the sale of plunder. Slaves captured by the pirates were sold to local plantation owners in hidden locations near New Orleans, while informants warned Laffite if they were in danger of attack.

When increased U.S. military presence in the delta made Barataria unsafe, Laffite moved to Galveston in Texas, which, for a few years, became a new safe pirate haven. Unlike New Orleans, Texas was a frontier region, operating outside the authorities of Spain or Mexico on the one hand and the United States and Texan rebels on the other. (In 1836 Texas won freedom from Spain and remained an independent state until 1845, when the U.S. took control.) While the four powers struggled for supremacy, piracy thrived along the remote Texan coasts.

There were several pirate havens, including Matagorda Bay and the Sabine estuary, although by 1817 the small town of Galveston became the supreme pirate base on the Gulf of Mexico. While Galveston Bay provided an escape route inland if Galveston Island was attacked, the town itself became a bustling and cosmopolitan market for pirates, frontiersmen, and Mexican traders. This success also invited the attention of the United States Navy. Attacks on American shipping from pirates based in Galveston provided the excuse to destroy the town, and it was captured and burned in 1820. At which point the axis of pirate activity moved to Cuba's northern coast, with its easy access to the busy shipping lane of the Straits of Florida. Relations between Spain and the United States were—at best—uneasy and Spanish colonial

The New Orleans region and Mississippi delta in a map from about the time of the pirate Jean Laffite. The river's width is exaggerated.

223

New Orleans at the end of the 18th century, with ships alongside the wharves lining the banks of the Mississippi.

officials turned a blind eye to pirate attacks, even actively encouraging piracy as a extra source of revenue. Corruption was rife and pirates, such as Charles Gibb found no problem in buying political protection by giving local authorities a shar of his plunder. American consuls reported that the Spanish mayors in the ports c Matanzas and Caibarién were in league with pirates, as was the governor of th western province of Pinar del Rio.

America countered the threat of Cuban piracy though a diplomatic initiativ that eventually obliged the Spanish authorities to crack down on corrupt officia who condoned piracy, while U.S. Navy forces patrolled the coast. By Decembe 1823, President Monroe was able to note with some satisfaction "the co-operatio of the invigorated administration of Cuba." For the Cubans, it was a less happy c smug outcome than the Americans enjoyed—dispossessed of the water, many pirat turned their back on the sea to become bandits on land. With Cuban plantatior under almost constant attack, it was the turn of the Spanish army rather than th navy to deal with the problem. The situation precipitated disaster for Charles Gibb as a cleaned up Cuba handed the pirate-brigand over to the American authoritie Tried in New York and hanged in 1831, he was one of the last pirates to use th Caribbean as a base.

Pirates, pirates everywhere

In the modern era, almost anywhere in the world can be a pirate haven, an wherever a substantial degree of political instability exists, there pirates will flourisl And yet for much of the 20th century it seemed as though piracy had been eradicate

n all but the most remote locations, generally small-time events involving old-fashioned sailing ships and junks, hardly a matter for any but schoolboys' stories. y the end of the 19th century, steam had replaced sail almost universally in the orld's merchant and military navies, and in the rapid development from boilers hat burned wood to those using coal and then oil, piracy appeared to have been utstripped by progress. The sheer size and speed of modern vessels was thought o preclude pirate attack, and the costs of fitting anything out of any reasonable apability as a pirate ship thought to be too high. This comfortable view prevailed ntil the 1980s, when everything changed and a fresh wave of pirate attacks swept he world's seas and oceans—around the Indonesian archipelago, off China, in the Caribbean, off Africa's coasts, in Brazil's ports and rivers, and even isolated incidents 1 the Mediterranean.

To the 21st-century mind, perhaps the most disturbing aspect of this renewed crime ave is the equal emphasis on seizing passengers as well as cargoes. A society increasingly sed to the extended comforts of packaged cruise-ship vacations is not one readily le to face up to the reality of pirate attack—the entire business feels so "medieval." either is retribution such an easy matter as it used to be in Woodes Rogers' day. The nited Nations' definition of piracy as "any illegal act of violence or detention, or act f depredation committed for *private ends* by the crew or the passengers of a private ship irected on the *high seas*" hinders any sensible response. Not only must victims prove that e attack was made for "private ends" but that the act was committed on the "high seas." his is no easy matter when by far and away the majority of modern piratical attacks take lace in easy sight of land, in territorial waters. Indeed, many "pirates" claim that they are

Photographed in 1991, on their fast outrigger boat, Filipino pirates wait patiently for some passing prey.

China's coastguards, at the forefront of anti-piracy in the South China Sea, have not always been innocent of pirate attacks on international shipping themselves.

really part of regional independence movements and, therefore, freedom fighters. And anyway, you have to catch them first. Many are local fishermen, but instead of fishing nets the crew carries automatic weapons. They operate fast outrigger craft, ideally suited for hit-and-run attacks on passing shipping in the confined coastal waters of Southeast Asia and the Philippines.

Corruption in olden days often denied justice, so it still can. Victims sometimes find that in laying a case before the local authorities, they are actually talking to the sponsors of the piracy. Still other attacks are conducted by representatives of the local government, as the sadly typical case of the Philippines coastguards who illegally seized a Japanese merchant ship in 1995 underlines. In that particular instance, however, the guilty were subsequently convicted in Manila of robbery. Filipino gangs have also been identified as the perpetrators of numerous attacks; regional, religious, and political tensions have given them the excuse to operate openly in Philippine waters. While most of these attacks are mounted against coastal fishermen operating in the Sulu, Mindanao, and Celebes seas, others are more daring: vacationers have been seized and held for ransom—sometimes for financial gain, more often for political leverage.

The South China Sea never really ceased to be a haunt of pirates, but in the 1990s Beijing had to admit that the naval arm of the Chinese Border Patrol might have joined their ranks. In its enthusiasm for pursuing pirates the over-zealous patrol had attacked non-Chinese ships in international waters. Singapore also reacted with severity when in the 1990s attacks began on ships passing through that old pirate haunt, the Strait of Malacca (however without finding excuses to strike out at innocent shipping). These were hit-and-run crimes by robbers using small but fast boats, where the perpetrators made off with money and valuables. In the main there were few casualties, but the fear that resistance might lead to murder was always present. Singapore's strict judicial system that combined corporal punishment with lengthy custodial sentences resulted in a marked decline in these incidents—but only for a brief period (see below).

As ever, political instability anywhere in the world creates the perfect environment for opportunistic piracy. The revolution in Jakarta in 1998 has left the archipelago with a legacy of guerrilla movements that have eroded the government's authority outside the major urban centers, and a fresh wave of pirate attacks have been reported in Indonesian waters. Similarly, on the other side of the world pirate attacks in the Caribbean have become increasingly common since the 1980s. The Colombian and Venezuelan drug barons—sometimes warring with their governments, sometimes with each other—have destabilized the region with their gun-running and drugs transhipments.

Brazil too suffered from a wave of lawlessness that led to widespread attacks on ships in her ports, principally in Rio de Janeiro. Since the mid-1990s the Brazilian authorities have been put under intense pressure to clean up their home waters but mariners still regard Brazilian ports as the most dangerous in the world. Similarly,

On the Mekong river, a Vietnamese river pirate smuggles black market cargoes.

attacks have been reported on the Amazon, which for miles from its mouth is more like an inland sea than a river.

In West Africa, the end of colonial rule sparked an eruption of coup d'états that led to unstable governments, tribal conflict, guerrilla fighting, and eventually civil war. The Nigerian Civil War (1967–70) and similar power struggles in other West African countries plunged the region into a period of anarchy and lawlessness which is not yet entirely over. The general chaos and violence provided a fertile pool for pirates, not all of them common criminals. Some attacks on international shipping were made by the very naval gunboats supposedly engaged in policing the Gulf of Guinea. In 1981 Nigeria's coast was declared the world's most dangerous. For a while, entrenched military rule seemed to curb the worst of the piracy, but conflicts over oil in the region have once again made the waters of the Bight of Benin a dangerous spot.

East Africa has fared no better. After the mid-1980s, as Ethiopia and Somalia became embroiled in their civil wars, ships sailing along the desert coasts of the Indian Ocean came under vicious attack—cargo and passenger vessels alike have suffered. The inhospitable shore between Djibouti and Mogadishu is ideal for hiding pirate bases and a no-go region for any police activity. Even ships using the Suez Canal and the Red Sea have suffered. In some cases liberation movements want to fund their activities, in others short-lived revolutionary government officials seize ships on the grounds that they are infringing territorial waters.

There are authoritative voices who make the case that piratical incidents have increased since the start of the 21st century to such an extent that today the world's seas are as unsafe as at any time in the past. Modern piracy is no longer the preserve of a relatively small number of dissident, dispossessed, or downtrodden outcasts of society but a global underworld industry whose machinery includes unscrupulous bankers as well as industrial muscle. Every year, an alarming number of the world's estimated 45,000 merchant ships disappear. They are not all sunk—most are taken by pirates, especially in the vulnerable Strait

The victims of Filipino pirates are often little more than fishermen. In these two photographs, pirates have captured such a vessel. In the top one the victims can be seen cowering down in the boat's bow. In the picture below, one of them begs a gunman for their lives.

The adolescent, trucculent posing for the camera disguises a real danger from these young men who live on poverty-stricken Bongao. The tiny Philippine island, which lies just of the northeastern tip of Borneo, has no industry, raises few crops of food, but nourishes piracy.

of Malacca, where they are boarded by sea dacoits using high-speed boats. The highjacked vessel is soon hidden in one of the numerous inlets of Sumatra, shielded from view by the dense jungle, where the dacoits go to work to give the ship a complete paint-job overhaul. In no time the pirated vessel is back at sea, re-registered with new, false paperwork and with a new crew, making big profits for the man who originally commissioned the pirates.

This sleight of hand is made possible by the so-called F.O.C. countries, those who offer the service of vessel registration—required by international law—in return for a fee and no questions asked. The ship is then said to be sailing under that country's flag, the so-called "flag of convenience" (F.O.C.), even though it may never visit the port of its registration. It is perhaps an irony that the two countries that pioneered the (relatively) inexpensive flag of convenience were Panama—so ravaged by buccaneers and pirates—and Liberia in West Africa—whose people were so victimized by piratical slavers. There are now tens of F.O.C. countries, and they are under little or no obligation to reveal the details of ship registrations, which makes it hard for the authorities to make checks on the ship's real (and probably illegal) owners. So the original details of the freighter seized by dacoits in the Strait of Malacca vanish into thin air, and new papers registered in a no-questions asked F.O.C. replace them, and no authority can track down the trail.

What can be done to combat this new rash of piracy is being done but it is little, for the cost of establishing even minimal control may run into the billions of dollars. The U.S. Department of State has forged links with other countries to aid in setting up international controls, and establishments have been opened in Hungary, Thailand, and Africa. Those in charge of ports are being urged to attend specialist courses at the renowned World Maritime University in Malmo, Sweden. Better awareness of the pirates' tricks has improved Brazil's previously appalling situation, where ships were regularly stolen from under the port authority's eyes. Greater pressure is being applied to F.O.C. countries to make sure they do not register stolen vessels, and in recognition of the weakness inherent in the United Nations definition given above, a recently agreed article in the Law of the Sea Convention provides a basis for boarding vessels flying questionable flags.

Nevertheless, so long as those in power are unwilling to crush piracy in their waters, the situation will endure and pirates will continue to thrive in the world's unstable regions. To the victims of these crimes, be they tourists on a cultural cruise, local fishermen, passing yachtsmen, or the crews of large merchant ships, modern piracy has no romanticism.

In Batam, Indonesia, pirates operating out of the Riau Islands practice boarding ships with a bamboo rod and grappling hook. Piracy is once again a big problem in the South China Sea, furthered by corrupt officials.

November 2005, the cruise liner *Seabourn Spirit* lies at anchor in the Seychelles after escaping an attack by Somali pirates off the East African coast. Reports suggested that at least two boats closed on the ship, the pirates firing automatic weapons and rocket-propelled grenades. Terrified vacationing passengers could only watch as the *Seabourn Spirit's* crew repelled the attackers without returning fire.

CHAPTER FOURTEEN

Myths, Manners, Codes

The pirate as popular culture and social reformer

Mythmaker—the frontispiece of the French edition of Exquemelin's buccaneer epic.

Treasure Island developed all the elements of the pirate myth for a mass market.

A quick poll conducted outside a dockside tavern in the author's home town showed that the majority of people named Blackbeard as the most readily identifiable pirate. That should not surprise; certainly in the Western mind, much of the popular image dates from the so-called "Golden Age" of piracy, that brief period between 1690 and 1730. Ask anyone to name a pirate and chances are they pick one from that short period, a pinprick of history. Piracy has existed since man first launched a dugout canoe, so why are we so obsessed with a few characters who lived in the early 18th century? The answer is publicity... and a good brand image.

We have already seen how 17th-century readers reveled in the atrocities and hardships, the heroism and cowardice contained in the pages of Alexander Exquemelin's *History of the Bucaniers of America*, which made figures like Sir Henry Morgan household names. Although his tales were lavishly embellished to help sales, Exquemelin provided the first portrayal of pirates for the general public. Only 40 years after Exquemelin's book appeared in its English edition, Captain Charles Johnson's *General History* provided his publisher with another runaway success—and the Golden Age had not even ended. Its contemporaneous biographical account of the lives of many pirates may have contained any number of inaccuracies, but it made its readers feel as though they owned the pirates described. It remains one of the most popular pirate books of all time and it says much about the enduring popularity of both titles that they remain in print today.

Johnson promoted the pirate brand even further when his play *The Successful Pyrate* opened at London's Drury Lane Theatre, a production based on the exploits of Henry Every. Piracy was being romanticized even while the criminals and their victims still lived. This process has continued until today. In the past three centuries since the Golden Age, a number of milestones have marked this enshrining of the pirate in popular culture. Early 19th-century romantic writers and composers found inspiration in piracy, the best-known examples of this romantic trend being Lord Byron's poem *The Corsair* (1814), Sir Walter Scott's novel *The Pirate* (1821), and Giuseppe Verdi's opera *Il Corsaro* (1848). These were rarefied entertainments with an appeal for the upper classes; it was the work of Scottish writer Robert Louis Stevenson (1850-94) that really raised piracy above the subject matter of romantic writers and placed it into the realm of popular culture. His *Treasure Island* (1883) exercised an enormous influence on the public's perception of pirates. Reprinted countless times in many languages, filmed four times, the subject of endless television adaptations, Stevenson introduced all the elements that are an indelible part of the irate myth: treasure maps, buried plunder, parrots, wooden legs, eye patches, and "Fifteen men on a dead man's chest." Most have no place in the reality of piracy.

In 1904 another Scotsman, J.M. Barrie (1860-1937), took the brand to the next level with his play of *Peter Pan and Wendy*, such a huge stage success that he next turned it into a book. *Peter Pan* has enchanted ever since, with its mix of fairytale and children's adventure story. Its pirates, described as evil incompetents, set a precedent followed in many later pirate portrayals—even Johnny Depp's Jack Sparrow has echoes of Captain Hook. *Peter Pan* also gave us pirate hats with skull and crossbones symbols on them, splitting reality and myth even further apart. Barrie's incipient humor (the Disney film made it full-blown) does not sabotage the sense of adventure in *Peter Pan*, but for many writers in the first half of the 20th century, action was the byword. Writers of this "Boy's Own" style of idealized adventure fiction often went back to Exquemelin and Johnson for inspiration, but updated the image with a new breed of pirate character: the clever hero who battles the evil pirates and beats the dastardly villains at their own game.

In the *Peter Pan Picture Book* of 1907, illustrator Alice B. Woodward caught all the camp frenzy of evil incompetent Hook, a model for later pirate portrayals, as Errol Flynn was the embodiment of super-able and moral pirates in *The Sea Hawk*.

The new brand was ideal for the silver screen and early Hollywood did not hang around. *Treasure Island* was released in 1920, followed four years later by *Captain Blood* and in 1926 by *The Black Pirate*, all silent movies. While the first two made an impact, the latter, starring Douglas Fairbanks Senior, created a new genre—the "swashbuckler," with sea fights, sword duels, sticking daggers into sails to slide down to the deck, pirate gentlemen rescuing fair maidens, and the righting of wrongs. These valiant pirate heroes were not Hollywood originals but screen adaptations of existing fictional characters, as often as not from the novels of Rafael Sabatini (1875-1950). While a noted master of boy's adventure tales, Sabatini never allowed historical record to stand in the way of a good yarn. His influence on the next-generation pirate portrayals of Errol Flynn and Tyrone Power is obvious. Messers Flynn and Power—among others—became stars in classics such as the remake of *Captain Blood* (1935), *The Sea Hawk* (1940), and *The Black Swan* (1942).

Among those of merit, there was also much dross in the flood of pirate epics that followed the coming of talking pictures, and in time the good pirate-bad pirate theme grew wearisome. When a portrayal of a historical pirate was made, his evil persona was invariably hammed up to provide the necessary demonic foil for the hero. There were some exceptions, particularly the screen portrayals of Sir Francis Drake in *Seven Seas to Calais* (1963) and Jean Laffite in *The Buccaneer* (1950), which were more flattering. By the 1950s, genres like the cowboy and pirate movies, suffering from over- exposure and increasingly flaccid plots, turned to comedy and soon became self-parodies, *The Crimson Pirate* (1952) being a prime example. Apart from the occasional appearance on television, classic piracy in the cinema seemed dead, although *Cutthroat Island* (1997) gave pirates a boost while following the same romantic approach, with the twist that the hero was a woman, played by Geena Davis. And more recently, the *Pirates of the Caribbean* franchise has revived the genre to unexpected levels.

In the past 15 years historians have been addressing the subject of piracy seriously but while the work of pirate historians such as David Cordingly, Robert Ritchie and Jan Rogozinski has tried to strip the fact from the fiction of piracy, they are swimming against the stream of popular culture. Since the early 18th century, the romantic view of piracy, running in tandem with an image of demonic cruelty personified by Johnson's Blackbeard, has proved too deeply ingrained to eradicate. We want our pirates to be swashbucklers who make their victims walk the plank.

Slops and the motley crew—pirate apparel

The stereotypical appearance of Hollywood pirates has been necessarily colorful. Bicorn hats adorned with a skull and crossbones plus a splendidly decorated long-tailed captain's coat are the standard attire for any pirate leader. His men tend toward head scarves, plain white shirts, and seamen's baggy trousers, adding ear-rings and tattoos for extra effect. In fact what pirates wore was largely dictated by fashions of their time and practicality. There are numerous instances during the Golden Age where pirate crews were passed off as privateer crews or as hands onboard a legitimate slave ship or merchant vessel. This implies that a pirate's appearance was identical to that of other early 18th-century seamen. They did not adopt a special uniform and retained the clothes—called "slops"—that they wore when they remained within the law.

Slops loosely defined a sailor's clothing, although it did not imply a uniform exactly. Even naval ratings during the early 18th century wore no special uniform, although naval captains frequently adopted one for their own barge crew or shore party. As early as 1628, the English Admiralty had established the minimum clothing for press-ganged sailors in the navy, and little had altered by the 18th century. At sea, slops consisted of canvas jackets or short woolen coats known as fearnoughts, usually made from a heavy blue or gray material and waterproofed with tar or wax, worn over a linen or cotton shirt. The shirts were usually white in color—or more realistically, very off-white—although striped or checkered blue and white shirts may be seen in contemporary illustrations.

Unless the weather was particularly bad, sailors often just wore a shirt or went bare-chested. Linen neck cloths and bandanas helped to absorb sweat. Canvas pants—the "sailors' petticoats"—were standard dress for seamen, although woolen breeches were also used. Footwear was generally reserved for

The motley crew, dressed for life at sea in whatever came to hand. While some captains banned rum at sea, there was no such restriction on land and many pirates escaped the hangman's noose by dying from alcohol abuse.

visits ashore—at sea, seamen usually went barefoot. The head was another matter and some form of head covering was a vital part of a sailor's dress, especially in the tropics. Typical headwear included head scarves, tricorn or "slouch" hats, and knitted "Monmouth" or montero caps. "Matching accessories" was not a concept the 18th-century seaman paid much attention to—multi-hued knitwear and mismatched items made a pirate band literally a motley crew.

Unlike other sailors, pirates had the opportunity to amass stolen clothing, and if the prize was carrying wealthy passengers this could be very fine stuff. It was also likely to be far less practical than normal pirate attire but there are instances cited when pirates went into action wearing fashion-plate items including silk shirts, brocaded jackets, and hats piled high with feathers. There was sometimes a reasonable excuse for pirate captains to look their best. Although elected from among the crew, and in theory dressed the same, captains also frequently had to pass themselves off as officers of a privateer or merchant ship. This meant wearing breeches, a waistcoat and a long blue "sea coat" (Edward England was described wearing "a short coat, but without shoes or stockings"). The best-dressed pirate of the Golden Age was Bartholomew Roberts. At his death, he was said to be wearing "a rich crimson damask waistcoat and breeches, a red feather in his hat, a gold chain round his neck, with a diamond cross hanging to it." Roberts probably looked more like the archetypal Hollywood swashbuckler than any other pirate leader. Blackbeard was wearing a plain sea coat when he was killed, and even the well-born Stede Bonnet was only dressed in "a plain gentleman's coat" at his capture. At sea, practicality took precedence over elegance.

For breaking any article of the code, pirates had to endure various tortures. A common punishment, known as "sweating," involved the prisoner running around the mainmast at spearpoint until he collapsed from exhaustion.

Honor among thieves—the pirate code

There may have been little discipline beyond that of practicality that governed what a pirate wore, but his conduct was frequently subjected to constraints, and not always restricted to how he behaved toward his messmates. For men living beyond the law, imposing a code of conduct seems a surprising aspect of pirate life, and yet it was a common practice, albeit more to prevent disputes over plunder than for any social motives, except for the provisions that offered recompense for injured comrades. For their time, charters like that drawn up by Henry Morgan before the assault on Panama were remarkable documents.

Addressing his army of 2000 men—"ragged, hungry, empty in pocket; their baggage only the clothes on their backs and the guns in their hands"—Morgan first laid out the payments for injuries sustained in action. For the loss of a hand or a foot 500 pieces of eight or six slaves, the choice to be his; the loss of both legs entitled him to 1500 pieces-of-eight or 15 slaves; for both hands 1800. One eye was worth 100 pieces-of-eight, both eyes 2000. No man was to take anything for himself; all booty would be held in common and divided after the campaign. Recompense for injuries would be paid first, and then rewards for various stipulated services and feats of bravery. After these deductions, Morgan would receive one-hundredth of the remaining booty, the rest to be divided equally among the men.

The Panama campaign was a large, land-based attack and no doubt required strict stipulations, but even small pirate crews drafted these tenets and lived by them. Of particular importance was the election of the captain, who could be removed if the crew disapproved of his actions, as happened to both Charles Vane and Edward England. Charters included rules against gambling, womanizing, fighting, and drinking; all pastimes that have traditionally been associated with pirates. Although many pirate charters are alluded to, the following example drawn up by Bartholomew Roberts after his second-in-command, Walter Kennedy, disappeared in the *Rover* is the most extensive of the few to survive.

Tied to a mast, an unfortunate captive is used for the crew's target practice with pistols and bottles.

1. Every man shall have an equal vote in affairs of moment. He shall have an equal title to the fresh provisions or strong liquors at any time seized, and shall use them at pleasure unless a scarcity makes it necessary for the common good that a retrenchment may be voted.

2. Every man shall be called fairly in turn by the list on board of prizes, because over and above their proper share, they are allowed a shift of clothes. But if they defraud the company to the value of even one dollar in plate, jewels, or money, they shall be marooned. If any man rob another he shall have his nose and ears slit, and be put ashore where he shall be sure to encounter hardships.

3. None shall game for money, either with dice or cards.

4. The lights and candles shall be put out at eight at night, and if any of the crew desire to drink after that hour they shall sit upon the open deck without lights.

5. Each man shall keep his piece, cutlass and pistols, at all times clean and ready for action.

6. No boy or woman to be allowed amongst them. If any man shall be found seducing one of the latter sex and carrying her to sea in disguise, he shall suffer death.

7. He that shall desert the ship or his quarters in time of battle shall be punished by death or marooning.

8. None shall strike another aboard the ship, but every man's quarrel shall be ended on shore by sword or pistol in this manner: at the word of command from the Quartermaster, each man being previously placed back to back, shall turn and fire immediately. If any man do not, the Quartermaster shall knock the piece out of his hand. If both miss their aim, they shall take to their cutlasses, and he that draws first blood shall be declared the victor.

9. No man shall talk of breaking up their way of living till each has a share of one thousand pounds. Every man who shall become a cripple or lose a limb in the service shall have eight hundred pieces of eight from the common stock, and for lesser hurts proportionately.

10. The Captain and the Quartermaster shall each receive two shares of a prize, the Master Gunner and Boatswain, one and one half shares, all other officers one and one quarter, and private gentlemen of fortune one share each.

11. The musicians shall have rest on the Sabbath Day only, by right, on all other days, by favor only.

This code is interesting in its emphasis on a far more equal division of plunder than was to be found in any other arm of seafaring at the time. Elected officers received a higher share, commensurate with their duties, as to be expected, but a fraction of the share found in naval service, where over half was allocated to the officers. Privateers operated a half-measure between the two forms of division, but a high percentage was retained for the financial backers, which soaked up much of the profit. This was part of the reason why William Kidd eventually succumbed to the demands of his crew to turn pirate, since his privateers' contract offered little financial reward for either him as master or any of the seamen. One notable aspect of both Morgan and Roberts's codes is the provision of financial aid for injured crewmen. At a time when it was common practice for injured naval ratings to be cast ashore to beg or starve, pirates looked after their own. In this respect, at least, pirate codes were revolutionary social charters for their time.

The degree to which pirates adhered to the articles of their codes can only remain a matter of speculation. Honor among thieves is a hard concept to swallow without some skepticism, and while it is easier to believe that buccaneers and privateers were bound by the greater weight of law behind their letters of marque, pirates probably interpreted the rules as suited the individual. Perhaps this is one instance where Hollywood has the truth of the matter, as Keira Knightley's Elizabeth in *Pirates of the Caribbean: The Curse of the Black Pearl* discovers when she insists on her rights under the pirate articles, only to be told by Geoffrey Rush's Captain Barbossa that they are "actually more what you might call a set of *guidelines* than an *actual* code."

How the treasure was divided, by Howard Pyle. According to the pirate code, crews divided the spoils of conquest between them in proportions that were agreed beforehand.

Index

The Prince – classic Golden Age romanticism by the master of pirate art, Howard Pyle.

238